Supercharge Excel
When You Learn to Write DAX for Power Pivot

by
Matt Allington

T0191316

Holy Macro! Books
PO Box 541731
Merritt Island, FL 32954

Supercharge Excel

Author: Matt Allington

Layout: Jill Bee

Copyediting: Kitty Wilson

Cover Design: Emrul Hasan & Shannon Travise

Cover Illustration: Freepik

Indexing: Nellie Jay

Published by: Holy Macro! Books, PO Box 541731, Merritt Island FL 32954, USA

Distributed by: Independent Publishers Group, Chicago, IL

First Printing: May, 2018

ISBN: 978-1-61547-053-2 Print, 978-1-61547-236-9 PDF, 978-1-61547-359-5 ePub, 978-1-61547-136-2 Mobi

Library of Congress Control Number: 2017961953

Table of Contents

Introduction iv

1: Concept: Introduction to Data Modelling 1

2: Concept: Loading Data 3

3: Concept: Measures 25

4: DAX Topic: SUM(), COUNT(), COUNTROWS(), MIN(), MAX(), COUNTBLANK(), and DIVIDE() 34

5: Concept: Filter Propagation 51

6: Concept: Lookup Tables and Data Tables 57

7: DAX Topic: The Basic Iterators SUMX() and AVERAGEX() 62

8: DAX Topic: Calculated Columns 71

9: DAX Topic: CALCULATE() 74

10: Concept: Evaluation Context and Context Transition 82

11: DAX Topic: IF(), SWITCH(), and FIND() 88

12: DAX Topic: VALUES() and HASONEVALUE() 91

13: DAX Topic: ALL(), ALLEXCEPT(), and ALLSELECTED() 98

14: DAX Topic: FILTER() 111

15: DAX Topic: Time Intelligence 120

16: DAX Topic: RELATED() and RELATEDTABLE() 144

17: Concept: Disconnected Tables 149

18: Concept: KPIs 164

19: Concept: Multiple Data Tables 167

20: Concept: Cube Formulas 175

21: Moving from Excel to Power BI 181

22: Next Steps on Your DAX Journey 191

Appendix A: Answers to Practice Exercises 193

Table of Here's How Sections 202

Index 203

Introduction

Power Pivot is a revolutionary piece of software that has been around since 2009. Despite its being more than eight years old at this writing, most people who could benefit from Power Pivot still don't know it exists. The good news is that you are not one of those people. If you are reading this, then you already know about Power Pivot, and chances are good that you already know enough about it to know that you are capable of supercharging Excel when you learn to write DAX.

Bill Jelen, aka MrExcel, has said, "Power Pivot is the best thing to happen to Excel in 20 years." I totally agree with Bill: Power Pivot is simply awesome. Power Pivot brings everything that is good about enterprise-strength business intelligence (BI) tools directly to you right inside Excel—and without the negative time and cost impacts you would normally expect from big-scale BI projects. In addition, it is not just the time and money that matter. The fact that you can do everything yourself with Power Pivot is very empowering. Analyses that you would never have considered viable in the past are now "can do" tasks within the current business cycle.

When you learn to write DAX, you will unleash enormous power, and you can use that power to supercharge your workbooks, skills, and career as never before.

Supercharge Power BI

Supercharge Excel: When You Learn to Write DAX for Power Pivot has been written specifically to teach Power Pivot and DAX using Power Pivot for Excel. I have written a sister book, Supercharge Power BI: Power BI Is Better When You Learn to Write DAX. These two books cover the same basic content but with a different user interface. Because the skills you will learn in this book are fully transferable to Power BI and vice versa, you really need only one of these books to secure the required skills. However, if you want to learn about the differences in the UI and practice what you have learnt, then reading Supercharge Power BI will certainly help you cement your learning across the different UIs.

Why You Need This Book

I am a full-time Power Pivot and Power BI consultant, trainer, and BI practitioner. I have taught many Excel users how to use Power Pivot and Power BI at live training classes, in online training classes, and on various Power Pivot/Power BI forums. This teaching experience has given me great insight into how Excel users learn Power Pivot and what resources they need to succeed. Power Pivot is very learnable, but it is very different to Excel; you definitely need some structured learning if you want to be good at using this tool. I have learnt that Excel users need practice, practice, practice. The book you're reading right now, *Supercharge Excel: When You Learn to Write DAX for Power Pivot*, is designed to give you practice and to teach you how to write DAX. If you can't write DAX, you will never be good at Power Pivot or Power BI.

I refer above to *Excel users*, and that is quite deliberate. I have observed that Excel professionals learn the DAX language (*DAX* stands for *Data Analysis Expressions*) differently than do IT/SQL Server professionals. IT/SQL Server professionals are simply not the same as Excel business users. SQL Server professionals have a solid knowledge of database design and principles, table relationships, how to efficiently aggregate data, etc. And, of course, there are some Excel users who also have knowledge about those things. But I believe IT/SQL Server professionals can take a much more technical path to learning DAX than most Excel users because they have the technical grounding to build upon. Excel users need a different approach, and this book is written with them in mind. That is not to say that an IT/SQL Server professional would not get any value from this book/approach; it really depends on your learning style. But suffice it to say that if you are an Excel professional who is trying to learn Power Pivot and DAX, this book was written with your specific needs in mind.

Incremental Learning

I am an Excel user from way back—a long way back actually. I'm not the kind of guy who can sit down and read a novel, but I love to buy Excel reference books and read them cover to cover. And I have learnt *a lot* about Excel over the years by using this approach. When I find some new concept that I love and want to try, most of the time I just remember it. But sometimes I add a sticky note to the page so I can I find it again in the future when I need it. In a way, I am incrementally learning a small number of new skills on top of the large base of skills I already have. When you incrementally learn like this, it is relatively easy to remember the detail of the new thing you just learnt.

It's a bit like when a new employee starts work at a company. Existing employees only have to learn the name of that one new person. But the new employee has to learn the name of every person in the entire company. It is relatively easy for the existing employees to remember one new name, but it's a lot harder for the new person to start from scratch and learn all the names. Similarly, when you're an experienced Excel user reading a regular Excel book, you already know a lot and need to learn only a few things that are new—and those new bits are likely to be gold. It is easy to remember those few new things because often they strike a chord with you. Even if you don't remember the details, the next time you face a similar problem, you'll remember that you read something about it once, and you'll be able to go find your book to look it up.

Well, unfortunately for seasoned Excel users, Power Pivot is a completely different piece of software from Excel, even though it is bundled with Excel. Power Pivot shares some things in common with Excel (such as some common formulas), but many of the really useful concepts are very different and completely new. They are not super-difficult to learn, but indeed you will need to learn from scratch, just as that new employee has to learn everyone's name. Once you get a critical mass of new Power Pivot knowledge in your head, you will be off and running. At that point, you will be able to incrementally learn all you want, but until then, you need to read, learn, and, most importantly, practice, practice, practice.

Passive vs. Active Learning

I think about learning as being either passive or active. An example of passive learning is lying in bed, reading your Power Pivot book, nodding your head to indicate that you understand what is being covered. When you learn something completely new, you simply can't take this approach. I read a lot of Power Pivot books early in my discovery, but the first time I sat in front of my computer and wanted to write some DAX, I was totally lost. What I really needed to do was change from a passive learning approach to an active approach, where I was participating in the learning process rather than being a spectator.

Passive learning on its own is more suited to incrementally adding knowledge to a solid base. Passive learning is not a good approach when you are starting something completely new from scratch. I'm not saying that passive learning is bad. It is useful to do some passive learning in addition to active learning, but you shouldn't try to learn a completely new skill from scratch using *only* passive learning.

How to Get Value from This Book

There are more than 40 "Here's How" worked-through examples and more than 70 individual practice exercises in this book. That gives you more than 110 opportunities to practice and learn more. Make the most of these opportunities to develop your skills; after all, that is why you purchased this book.

If you think you can get value from this book by reading it and not doing the practice exercises, let me tell you: You can't. If you already know how to complete a task, and you have done it before, then just reading is fine. However, if you don't know how to do a task or an exercise, then you should practice in front of your computer. First try to do an exercise without looking at the answers. If you can't work it out, then reread the worked-through examples (labelled "Here's How") and then try to do the exercise again. Practice, practice, practice until you have the knowledge committed to memory and can do it without looking.

Don't Treat This Like a Library Book

When we were kids going to school, most of us were taught that you should not write in library books. And I guess that is fair enough. Other people will use a library book after you are finished, and they probably don't want to read all your scribbles. Unfortunately, the message that many of us took away was "Don't write in *any* book *ever*." I think it is a mistake to think that you can't write in your own books. You bought it, you own it, so why can't you write in it? In fact, I would go one step further and say *you should* write in the reference books you own. You bought them for a reason: to learn. If you are reading this book and want to make some notes to yourself for future reference, then you should definitely do that.

But I guess I am forgetting the eBook revolution. I know you can't write in an eBook, but I know you can highlight passages of text in a Kindle, and I assume you can do something similar with other eBook formats. You can also type in your own notes and attach them to passages of text in many eBooks. There are lots of advantages to eBooks, and the one that means the most to me is the fact that I can have a new book in front of me just moments after I have decided to buy it.

Personally, I find that eBooks are not a great fit as reference books. I prefer to have a tactile object so I can flip through the pages, add sticky notes, and so on. But that is just me, and we are all different. I am sure there are plenty of people in both camps. On the upside, eBooks are usually in colour, and printed books (like this one) are more often in black and white. Whichever camp you are in—eBook or physical book—I encourage you to write in this book and/or make notes to yourself using the eBook tools at your disposal. Doing so will make this book a more useful, personalised tool well into the future.

Refreshing Your Pivot Table Skills

This is not a book about how to use pivot tables. Pivot tables have been around for more than 20 years and are some of the best summarisation and visualisation tools available for large data sets. This book assumes that you already know how to use a pivot table and are reasonably competent in doing so. The assumed skills include:

- How to create a pivot table from a standard Excel list
- How to add data to rows, columns, and filters for a pivot table

If you don't know how to do these things well, I suggest you brush up on your skills now before you move forward. There are lots of really good tutorial videos available on YouTube.

Setting Up a Pivot Table

One important concept that is repeated throughout this book is that I recommend you always set up a pivot table before you create your DAX formulas. This is especially important for Excel users as it provides context for the formulas you will write (more on this later).

You use five areas of the PivotTable Fields list to create or update a pivot table: Filters (see #1 in the figure below), Columns (#2), Rows (#3), Values (#4), and Slicers (#5). Say that the instructions in this book tell you to set up a pivot table with `Products[Category]` on Rows, `Customers[Gender]` on Columns, `'Calendar'[CalendarYear]` on Filters, `Customers[Occupation]` on Slicers, and a measure such as `[Total Sales]` on Values. In that case, you should use the PivotTable Fields list (shown on the right in the figure below) to build the pivot table (shown on the left below) as instructed. If you are not clear on how to do this, then you should definitely brush up on building pivot tables before proceeding.

> **Note:** *Calendar* is a reserved word in Power Pivot. Therefore, if you use the word Calendar as a table name, it must be enclosed in single quotes to differentiate between the reserved word and the name of the table (e.g., `'Calendar'[CalendarYear]`). The same is true for other keywords, such as `'Date'` and `'Month'`.

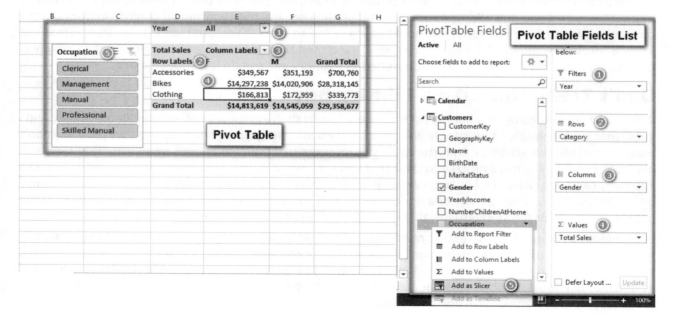

Note: There are a few ways to add a slicer to a pivot table. In the PivotTable Fields list (on the right in the image above), you can right-click on any column in any table and then select Add as Slicer (see #5 above). You can also navigate to the Excel Insert tab and click the Slicer button there. Just make sure you first select the pivot table before trying to insert a slicer.

Exercise Data

It is surprisingly difficult to create your own database of meaningful data to use for data analysis practice. Think about the data that exists in a commercial retail business, for example; it may include customer data, finance data, sales data, products, territories, etc. And it is not a simple task to create a meaningful quantity of realistic data from scratch; it is a lot of work. Microsoft has created a number of sample databases that anyone can download and use for free. I use a modified version of the Microsoft AdventureWorks database throughout this book, provided to you in Microsoft Access format. You can download a copy of it by going to http://xbi.com.au/learndax. (Note that you do not need to have Microsoft Access installed to use this database.) This is the same sample database I use in my live training classes.

AdventureWorks contains sample data for a fictitious retail bicycle company that sells bikes and accessories in multiple countries. The data consists of the customers, products, and territories for the AdventureWorks business, along with five years of transactional sales history. The examples I use in this book therefore focus on reporting and analysis that would apply to a retail business, including such things as sales results, profit margins, customer activity, and product performance.

Clearly, not everyone who wants to learn to write DAX will operate in a retail environment. However, the retail concepts covered in this book should be familiar to everyone. So it doesn't matter if your specific BI needs are for something other than retail. The scenarios in this book are explained throughout, and you don't need to be a retail expert to complete or understand the exercises.

Getting Help Along the Way

Hopefully you will be able to complete the practice exercises in this book on your own. But sometimes you might need to ask someone a question before you can move forward. I encourage you to become a member of http://powerpivotforum.com.au and participate as someone who asks questions and also as someone who helps others when they get stuck. Answering questions for other people is a great way to cement your learning and build depth of knowledge. You will notice from the URL that this is an Aussie forum, but it is open to everyone. At this writing, only 15% of all traffic at the forum is from Australia, with the balance coming from more than 130 other countries around the world. I suggest that you sign up and get involved; your DAX will be better for it.

You can find a subforum dedicated to this book at http://xbi.com.au/ldf. In the unfortunate event that there are errors in this book, details of the errors will be posted at this subforum.

How This Book Is Organised

I've organised this book to make sense to a new Excel user. The general structure of the chapters is as follows:

- Each chapter title begins with either "DAX Topic" or "Concept." The former type covers one or more specific DAX formulas, including the syntax and usage; the latter type covers one or more principles that you need to understand in order to be competent with Power Pivot. I've ordered the chapters so that you can learn incrementally.

- Each "Concept" chapter starts with a description of the concept, and each "DAX Topic" chapter starts with some information about the DAX language to help you understand the topic.

- Almost every chapter provides at least one worked-through example. When you see "Here's How," you know you're reading one of those, and it's time to sit in front of your computer and follow along with me as I explain the concept.

- Almost every chapter includes a number of practice exercises that help you practice what you have learnt. You will find guidelines to complete the exercises, and you can also find the answers in Appendix A, at the end of the book. I recommend that you complete the exercises first and only then look at the answers to check that you got the correct results. This way you can cement the learning you are getting from this book.

- DAX is a lot like Excel in that there is often more than one way to do something. If you do an exercise differently than I show how to do it, as long as you get the correct/same answer, all is good.

Naming Conventions

This book uses best-practice naming conventions for Power Pivot and Power BI:

- There are no spaces in table names, like this:

    ```
    TableName
    ```

- Columns in tables *always* include the table name followed by the column name in square brackets, like this:

    ```
    TableName[ColumnName]
    ```

- Measures *never* include a table name, they often include spaces, and they are wrapped in square brackets, like this:

    ```
    [MeasureName]
    ```

- Measure and column formulas are written with the name (without the square brackets) followed by the formula, like this:

    ```
    Total Sales = SUM(Sales[ExtendedAmount])
    ```

Note: Another convention may be used in Power Pivot for Excel when writing a formula in the Power Pivot window. It involves using a : (colon) immediately before the = (equals sign). I don't use that convention in this book, but if you see a formula in the Power Pivot window, you will see the extra colon.

1: Concept: Introduction to Data Modelling

The *data modelling engine* that is used inside Power Pivot for Excel is the same one used in Power BI. *Data modelling* is not a term that is often familiar to business users as it is normally the domain of IT BI professionals. But this is no longer the case, thanks to the introduction of Power Pivot for Excel and Power BI.

What Is Data Modelling?

Data modelling is the process of taking data from various sources; loading, structuring, and relating data logically to other data; and enhancing, embellishing, and generally preparing the data for use. The objective is to be able to use the data without having to write a custom query every time you want to look at a different subset of data.

The data modelling process includes:

- Determining the optimal structure and shape of the source data to analyse, including whether to bring in all the data, full data, or summary data.
- Loading the data from the source into the data model (Power Pivot for Excel in this case).
- Defining the logical relationships between the various tables (which is similar to what you do with `VLOOKUP()` in Excel, except the data stays in the source table in Power Pivot).
- Defining data types (e.g., specifying whether a column of data is numeric or a column of currency values or a column of text fields).
- Creating new insights from the source data so that you can analyse concepts that don't exist natively in the source data but that can be calculated or created inside the data model. For example, if you have a table of transactional data with cost price and sell price, you can extend the data model to include calculations for margin, margin percentage, etc., even though these concepts are not explicitly in the source data. Once you have modelled these new facts in the data model, they can be reused over and over by people using your workbook.
- Giving meaningful names to your new business insights (i.e., to your measures).

When you learn the DAX language and join your tables of data in Power Pivot for Excel, you are actually learning data modelling. The term *data modelling* can be a little bit scary, but there is no reason to be concerned. By the time you have finished this book, you will be well on your way to being an accomplished data modeller using Power Pivot. Just use the techniques covered in this book and keep in mind that what you are actually doing is learning to be a data modeller. Having said that, however, I should also point out that there is a big difference between being able to do it and being an expert. Becoming an expert takes years of practice, experience, and lifelong learning.

Pivot Tables vs. Power Pivot

Some people wonder what the difference is between Power Pivot and pivot tables, so I'm going to start by explaining. Read on, and you'll have it sorted out in no time.

What Is a Pivot Table?

A *pivot table* is a summarisation and visualisation tool. The job of a pivot table is to connect to a data source and create on-the-fly totals and subtotals to help you and others make sense of data. The larger the set of data and the more granular the data, the more useful a pivot table becomes. Because pivot tables are embedded right inside Excel, with them you get all the other benefits of Excel as well.

Data Sources for Pivot Tables

Historically, there have been two main types of data sources that you can connect to with a pivot table: flat tables and data cubes.

Connecting to a Single Flat Table

To connect to a single flat table inside Excel, click in the table, select Insert, PivotTable, and off you go. There are some limitations with this approach, however:

- It is very common to have to do a lot of VLOOKUP()s (or similar operations) to be able to join data from different data sources into a single flat table.
- Excel has a 1 million row limit. In fact, though, if you are using lots of VLOOKUP()s in a single flat table, you will reach performance limits well before you ever hit 1 million rows.

These two issues have historically prevented Excel from being a scalable BI tool. But Power Pivot changes that, as you'll see in a few moments.

Connecting to a Data Cube

A less common but very powerful use of pivot tables is to connect directly to a reporting cube such as a SQL Server Analysis Services multidimensional cube directly from Excel. Many large enterprises have multidimensional data cubes available for reporting. Allowing Excel users to connect directly to a cube and use a pivot table for reporting is super easy and convenient. But this is a relatively rare use case compared to the general use of Excel and the more common single-table use of pivot tables.

Enter Power Pivot

Power Pivot doesn't change anything about pivot tables, but it changes everything when it comes to the data that pivot tables connect to. Power Pivot adds a third (and, in my view, the best) method of connecting to source data. Excel has limited ability to manage large sets of data for reporting purposes, whereas Power Pivot has no theoretical database size limit.

Power Pivot is a data modelling tool that allows you to prepare your data in a way that pivot tables can use. *Data modelling* is the process of preparing data so it can be used in reporting tools (such as a pivot table) without the need to write new database queries every time.

Power Pivot is a Microsoft SQL Server Analysis Services tabular database that is bundled with Microsoft Excel via a COM add-in. Excel manages Power Pivot databases, so the experience is seamless and transparent to the end user. You can use a user interface in Excel to build Power Pivot databases directly inside Excel.

Power Pivot allows you to:

Import data from many different data sources.

Logically join separate tables of data together so the data works together without the need for VLOOKUP() formulas.

Enhance the underlying raw data so that you can create new derived concepts (measures) from that data. For example, if the source data has sell price and cost price, it is possible to create the measures Margin $ and Margin % and make them available for use in reports.

Assign appropriate business names to the measures.

Apply to the data business formatting that will be applied throughout the data model.

Once a Power Pivot data model has been built and configured, the end user can use the data repeatedly to quickly build multiple pivot table reports inside Excel.

2: Concept: Loading Data

Before you can start to write DAX and use Power Pivot, you need to load some data. Power Pivot always loads a complete copy of the source data into the data model as the first step in the process. Once it's loaded, you can share your workbooks with others, and there is no need for anyone else to have direct access to your source data.

When you load data, you have to decide which data to import, including which tables, which columns in each table, and also what "shape" the data should be when imported. In the following "Here's How," you will simply load data that has been prepared for you. But you need to be aware that the process of deciding which data to load is an important part of the data modelling process. This decision has been made for you for this book.

Preparing for Data Load

You can download a copy of the sample AdventureWorks database used in this book from http://xbi.com.au/learndax. You should download the database now, unzip it, and place it in a location that is easy for you to find.

Here's How: Enabling Power Pivot in Excel

The Power Pivot menu may or may not be visible in your version of Excel. Follow these steps to see if it is visible and, if not, enable it:

1. Open a new Excel workbook. Look for the Power Pivot tab in the ribbon, shown in the figure below. If you see it, you don't need to follow the rest of these steps.

2. If you don't see the Power Pivot tab, select File, Options, Add-Ins.

3. Scroll to the bottom of the window and select COM Add-ins from the Manage list. Then click Go.

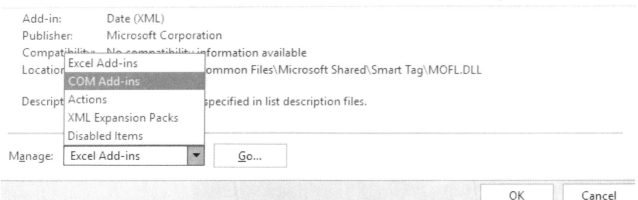

4.   In the COM Add-ins dialog that appears, check the Microsoft Power Pivot for Excel check box and then click OK.

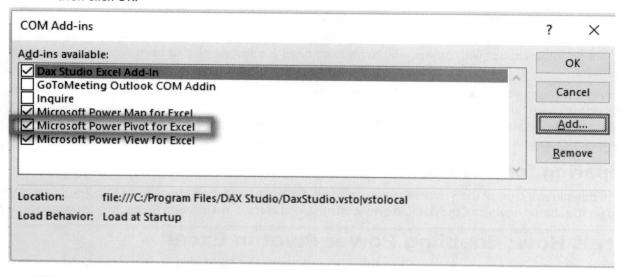

What if I Can't Find the Power Pivot Add-in? If you are using Excel 2013 or later and you can't see the Power Pivot add-in, then I have some bad news for you: Your version of Excel does not include Power Pivot, and you will need to purchase a different version of Excel to get it. For more information about Power Pivot versions, go to http://xbi.com.au/versions.

5.   On the PowerPivot tab, click Manage.

Take a moment to look at the Windows taskbar, shown in the figure below. Hover your mouse over Excel in the taskbar and notice that there are now two separate windows: the traditional Excel window (see #1 below) and the Power Pivot window (#2).

Note: Power Pivot is a separate application that is completely embedded inside Excel. Throughout this book, I often tell you to switch between Excel and Power Pivot. When I say this, I mean you should switch between the two windows shown above. If at any time you can't see the Power Pivot window because it is not open, you can open it by going to the Power Pivot tab in Excel and clicking Manage.

Direct Load to Power Pivot or Power Query?

Power Pivot for Excel has always allowed you to load data directly into the Power Pivot data model from within the Power Pivot window, as shown below.

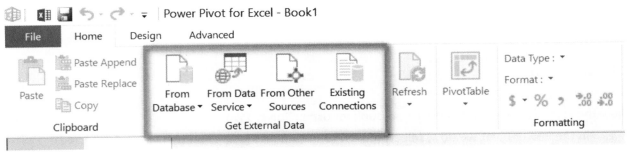

Since Excel 2016, Microsoft has embedded Power Query directly in Excel, under the Data, Get & Transform Data menu.

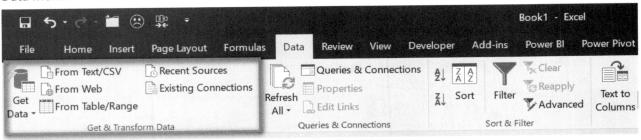

> **Note:** At this writing, there are several software builds of Excel 2016 available, and your version may look different to the image above. If your Data tab looks different to what is shown here, just take a few moments to look more closely at it and become clear about where the Power Query features are located.

This change of name to Get & Transform Data is unfortunate, in my view, and I prefer to use the name Power Query.

> **Note:** I use the term *Power Query* in this book, but remember that you launch Power Query from the Get & Transform Data menu.

With the introduction of Power Query, you have a choice to either load data directly into Power Pivot using the legacy Power Pivot approach or use Power Query (from the Get & Transform Data menu) instead. There are a couple reasons to prefer using the newer Power Query approach over the legacy approach:

- When you load data using the legacy Power Pivot approach, it is not possible to change a data source. For example, if you load data into a table in Power Pivot from a spreadsheet and later decide to source the data from SQL Server instead, it is not possible to simply repoint the table to the new and different type of data source. Instead, you must first delete the table and then re-import the data from the beginning. This doesn't sound so bad at first, but it means that all the relationships need to be re-created and that any measures stored in the table will be lost—and these are big problems.

- Power Query allows you to easily manipulate data during load in ways that are not possible using the legacy Power Pivot approach.

> **Note:** As of this writing, loading data using Power Query takes longer than loading the same data using the legacy Power Pivot approach. It is not so long that it is unworkable, but it can take 15 to 20 seconds longer to load for some reason.

The next "Here's How" section describes how to load data using the legacy Power Pivot approach. I suggest you read it and follow along on your machine so you know how. For the rest of this book (and when you start building your own data models), I recommend that you use the Power Query data load approach, which is described in a later "Here's How" section.

Here's How: Data Load Using Power Pivot

This section describes how to load the following tables from the AdventureWorks Access database using the legacy Power Pivot data load approach:

- Sales
- Products
- Territories
- Calendar
- Customers

Follow these steps to load data into a workbook for use in Power Pivot:

1. In the Power Pivot window, select Home, From Database (see #1 below), From Access (#2).

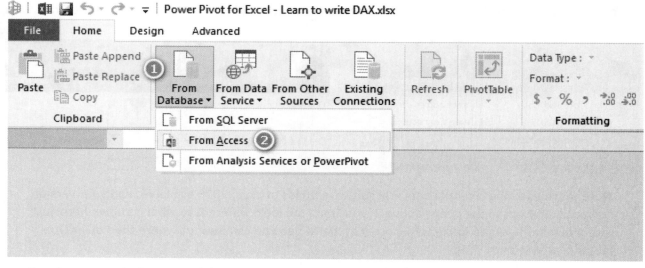

2. Browse to the location of the sample database you downloaded and unzipped earlier in this chapter and then click Next.

3. Accept the default option in the Table Import Wizard dialog (as shown below) and then click Next.

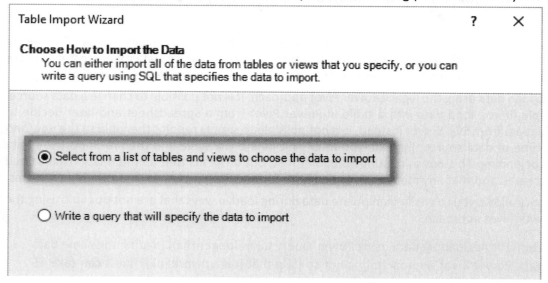

4. Select the five views at the bottom of the list by placing a check mark in the box next to each one. (Note the different icons for queries/views and for tables.)

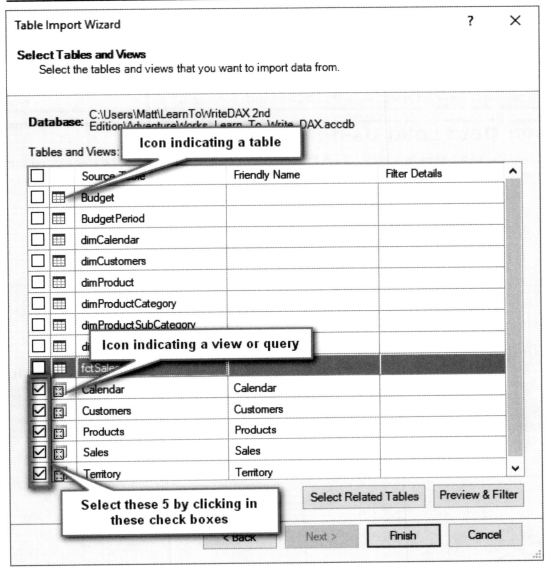

5. Click Finish, and the wizard imports your data.

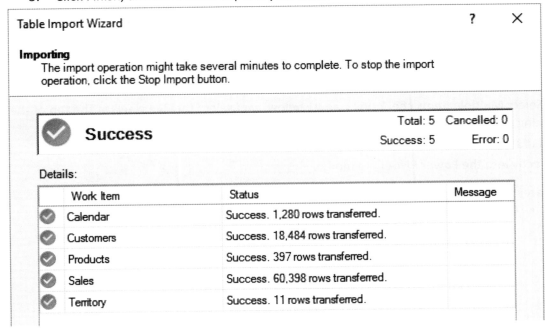

When you close the Table Import Wizard, you see the five tables you have just imported in the Power Pivot window. There should be five new tabs, one for each of the tables you just imported. Each of the tables is a complete copy of the data you imported from the source files (an Access database, in this example). You don't need the source files again until you are ready to refresh the data—typically when the data changes at some time in the future. This is one of the many great things about Power Pivot: You can simply refresh the data when the data changes, and your workbooks are updated with the new data.

Here's How: Data Load Using Power Query

This section describes how to load the following tables from the AdventureWorks Access database using the Power Query data load approach:

- Sales
- Products
- Territory
- Calendar
- Customers

Then you will prepare these tables for use in Power Pivot.

Follow these steps to load data into a workbook for use in Power Pivot using Power Query:

1.   If necessary, open another new blank Excel workbook.

2.   Click Data (see #1 below), Get Data (#2), From Database (#3), From Microsoft Access Database (#4).

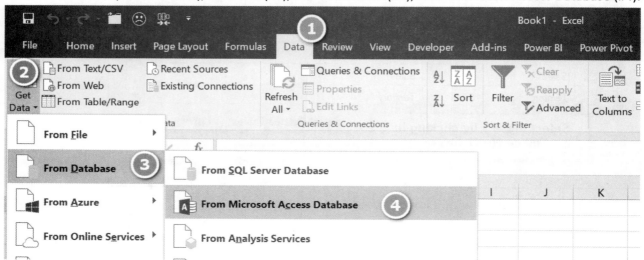

3.   Browse to the location of the sample database you downloaded and unzipped earlier in this chapter and then click Import.

4.   Click the Select Multiple Items check box (see #1 below) and select the five views at the top of the list by placing a check mark in the box next to each one (#2).

5.   Click Load (#3).

The data loads directly into the Power Pivot data model.

> **Note:** There are different icons for queries/views and for tables. The icons at the top of the list in the figure below (e.g., next to Calendar and Customers) indicate views/queries, and the icons at the bottom (e.g., next to Budget and BudgetPeriod) indicate tables.

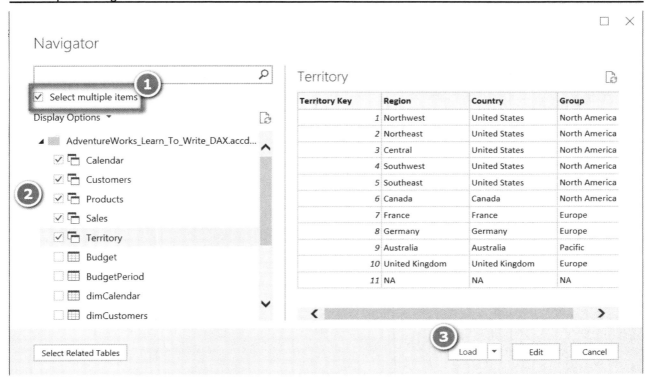

There is also a Load To option, as shown in the image below. If you select this option, you have a number of choices for loading the data to the data model, to an Excel table, or both. You can do the exercise again if you want to see how this works.

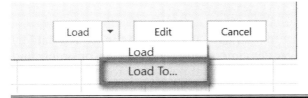

Tip: The sample data in this book has been well prepared for learning how to use Power Pivot. However, you should not assume that any other source database has the correct table structure for Power Pivot; in fact, few databases do.

Note: If you click the Edit button instead of Load (as shown in the image above), you launch into the Power Query Editor, where you can transform the data prior to loading it into Power Pivot. Power Query is beyond the scope of this book, but I have a comprehensive online training course specifically designed to teach you how to use this powerful tool. You can learn more about that training course at http://xbi.com.au/powerquerytraining.

Also notice that the tables at the bottom of the import navigator shown above have names like `dimProduct` and `fctSales`, where `dim` indicates *dimension*, and `fct` indicates *fact*. It is very common for database tables to have prefixes like this. Business users can think of a dimension table as a lookup table and a fact table as a data (or transactions) table. The fact that there are two different types of tables—lookup tables and data tables—is a very important concept in Power Pivot, and you will learn a lot more about this as you work through this book.

It is best practice for Excel users to remove the `dim` and `fct` prefixes from the table names before importing these tables into Power Pivot. These prefixes have meaning to IT folk and help identify the type of table, but given that these table names will be visible to business users who use your Power Pivot reports, it is a good idea to remove the prefixes during import.

After completing the import, you should see the Queries & Connections pane appear, confirming that the data has been loaded into tables in Power Pivot.

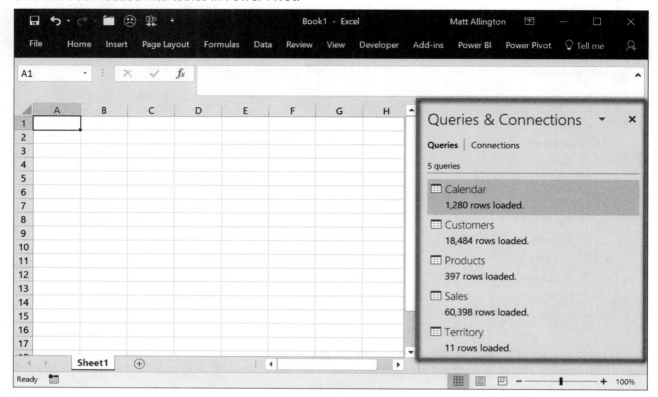

Using Your Data in Power Pivot

Regardless of whether you used Power Query or Power Pivot to load data, you can see the loaded data by navigating to the Power Pivot window. In Excel, go to the Power Pivot menu and click Manage, or simply find and select the Power Pivot window in the taskbar (if it is already open). After navigating to the Power Pivot window, ensure that you are in Data view by selecting Data View on the ribbon in the Power Pivot window (see #1 below). There is a second view of the data (Diagram view; #2 below) that shows the relationship between tables. (More on that shortly.)

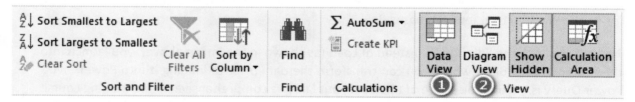

You should now see the five tables you have just imported in the Power Pivot window. There should be five new tabs, one for each of the tables you just imported. Each of the tables is a complete copy of the data you imported from the source files (an Access database, in this example). You don't need the source files again until you are ready to refresh the data—typically when the data changes at some time in the future. This is one of the many great things about Power Pivot: You can simply refresh the data when the data changes, and your workbooks are updated with the new data.

Here's How: Renaming Tables and Columns

It is good practice to make any changes to table and column names early. This renaming of tables is part of the data modelling process. If you loaded data using the legacy Power Pivot data load approach, you can rename a table directly inside the Power Pivot window by following these steps:

1. In the Data view, double-click the Territory tab and rename it Territories for consistency.

2. If you have loaded data using Power Query, you get the error message shown below when you try to rename a table.

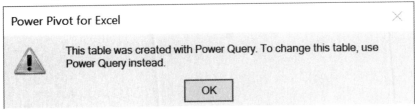

3. To rename a table that was loaded with Power Query, you need to go back to the Excel window. Right-click the Territory table/query in the Queries & Connections pane (see #1 below). Click Rename (#2) and give the table the new name *Territories*.

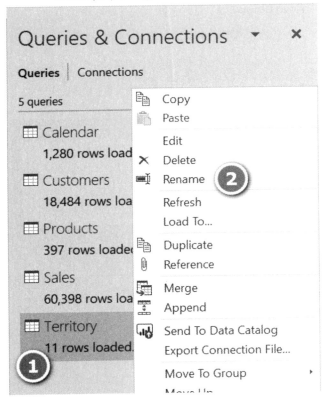

4. You then see the warning shown below.

Rename Query

Renaming this query will remove and recreate the associated Data Model table when the query is refreshed. Any customizations or references you made to the Data Model table will be lost. Are you sure you want to continue?

Rename   Cancel

5. Go ahead and click Rename. Hopefully you can see why it is good practice to make these changes early.

Note: The next stage of the data modelling process involves creating the logical relationships between the tables.

6. If necessary, switch back to the Power Pivot window.

7. Switch to Diagram view by clicking the Diagram View button on the ribbon.

8. If you can't see all five tables on the screen, click the Fit to Screen button at the bottom of the window to reveal the hidden tables.

9. Position the tables so that any data tables (there is only one in this case) are at the bottom of the screen and the lookup tables are at the top, as shown below.

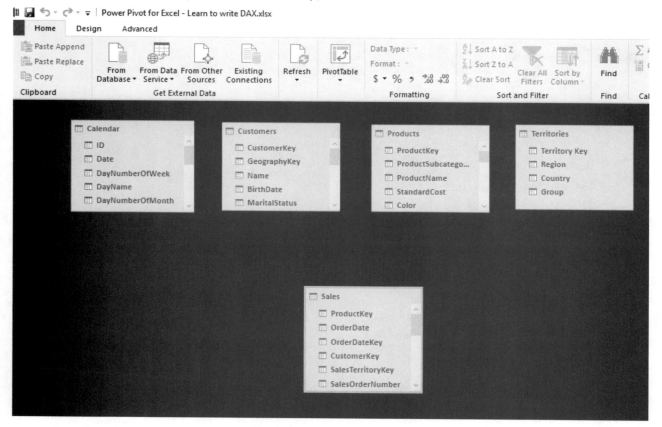

Note: A data table contains transactional information—in this case sales transactions. Lookup tables contain information about logical groups of objects, such as customers, products, time (calendar), etc. In the old world before Power Pivot, an Excel user needed to create one big flat table in Excel before creating a pivot table. Often that meant writing VLOOKUP() formulas to bring in other data from other tables into the one allowed big flat table. These other tables containing the extra data needed are the lookup tables in Power Pivot. Each of these tables must have a unique ID column, such as ProductNumber, CustomerNumber, etc. These unique columns are sometimes called *keys*.

When you've completed the preceding steps, you need to join the data table(s) to the lookup table(s), as described in the next "Here's How."

> **Note:** The relationship between tables in Power Pivot is always of the type "one to many," and there can be only one active relationship. Unlike in other database programs (Power Pivot is actually a database), there is no other type of table join available in Power Pivot (for versions up through Excel 2016 anyway). The data table may contain none, one, or many rows of data for each row in the lookup table. The following "Here's How" shows how to join tables.

Here's How: Joining Tables in Power Pivot

A customers table typically has a list of all customers that a business has on file. But some of these customers may have never purchased anything from the company. Some customers may have made only a single purchase, and some customers may have made many purchases. So for each entry in the Customers table, the Sales table has either zero, one, or many rows.

The Sales table can be joined logically to the Customers table by using the customer key (often called customer number or ID). When these tables are joined on the customer key, there is a one-to-many (Customers-to-Sales) relationship between these two tables.

To join a lookup table to a data table in Power Pivot, follow these steps:

1. Select a column from the data table (the table at the bottom of the Power Pivot screen, as shown below). In this case, click the OrderDate column in the Sales table (see #1 below) and hold down the mouse button.

2. Drag the column up and hover over the matching key in the lookup table (in this case, the Date column in the Calendar table; see #2).

3. Release the mouse button to complete the join.

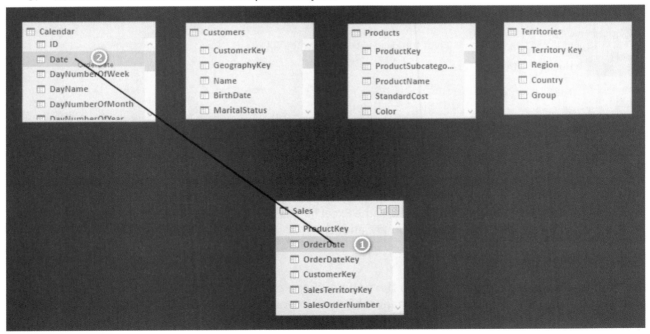

4. Complete the same process for the other three tables. See if you can work out on your own which are the correct columns to join before you look at the answers below:

Data Table	Column	Lookup Table	Column
Sales	ProductKey	Products	ProductKey
Sales	CustomerKey	Customers	CustomerKey
Sales	SalesTerritoryKey	Territories	TerritoryKey

Because the relationships are always one-to-many, the joins are specifically single-directional. Always drag from the data table up to the lookup table, not the other way around (as you would if you were writing a VLOOKUP() in Excel).As you can see in the image below, there is an asterisk (see #1 below) at the end of the relationship that points to the data table, there is a 1 (#2) at the end that points to the lookup table, and there is an arrow (#3) that points toward the data table. (More on these arrows later.)

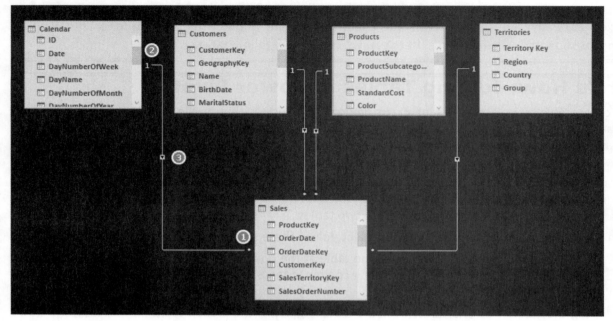

5.   By putting the data table at the bottom, you get a visual clue that the tables at the top of the screen are lookup tables. (Get it? You have to "look up" to see the lookup tables.)

6.   Save the workbook by clicking the Save icon (see #1 below).

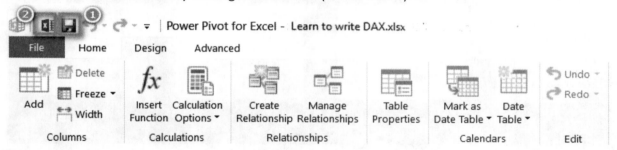

When you click the Save icon, you save both the Excel workbook and the Power Pivot data model at the same time (just as happens when you click the Save button in Excel). The Excel workbook and the Power Pivot data model are always saved together inside the same Excel file (.xlsx, .xlsb, .xlsm, etc.). If you want to switch back to the Excel window, click the Excel button (#2 above).

Shaping Data

It's time to pause for a minute to discuss the optimal shape of data for Power Pivot. When I say "shape" of data, I am talking about things like how many tables you import, how many columns are in each table, which columns are in each of the tables, etc.

Shaping data is a huge topic, and it is not in scope to cover it fully in this book. But I do want to give some foundational advice to get you started. One reason this advice is important is because the shape of data in transactional systems (or relational databases) is seldom the ideal shape for Power Pivot. When the IT department executes an enterprise BI project, one of the important first steps is to shape the data so it is optimal for reporting. This step is normally completely transparent to the end user (i.e., you), and hence the end user is shielded from the need to do this. But I am sharing this important information with you here and now because you need to understand data shaping if you want to have efficient and effective Power Pivot data models. Just copying what you have in your source data is unlikely to be optimal.

Choosing a Schema (Table Structure)

The generally accepted approach for bringing data into Power Pivot is to bring in the data in what's known as a *star schema*. This is a technical term that comes from the Kimball methodology (also known as *dimensional modelling*; you can look it up online if you're interested) and describes the logical way data should be structured for optimal reporting performance. The objective of dimensional modelling is to allow the user to visualise the data without the need to write a new query over the database for each report. The visual layout of the tables in the following image (which includes exactly the same data you just imported) helps you see why it is called a star schema.

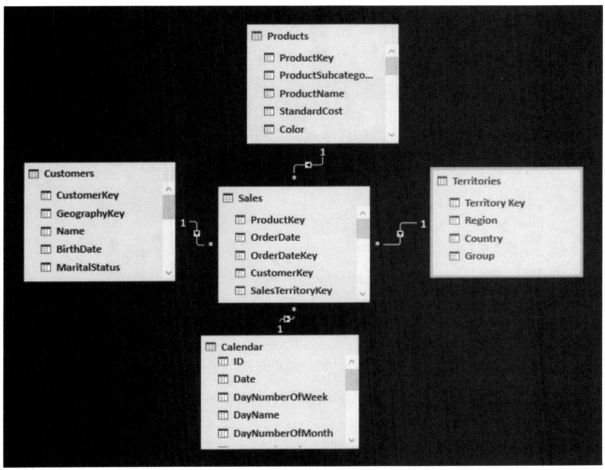

In this schema, data tables (only one, `Sales`, in this example) are surrounded by lookup tables (`Customers`, `Products`, `Territories`, and `Calendar` in this example), and together they visually make a star shape. You can find more comprehensive coverage of this topic in Chapter 6.

The Visual Layout of Tables in the Diagram View

When it comes to visually positioning tables in the Power Pivot Diagram view, I teach Excel users to position the tables in such a way that the lookup tables are located at the top of the window and the data tables are located at the bottom of the window (as shown below).

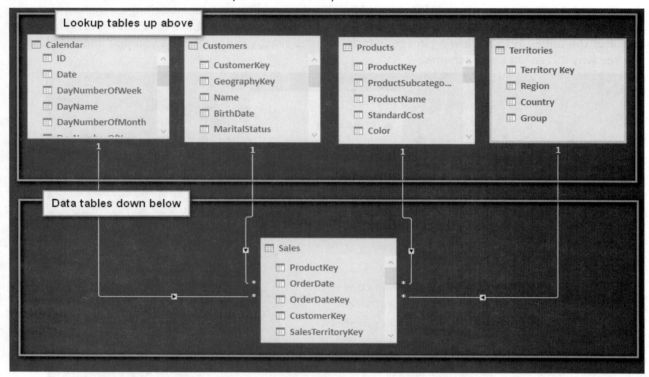

Note: There is no one correct way to shape your data, but using the star schema is the recommended approach. However, other shapes work, too. For example, you can use a snowflake schema (Google it), with secondary lookup tables joined to the primary lookup tables; however, the extra relationships can come at the cost of degraded performance and possibly also confusion to users, particularly if they are building their own reports using your data model.

If you compare the last two images above, you will see that they have exactly the same logical relationship (links) between the tables: *They are both star schemas*, even though they have different visual layouts.

The visual layout in the second image, the one just above, is the one developed and recommended by Rob Collie, and I call it the "Collie layout methodology." The Collie layout methodology involves placing the lookup tables at the top of the window and the data tables at the bottom. The importance of this for business users learning Power Pivot will become evident later in the book. For now, just trust me and do follow the Collie layout methodology.

Understanding the Two Types of Tables: Lookup Tables and Data Tables

In the IT world, lookup tables are referred to as *dimension tables*, and data tables are called *fact tables*. For business users, though, I suggest using the terminology *lookup tables* and *data tables*.

A data table contains transactional information. In this book, the data table contains sales transactions. Lookup tables contain information about logical groups of objects, such as customers, products, time (`'Calendar'`), etc.

Before Power Pivot and Power BI, an Excel user needed to create one big flat table in Excel before creating a pivot table. Often that meant writing VLOOKUP() formulas to bring data from other tables into the one allowed big flat table. It is no longer necessary to bring data from the lookup tables into the data tables by using VLOOKUP(). Instead, you can simply load the lookup tables and join them with a relationship.

Lookup Tables

You should have one lookup table for each "object" that you need for reporting purposes. For example, in the data being used here, these objects are customers, products, territories, and time (i.e., the Calendar table). A key feature of a lookup table is that it contains one and only one row for each individual item in the table, and it has as many columns as needed to describe the object.

So, there is only one row for each unique customer in the Customers table. The Customers table has lots of columns describing each customer—such as customer number (key), customer name, customer address, etc.—but there is only one row for each customer. Each row is unique, based on the customer number, and no duplicates of customer number (key) are allowed.

Data Tables

It is possible to have many data tables, but there is only one in this example: the Sales table. This data table contains lots of rows (more than 60,000 in this case) and all the transactional records of sales that occurred over several years. Importantly, the data table can be joined to each of the lookup tables. In this case, the Sales table contains one column (technically called a *foreign key*) that matches each of the keys in each lookup table (technically called a *primary key*). Stated differently, the Sales data table has four foreign key columns: a date, a customer number, a product number, and a territory key. These columns allow the Sales data table to be logically joined to each of the lookup tables.

Ideally, data tables should have very few columns but as many rows as needed to bring in all the data records. Data tables normally have lots of rows (sometimes in the tens of millions or even billions).

The Shaping Bottom Line

When it comes to shaping data, you need to remember the following:

- There are two types of tables: *data tables*, which contain the data you want to analyse, and *lookup tables*, which contain metadata about the objects you are going to analyse, such as the name, address, and city of each customer.

- The rule of thumb is to load one table for each object. This is both efficient for the database to process and easy for users to understand.

- The optimal way to shape your data is to use a star schema, but other schemas, such as a snowflake schema, can work, too, though they may be less efficient.

- For business users, it is best to position tables in Power Pivot Diagram view, using the Collie layout methodology. (You'll learn more about why you should do this in Chapter 5.)

Here's How: Making Changes to a Table That Is Already Loaded

Say that you want to make two changes to the Calendar table. First, you only want to bring in dates for the years 2002 and 2003. Second, you want to remove the fiscal date columns from the table. The following steps walk you through how to use Power Query to make changes like these to a table that is already loaded:

1. If necessary, navigate to the Excel window and locate the Queries & Connections pane on the right side of the window. If you can't see it, you can make it visible by clicking Data (see #1 below), Queries & Connections (#2).

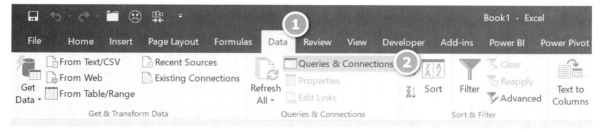

2. In the Queries & Connections pane, right-click the Calendar table and select Edit. The Query Editor window opens.

3. Locate the `CalendarYear` column (see #1 below). Deselect years 2001 and 2004 (#2 and #3) and then click OK.

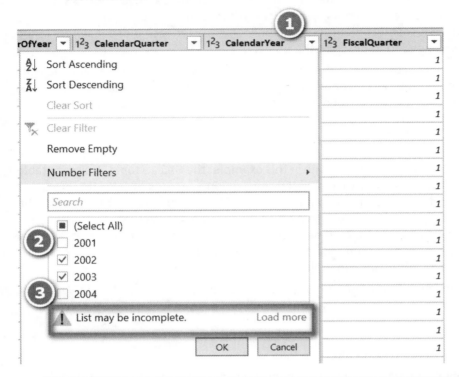

Note: Note the message "List may be incomplete" and also the Load More hyperlink. It is very common to see this in Power Query. Power Query only ever loads a sample or records; hence, it provides a warning that there may be other options that are not visible on the screen (calendar years, in this case). You can click the Load More hyperlink to force Power Query to load all possible records, but it may take a few seconds (or even minutes) to load all the possible values.

4. Remove the columns `FiscalQuarter` and `FiscalYear`. To do so, multi-select these two columns (see #1 below) by holding down Shift or Ctrl, right-clicking, and selecting Remove Columns (#2).

5. Click OK.

6. Navigate to the `FiscalYear` column, right-click (see #1 below), and then select Remove Columns (#2).

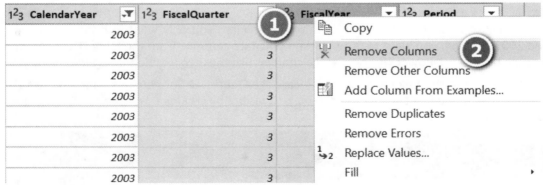

7. Click Close & Load.

8. Save the workbook.

Note: In this section and for the rest of this book, whenever I show changes to the loaded data, I always use the Power Query data load method.

Here's How: Deleting Steps in a Query

Now that you've seen how to make changes to a table that you have previously imported using Power Query, you're ready to get some practice. Go back and clear the filters you applied on the `CalendarYear` column because you need all the rows in the `Calendar` table for the practice exercises in this book. Clearing the filters is quite easy to do:

1. Edit the query for the `Calendar` table as before, by right-clicking the table and selecting Edit Query.
2. Click the X next to Filtered Rows under Applied Steps, as shown in the image below, to remove the step.
3. Click Delete when prompted.
4. Click Close & Load and then save the workbook.

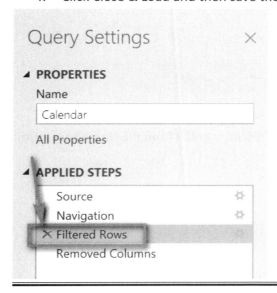

Here's How: Importing New Tables

The purpose of this exercise is to show you how to add new tables of data when needed. In this exercise, you will use Power Query to bring in the `ProductSubCategory` table from the original Access database and join it to your data model. Follow these steps:

1. In the Excel window, on the Data tab (see #1 below), click Recent Sources (#2) and then select the AdventureWorks Access database from the list and click Connect.

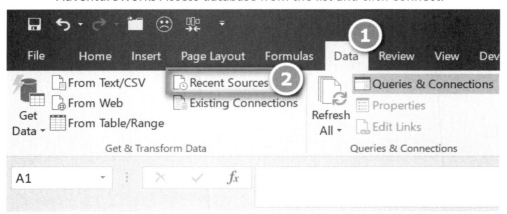

2. Select the `dimProductSubCategory` table (see #1 below) and click Edit (#2).

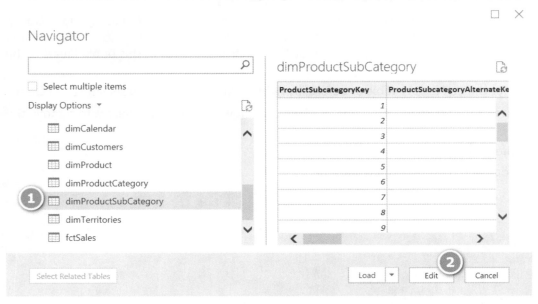

3. In the Query Settings pane on the right, remove the `dimProduct` prefix from the Name box, so you are left with the friendly name `SubCategory`.

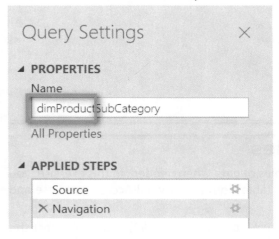

4. This time, instead of clicking Close & Load, click Close & Load To.

5. In the dialog that appears (shown below), select Only Create Connection (see #1 below), select Add This Data to the Data Model (#2), and then click OK.

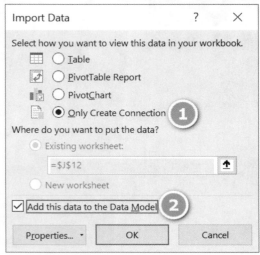

Note: At this writing, the load experience is different (and inconsistent) depending on whether you have checked Select Multiple Items or not and whether you then click Load or Edit. If at any time you want to change where the data is loaded, simply right-click the query (in the Query and Connections pane on the right of Excel), select Load To, and then change the load parameters in the dialog, as shown above.

6.   Switch to the Diagram view of the Power Pivot window. `SubCategory` is a lookup table of the `Products` table, so if you're using the Collie layout methodology, place the `SubCategory` table above the `Products` table, as shown below. Create a relationship between `Products[Product-SubcategoryKey]` and `SubCategory[ProductSubcategoryKey]`.

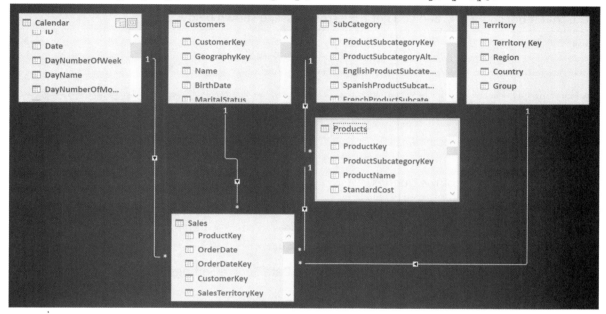

7.   Save the workbook.

Note: Now that there is a second lookup table (`SubCategory`) connected to another lookup table (`Products`), this is technically a snowflake schema. It will work, but it can be less efficient than a star schema. In addition, this shape can be confusing to users of the report because it does not follow the "one object, one table" rule; there are two tables that contain information about products. It is not wrong to do it this way. It is just a guideline to try to build models that follow the "one object, one table" rule where possible to keep things fast and easy to understand.

8.   Delete this `SubCategory` table now because you won't need it again. To do so, switch back to Excel, navigate to the Queries & Connections pane, right-click the `SubCategory` query, and select Delete.

Here's How: Changing the File Location of an Existing Connection

It's important to know how to move an Access database to a new location and then point the existing data connection to the new location. You need to do this, for example, if you ever send an Excel workbook that used Power Query as well as the data source to another user or if you need to change your file locations on your own computer.

The data connections you create in Power Query are relative to your computer. When you send a workbook and data source to another user, that person will have to edit the data connection so that it will work on his or her own PC.

Note: You need to follow the steps in this section only if you send *both* a workbook *and* a data source to another user. But that is not normally what you do. Normally you just distribute a workbook and not the data source.

To simulate what can happen when a file location changes, first move the Access database to a new location so the existing query cannot find it. Then you can proceed to change the file location of the existing connection to the new location. Follow these steps:

1.   In Windows Explorer, create a new folder.

2.   Navigate to your Access database and move it into the new folder you just created.

3.   Try to refresh one of your queries in the Queries & Connections pane, right-click, and select Refresh. Note that it doesn't work, and you get the error message shown below.

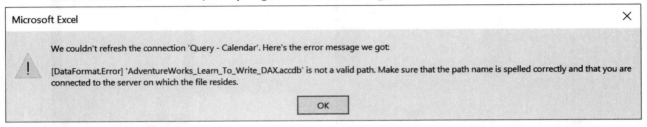

4.   Click OK.

5.   Right-click and edit one of the queries.

Note: The Query Editor keeps a cached copy of the data in the tables. When you first go into the Query Editor, the tables may seem fine. If you click Refresh Preview, Refresh All, the Query Editor tries to refresh the cache, and then you see error messages.

6.   Click File (see #1 below), Options and Settings (#2), Data Source Settings (#3).

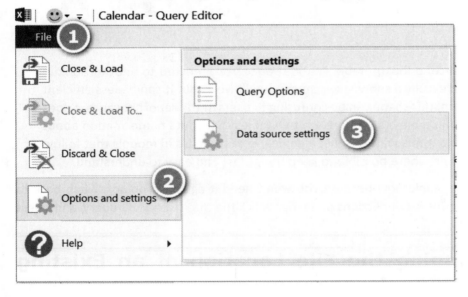

7. Select the data source that relates to the Access database (see #1 below) and then click Change Source (#2).

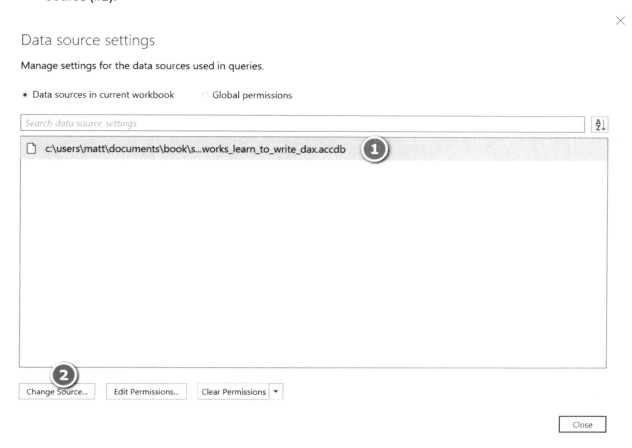

8. Click Browse (see #1 below), locate the new file location, and then click OK (#2) when you're done.

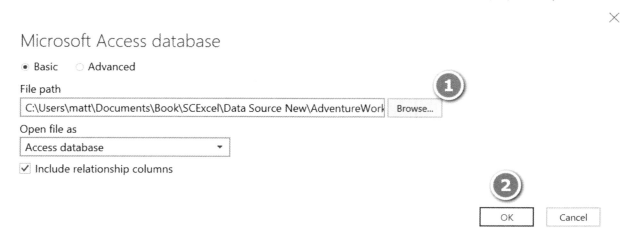

9. Click Close and then click Close & Load.

10. When the queries finish refreshing, save the workbook.

Here's How: Inserting a New Pivot Table

Now that you have data loaded into the Power Pivot data model, it is time to create a simple report. This is normally done via a pivot table. Follow these steps to insert a new pivot table:

1.   In the Excel window, select Insert, Pivot Table.

2.   In the Create PivotTable dialog box, make sure that Use This Workbook's Data Model is selected (see #1 below) and then click OK (#2).

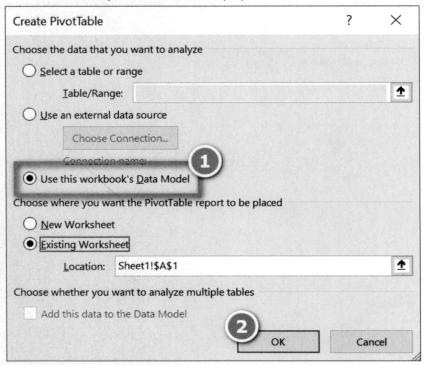

3.   The PivotTable Fields list appears on the right of the Excel worksheet that contains the new pivot table. Note that multiple tables are visible in the PivotTable Fields list. This is an indication that the pivot table is connected to a data model. A traditional Excel pivot table has only a single table visible in the PivotTable Fields list.

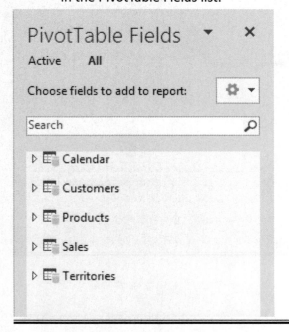

3: Concept: Measures

Measures have been around for many years in the enterprise versions of Microsoft BI tools, such as SQL Server Analysis Services. There is nothing confusing or hard to learn about measures. A *measure* is simply a DAX formula that instructs Power Pivot to do a calculation on data. In a sense, a measure is a lot like a formula in a cell in Excel. The main difference, however, between a formula in a cell in Excel and a measure is that a measure always operates over the entire data model, not over just a few cells in a spreadsheet. You'll learn more about this later, but for now you can just think of a measure as a formula that calculates a result from the loaded data.

> **Note:** The term *measure* has a bit of a chequered history in Power Pivot for Excel. In Excel 2010, which provided the first release of Power Pivot, Microsoft used the term *measure*. In Excel 2013, the second release, Microsoft changed the name *measure* to *calculated field*. Thankfully, in Excel 2016, Microsoft reversed its decision and used the term *measure* again, and it seems to be sticking with that.

Techniques for Writing DAX Measures

There are three places you can write DAX measures:

- You can write a measure in the formula bar in the Power Pivot window, as shown below. If you use this method, you must specify the measure name followed by a colon and then the formula. Note that there can be no spaces between the measure name, the colon, and the equals sign.

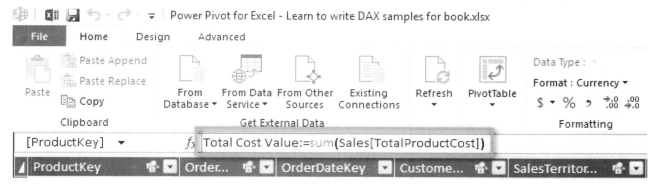

- You can write and edit measures in any empty cell in the calculation area at the bottom of the Power Pivot window, as shown below. Note that you need to use a colon here, too.

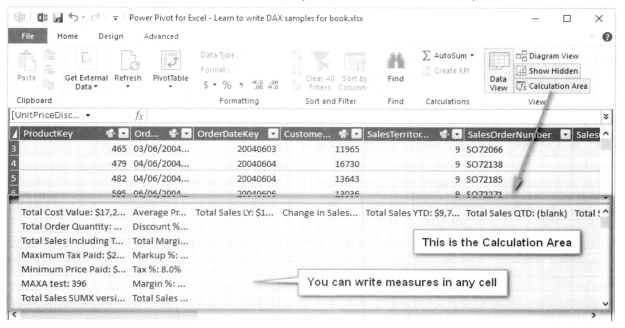

- You can write measures in the Measure dialog in Excel, as shown below. You can open this dialog from within Excel by navigating to the Power Pivot tab (see #1 below) and clicking on the Measures button (#2) and then New Measure (#3).

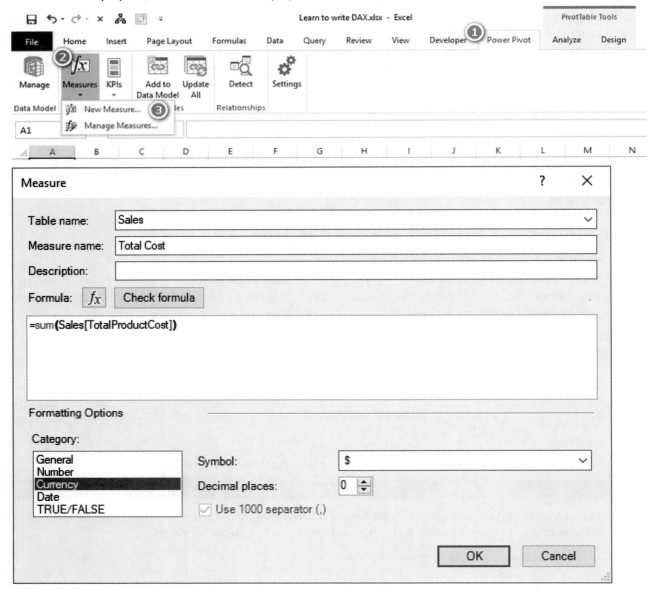

In general, Excel users should write DAX in the Measure dialog box in Excel. And it is normally best to first create a pivot table that provides some context for a measure you are about to write. If you do it this way, you immediately see the measure in a pivot table when you click OK, which gives you immediate feedback about whether the formula is written correctly (i.e., it gives you the results you are expecting).

Here's How: Writing Measures

The approach to writing new measures described here is what I recommend for Excel users. Until you get the hang of it, this procedure for creating measures will be foreign, so be sure to practice. Follow these steps:

1. Create a new blank pivot table connected to your data model (or use an existing one if you already have something appropriate).

2. Add some relevant data to the rows in your pivot table. For the sample database used in this book, I suggest that you go to the Products table and place [Category] on Rows in the pivot table (see #1 below).

3. Click inside the pivot table, navigate to the Power Pivot tab, click the Measures button (#2), and then select New Measure (#3). The Measure dialog appears.

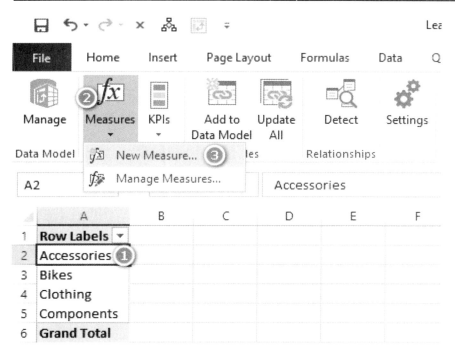

Tip: You should use the following steps and the Measure dialog shown below as a process flow/guide. If you don't do this, you risk missing one or more of the steps. Missing a step will end up costing you time and causing rework. Get in the good habit of following the process steps I describe here, using the dialog to remind you of all the steps. Always follow the order outlined here.

4. In the Table Name drop-down (see #1 below), select where your measure will be stored. You should place the measure in the table the data comes from. In this case, the "data" you are using is in the `Sales[ExtendedAmount]` column, which is in the `Sales` table, so select Sales from the Table Name drop-down.

5. In the Measure Name text box (#2), give the new measure a meaningful, unique name, such as `Total Sales`.

Note: In the examples in this book, you should use the names I tell you to use. When you are writing your own DAX with your own data in the future, you should use descriptive, meaningful names (including spaces). Don't try to abbreviate a name like `Total Sales` as `TS` as doing so will cause you or others confusion down the track.

6. In the Formula box (#3) write the DAX formula.

7. Click Check Formula (#4) to check whether the formula you wrote is syntactically correct. Fix any errors, if needed.

8. Select an appropriate formatting option from the Category list (#5) and make suitable selections for Symbol and Decimal Places in the area to the right of the Category list.

9. Click OK to save the new measure (#6).

Note: I generally don't enter anything in the Description box, but it is there for you to use if you like. It's for reference only and doesn't impact the behaviour of the formulas.

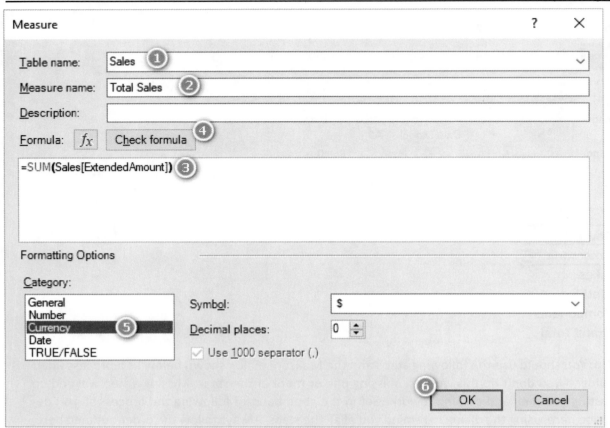

10. After you click OK, you get immediate feedback about whether everything is working as you expect, as shown below.

	A	B
1	**Row Labels** ▾	**Total Sales**
2	Accessories	$700,760
3	Bikes	$28,318,145
4	Clothing	$339,773
5	**Grand Total**	**$29,358,677**

Remember that following this step-by-step procedure will save you time because you will not have to go back and fix things you missed. Practice doing it this way right from the start, and you will develop good habits that will serve you well in the future.

Avoiding Implicit Measures

You can create a measure by dragging a column from a table and dropping it in the Values section of the Pivot-Table Fields list, as shown below. When you do this, you create what is called an *implicit measure*. This is the way you always had to do it with traditional pivot tables; there was no other option. However, I recommend that you avoid doing this when using Power Pivot.

There are several reasons to avoid creating implicit measures:

- The name of the implicit measure that Excel generates for you is not very helpful. For example, as shown below, Excel generates the field name [Sum of ExtendedAmount], which is not nearly as helpful or clear as a name like [Total Sales] that you explicitly write yourself.

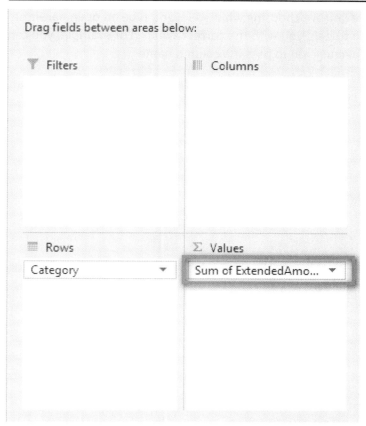

- No formatting is applied when you drag to create an implicit measure.
- Drag and drop works only with SUM and COUNT (i.e., the count is automatically applied when you drag and drop a text column into the Values section). If you want anything else (e.g., AVERAGE), you have to edit the settings anyway.
- You won't learn how to write good DAX if you let Excel create implicit measures for you.

So, do yourself a favour and don't drag and drop your table columns when writing DAX. Of course, if you just want a quick look at a field for some testing, then doing this is fine. But undo the change immediately after you have taken a look. If you want to keep a measure, write it from scratch using your DAX skills.

Here's How: Using IntelliSense

When you type in a DAX formula in the Measure dialog, I recommend that you learn to leverage the IntelliSense tooltips that appear. The following steps show how this works:

1. Click in an existing pivot table (the one you created earlier is fine, or you can create a new one) and then create a new measure and name it Test.

2. In the Formula box, click just after the equals sign (which is already there by default).

3. To enter the SUM function, start typing **sum** (case doesn't matter here). After you have finished typing these three letters *but before you type a parenthesis*, Excel displays an IntelliSense tooltip that provides a description of the function (see below). These tooltips often contain information that is valuable, particularly while you are learning.

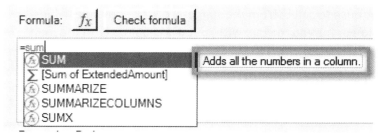

4. After reading the tooltip and making sure you are choosing what you want, type an open parenthesis, (, or press Tab. A new tooltip pops up to help you with the correct syntax. For example, you can see that the function shown below is expecting you to pass it a column name.

Measure

Table name:	Sales
Measure name:	Test
Description:	
Formula:	f_x Check formula

=sum(
SUM(**ColumnName**)

5. Start to type in the name of the column—in this case, **Ex** for ExtendedAmount. You see two columns appear in the tooltip list, as shown below.

Measure   ?   ✕

Table name:	Sales
Measure name:	Test
Description:	
Formula:	f_x Check formula

=SUM(ex
SUM(**ColumnName**)
   [ExtendedAmount]
   Sales[ExtendedAmount]

6. In this case, the two items in the tooltip list are the same column but expressed differently in the list; they are both the ExtendedAmount column in the Sales table. It is best practice in DAX to always type the table name before every column name inside your formulas, so use the up and down arrow keys to select the second item in the list, Sales[ExtendedAmount].

Note: Personally, I think this is poor design in the UI. You should never refer to a column name without specifying the table name. As a result, the UI should never allow you to select the column name without the table name. Maybe Microsoft will fix this someday.

7. Press Tab to select the column that includes the table name.

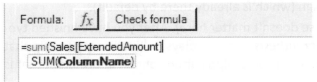

Formula: f_x Check formula

=sum(Sales[ExtendedAmount]
   SUM(**ColumnName**)

Tip: Try to use the keyboard and not the mouse to select from the suggested list of possible values, particularly if the list is short. It may be slower for you to start with, but it will be faster in the long run if you learn to do it this way.

8. Close the formula by typing **)** and then click Check Formula.

If you practice writing your DAX this way, you will become very fast very quickly. Stick with it until doing this seems like second nature.

Here's How: Editing Measures

It is easy to go back and edit (or simply review) measures after you have written them. Follow these steps from within Excel:

1. On the Power Pivot tab, click Measures (see #1 below) and then Manage Measures (#2) to see a list of all of the measures you have created.

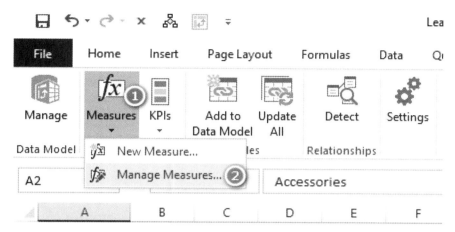

2. The Manage Measures dialog appears, as shown below.

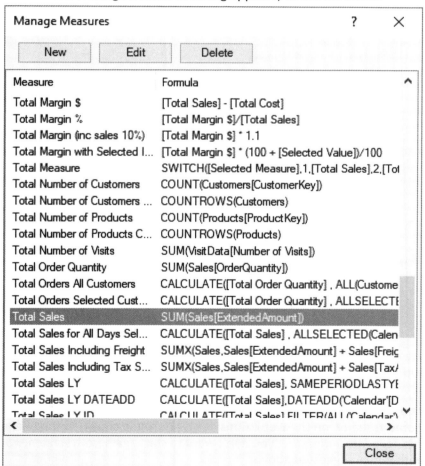

3. Use the Manage Measures dialog to create, edit, and delete any measures, as needed.

> **Note:** You can also edit an individual measure quickly by finding the measure in the PivotTable Fields list, right-clicking it, and selecting Edit.

What to Do When Something Goes Wrong Writing DAX

At some point, you will start the process of creating a new measure, and something will go wrong. For one reason or another, you will need to stop what you are doing and go back into Excel. This can be a problem for two reasons:

- The Measure dialog box is *modal*, so while it is open, you can't do anything else until you dismiss this box.
- The formula you add must be valid DAX; otherwise, it can create problems. Sometimes you can't even close the dialog if the DAX is not valid.

In such cases, you may lose the work you have already done (e.g., the steps you have already completed, such as selecting the table, typing the name of the formula, selecting the formatting), and you may even have the DAX formula half written. But because the formula is incorrect, you can't save it! There are two tricks to handling this problem, depending on how deep you are in the process.

The first trick can be used when you don't have any meaningful DAX that you want to save but you have already selected the table, typed the name of the formula, etc. In this case, simply enter =1 in the formula section, as shown below.

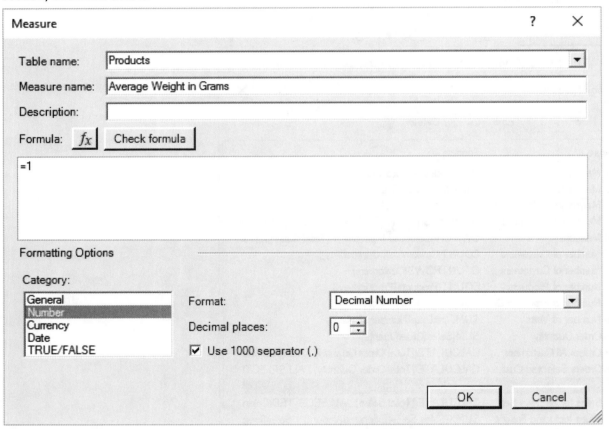

When you do this, the formula is saved with the name, table selection, and formatting. You can come back any time you are ready and edit the formula.

You use the second trick when you are having problems writing your formula, and you want to come back to it later (e.g., maybe you need to do some research on the web). Consider the formula shown in the image below as an example. Once you are this deep into a measure, you don't want to start again from scratch, nor do you want to replace the formula with =1, as suggested above.

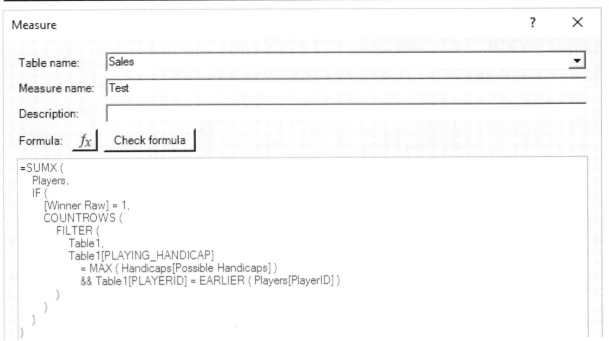

There is a simple solution to this problem, and it leverages the fact that DAX can return text results to a pivot table. If you need to suspend writing this measure midstream, simply wrap the formula in double quotes, as shown below.

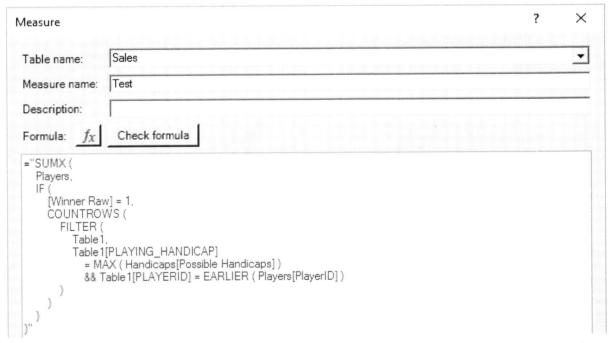

DAX then treats the entire formula as a text constant and allows you to save the formula. You can later come back and change the formula after you have had a chance to do your research.

The only time this doesn't work is when you have a genuine need to use double quotes in the formula, as in this example:

```
=CALCULATE([Total Number of Customers], Customers[Gender] = "M")
```

In this case, you can temporarily replace the double quotes in your formula with single quotes and then wrap the whole thing in double quotes, like this:

```
="CALCULATE([Total Number of Customers], Customers[Gender] = 'M')"
```

You can reverse these changes when you are ready to re-edit the measure.

4: DAX Topic: SUM(), COUNT(), COUNTROWS(), MIN(), MAX(), COUNTBLANK(), and DIVIDE()

This chapter starts out with some basic DAX formulas to get you started. Most of the DAX functions in this chapter accept a column as the only parameter—for example, =FORMULA(*ColumnName*). The exceptions are =COUNTROWS(*Table*), which takes a table (not a column) as the parameter, and DIVIDE(), which I cover later in the chapter.

All the functions in this chapter except DIVIDE() are *aggregation functions*, or *aggregators*. That is, they take inputs from a column or table and somehow aggregate the contents (differently for each formula).

Think about the column Sales[ExtendedAmount], which has more than 60,000 rows of data. You can't simply put the entire column into a pivot table because the pivot table can't "fit" a column with more than 60,000 values into a single cell on the spreadsheet.

The following example shows a DAX formula that uses a "naked" column, without any aggregation function. This does not work when you're writing a regular measure, as indicated by the error message shown below.

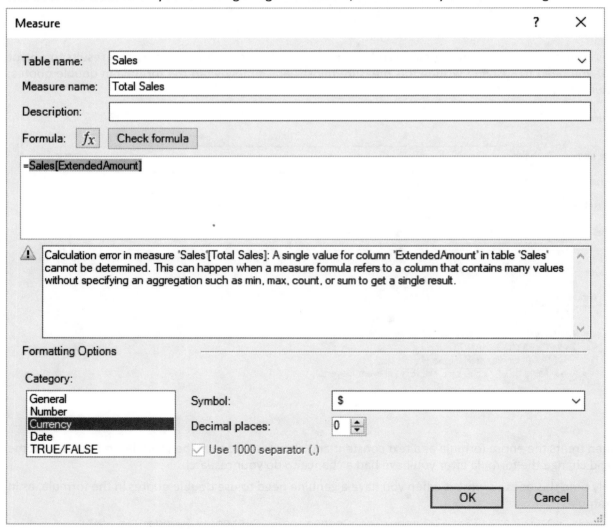

You have to tell Power Pivot how to aggregate the data from this column so that it returns just a single value to each cell in the pivot table. All the aggregators in this chapter effectively convert a column of values into a single value.

The correct way to write this measure is shown below.

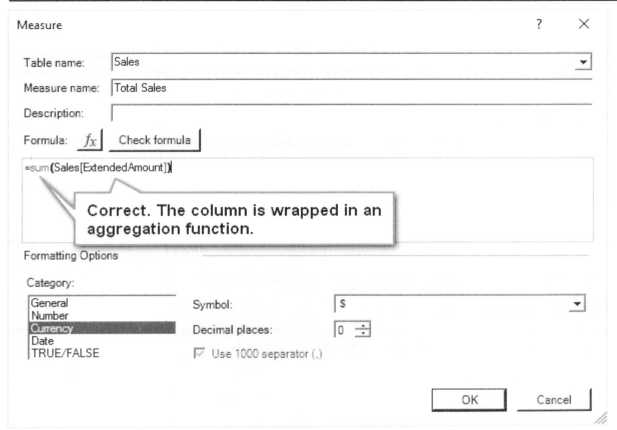

Did you notice that this example uses the table name and the column name in the formula? Remember that this is best practice.

Note: Always refer to the table name *and* the column name when writing DAX. Never refer to a column without specifying the table name first. You will understand why I say this shortly.

Reusing Measures

One important capability in DAX is that you can reuse measures when writing other measures. Say that you create a new measure called [Total Sales]. Once this measure exists in the Power Pivot data model, it can be referenced and reused inside other measures. For example, after creating the measure [Total Sales], you could use the following formula to create a new measure for 10% tax on the sale of goods:

```
Total Tax = [Total Sales] * 0.1
```

Note that the new measure [Total Tax] is a calculation based on the original measure [Total Sales] multiplied by 0.1.

It is good practice to reuse measures inside other measures.

Note: I did not add the table name in front of the measure name above. That is, I wrote [Total Sales] and not Sales[Total Sales]. Although you should always add the table name in front of a column (for example, Sales[ExtendedAmount]), it is best practice to omit the table name before a measure. The reason for doing it this way is that a reader can look at Sales[ExtendedAmount] and [Total Sales] and immediately tell that the first is a column and the second is a measure simply by the existence (or not) of the table name.

Writing DAX

It's time to start to write some DAX of your own to get some practice. When I say *write*, I mean sit in front of your PC, open your workbook with the data from Chapter 1 loaded, and really write some DAX. Especially if you have never written formulas using these functions, you should physically do it now, as you read this section. Imagining yourself doing it is not enough.

If you haven't already done so, go ahead and load the test data by following the steps in Chapter 1. Once it is loaded and prepared, you are ready to create the new measures in the following practice exercises. The first measure you will write is the same one from "Here's How: Using IntelliSense" in Chapter 3.

Practice Exercises

Periodically throughout the rest of this book, you will find practice exercises that are designed to help you learn by doing. You should complete each exercise as you get to it. The answers to all these practice exercises are provided in Appendix A.

Practice Exercises: SUM()

Try to write DAX formulas for the following measures without looking back at how to do so. If you can't do it, refer to Chapter 3 and then give it another go. Remember that you are here to practice! You can find the solutions to these practice exercises in Appendix A.

Write DAX formulas for the following columns, using SUM() for each one.

1. [Total Sales]

You should have already written this measure earlier in this book. If not, write a new measure that is the total of the sales in the ExtendedAmount column from the Sales table now.

	A	B
1	Row Labels ▾	Total Sales
2	Accessories	$700,760
3	Bikes	$28,318,145
4	Clothing	$339,773
5	**Grand Total**	$29,358,677

2. [Total Cost]

Create a measure that is the sum of one of the cost columns in the Sales table. This measure uses exactly the same structure as the [Total Sales] measure from Practice Exercise 1, but it adds the cost of the product instead of the sales amount. You can use any of the product cost columns in the Sales table; all the cost columns are the same in this sample database.

3. [Total Margin $]

Create a new measure for total margin, which is total sales minus total cost. Make sure you reuse the two measures you created above in this new measure.

4. [Total Margin %]

Create a new measure that expresses the total margin from Practice Exercise 3 as a percentage of total sales. Once again, reuse the measures you created above. I don't cover the DIVIDE() function until later in this chapter, but you can try to work out how to use it with the help of the IntelliSense if you like.

5. [Total Sales Tax Paid]

Create a measure for total sales tax paid. Look for a tax column in the Sales table and add up the total for that column.

6. [Total Sales Including Tax]

The [Total Sales] measure from Practice Exercise 1 excludes tax, so you need to add two measures together to get this total.

7. [Total Order Quantity]

This is similar to the other measures, but this time you add up the quantities purchased. Look for the correct column in the `Sales` table.

How Did It Go?

As you worked through the practice exercises, did you do the following?

- Did you create a pivot table first and put `Products[Category]` on Rows in your pivot table (or something else on Rows that is appropriate for these measures)? This is best practice for Excel users because you get immediate feedback after you write your measure; you can *see* the results.

- Did you reference all columns in your measures in the format *TableName[ColumnName]* (i.e., always reference the table name)? You should never reference a column in DAX without first specifying the table name; always use the table name and the column name.

- Did you use the Measure dialog box as your process flow prompt, filling each step along the way without skipping any steps? Using this dialog box, shown again below, is a great way to make sure you don't miss anything.

- Did you click the Check Formula button before clicking OK? At this writing, Power Pivot is a bit clunky and sensitive to incorrect syntax. Clicking OK when there is an error with the formula can create errors in your workbook, including pivot table errors and even workbook corruption. It's much better to get it right before you click OK, so get in the habit of *always* using the Check Formula button, even for very basic formulas.

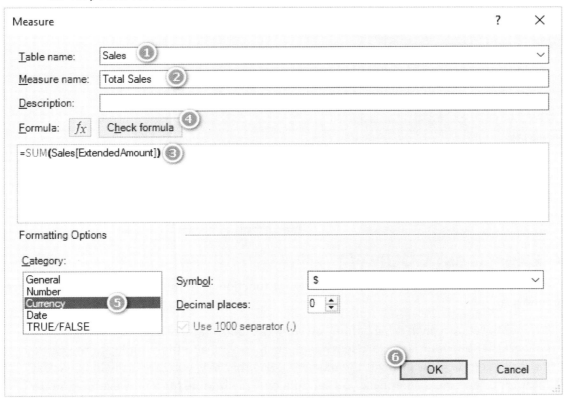

- Did you put the measures in the `Sales` table? The rule is that you should always put a measure in the table the data comes from. As you can see above, `[Total Sales]` is a formula that adds up the column `Sales[ExtendedAmount]`. This column of data is in the `Sales` table, so this is where you put the measure.

- Did you use the keyboard and look at the IntelliSense when you typed the measures? Try not to use the mouse. It may be faster now (for some people), but relying on the mouse will prevent you from getting faster in the future. Learn to use the keyboard and follow the process covered in the section "Here's How: Using IntelliSense."

Remember that the answers to all the exercises in this book are available in Appendix A. Try to avoid peeking at the appendix when you should be thinking and typing. If you do the thinking now, you will learn how to do it, and that will pay you back in spades in the future.

Okay, it's time to move on with a new DAX formula.

The COUNT( ) Function

As you write the formula shown below using COUNT(), take the time to look again at how IntelliSense can help you write DAX.

Remember that whenever you type a new formula, you can pause, and IntelliSense shows the syntax for the function, along with a description of the function. The description includes some very useful information. For example, in the figure below, the tooltip says that this function "counts the numbers in a column." This gives you three very useful pieces of information. You've probably already worked out the first one: It counts. In addition, this tooltip tells you that the function counts *numbers* and also that the numbers need to be in a *column*. This should be enough information about the COUNT() function for you to write some measures using it.

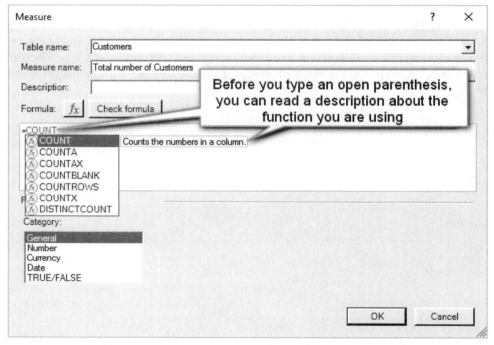

Practice Exercises: COUNT( )

Now it is time to write some DAX formulas using the COUNT() function. Find the solutions to these practice exercises in Appendix A.

> **Note:** Don't forget to set up a pivot table before you work the following exercises. A good approach is to give the worksheet in your last exercise a name, such as SUM, and then duplicate the worksheet for this next exercise, now giving it the name COUNT. This way, you can easily look back at your work later for a refresher. Whenever you set up a new pivot table for a new exercise, make sure you have something meaningful on Rows, such as Products[Category].
>
> Look at the image in "How Did It Go?" after the practice exercises below if you are not sure how to set up the pivot table.

8. [Total Number of Products]

Use the Products lookup table when writing this measure. Just count how many product numbers there are. Product numbers and product keys are the same thing in this example.

9. [Total Number of Customers]

Use the `Customers` lookup table. Again, just count the customer numbers. Customer numbers and customer keys are the same thing in this example.

How Did It Go?

Did you end up with the following pivot table?

	A	B	C
1	Row Labels ▾	Total Number of Customers	Total Number of Products
2	Accessories	18,484	35
3	Bikes	18,484	125
4	Clothing	18,484	48
5	Components	18,484	189
6	**Grand Total**	**18,484**	**397**

If not, check your answers against those in Appendix A.

> **Note:** The pivot table above is a bit confusing because [Total Number of Customers] doesn't seem to be correct. It is returning the same value for every row in the pivot table, and this is not something you are used to seeing. But if you think about it, it actually does make sense. You are not counting how many customers purchased these product categories; you are counting the number of customers in the customer master table, and the number of customers doesn't change based on the product categories; the customers are either in the master table or not. (You'll learn more about this in Chapter 5.)

Did you get any errors that you weren't expecting? Did you use the correct column(s) in your measures? Remember from the tooltip above that the COUNT() function counts numbers. It doesn't count text fields, so if you try to count the names or descriptions, you get an error.

The COUNTROWS() Function

Let's move on to a new function, COUNTROWS(). I personally prefer to use COUNTROWS() instead of COUNT(). It just seems more natural to me. These functions are not exactly the same, even though they can be used interchangeably at times. If you use COUNT() with *TableName*[*ColumnName*] and the column is missing a number in one of the rows (for some reason), then that row won't get counted. COUNTROWS() counts every row in the table, regardless of whether the columns have a value in every row. So be careful and make sure you select the best formula for the task at hand.

Practice Exercises: COUNTROWS()

For these exercises, rewrite the two measures from Practice Exercises 8 and 9 using COUNTROWS() instead of COUNT(). Find the solutions to these practice exercises in Appendix A.

10. [Total Number of Products COUNTROWS Version]

Count the number of products in the `Products` table, using the COUNTROWS() function.

11. [Total Number of Customers COUNTROWS Version]

Count the number of customers in the `Customers` table, using the COUNTROWS() function.

How Did It Go?

Not surprisingly, for Practice Exercises 10 and 11, you should get the same answers you got with COUNT (),
as shown below.

	A	B	C
1	Row Labels ▼	Total Number of Customers COUNTROWS version	Total Number of Products COUNTROWS version
2	Accessories	18,484	35
3	Bikes	18,484	125
4	Clothing	18,484	48
5	Components	18,484	189
6	Grand Total	18,484	397

A Word on Naming Measures

You may have noticed that I sometimes use very long and descriptive names for measures. I encourage you
to make measure names as long as they need to be to make it clear what the measures actually are. You
will be grateful you did down the track, when you are trying to work out the fine difference between two
similar-sounding measures.

Here's How: Changing Display Names in Pivot Tables

It is possible to change the display name of a measure once it is in a pivot table. Here are the steps:

1. Select the measure name in the pivot table (see #1 below).

2. Change the name in the formula bar in Excel (#2). Doing this does not change the name of the actual
   measure, just the name that is displayed in your pivot table.

| B1 | ▼ | : | × | ✓ | fx ② Total Number of Customers COUNTROWS version |

	A ①	B	C
1	Row Labels ▼	Total Number of Customers COUNTROWS version	Total Number of Products COUNTROWS version
2	Accessories	18,484	35
3	Bikes	18,484	125
4	Clothing	18,484	48
5	Components	18,484	189
6	Grand Total	18,484	397

3. If you have renamed your measures Total Customers and Total Products, this is what you now see:

	A	B	C
1	Row Labels ▼	Total Customers	Total Products
2	Accessories	18,484	35
3	Bikes	18,484	125
4	Clothing	18,484	48
5	Components	18,484	189
6	Grand Total	18,484	397

4. After you have changed the display name, you can change it back by right-clicking on the name (see
   #1 below) and selecting Value Field Settings (#2).

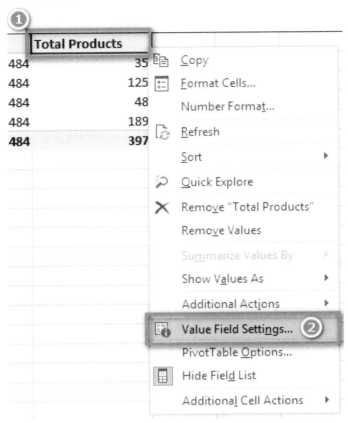

Then, in the Value Field Settings dialog, you can change the custom name back to the original name by setting the Custom Name text box to the same value as the Source Name text box above it—or any other name, for that matter.

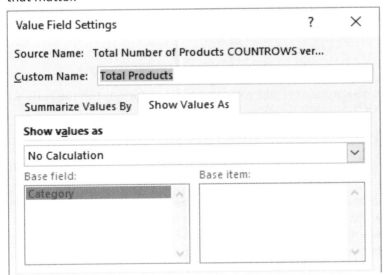

The method you've just seen is useful when you want a shorter name to appear in your pivot table. Sometimes the name of a measure will make sense only in certain situations (i.e., in certain pivot table layouts) and not in other pivot tables. However, if you want to keep using a longer descriptive name but just want to make it fit in the pivot table, you could use the VBA macro that Rob Collie has shared on his website to automatically wrap the names so they are more readable. Just go to http://powerpivotpro.com and search for "more readable pivots," and you will find it. I have this VBA code on my PC and a button on the Quick Access Toolbar to run the VBA code. This is a must-have Quick Access Toolbar button for serious Power Pivot users. **Note:** If you don't know how to use VBA tools that others make available, take a look at the blog post I wrote on this topic at http://xbi.com.au/vba.

The DISTINCTCOUNT() Function

DISTINCTCOUNT() counts each value in a column once and only once. If the value appears more than once in a column, it is still counted only once. Consider the Customers table: In this case, the customer key is unique, and by definition each customer key appears only once in the table. (Note that customer key and customer number are the same in this case.) So in this case, DISTINCTCOUNT() of the customer key in the Customers table gives you the same answer as COUNTROWS() of the Customers table. But if you were to do a DISTINCTCOUNT() of the customer key in the Sales table, you would actually be counting the total number of customers that had ever purchased something—which is not the same thing and may or may not give the same answer.

Practice Exercises: DISTINCTCOUNT()

To practice using DISTINCTCOUNT(), create a new pivot table and put Customers[Occupation] on Rows in the pivot table and [Total Sales] on Values. Then write the following measures using DISTINCT-COUNT(). Find the solutions to these practice exercises in Appendix A.

12. [Total Customers in Database DISTINCTCOUNT Version]

You need to count a column of unique values in the Customers table. Go ahead and write the measure now. When you are done, add the [Total Number of Customers] measure you created earlier to the pivot table as well. You should end up with a pivot table like the one below.

Row Labels ▼	Total Sales	Total Customers in Database Distinctcount version	Total Number of Customers
Clerical	$4,684,787	2,928	2,928
Management	$5,467,862	3,075	3,075
Manual	$2,857,971	2,384	2,384
Professional	$9,907,977	5,520	5,520
Skilled Manual	$6,440,081	4,577	4,577
Grand Total	$29,358,677	18,484	18,484

How Did It Go?

Did you get the same answer as above in the new measure? Did you remember to format the measure to something practical (e.g., a whole number with thousands separator)?

13. [Count of Occupation]

Create a new pivot table and put Customers[YearlyIncome] on Rows in the pivot table. Then create the measure [Count of Occupation].

Use DISTINCTCOUNT() to count the values in the Occupation column in the Customers table. You end up with a pivot table like the one shown below left. The way to read this pivot table is that there are customers in three different occupations that have incomes of 10,000, there are customers across four occupations that have incomes of 30,000, etc. (You'll learn about the conditional formatting shown below right in the next "Here's How.")

Row Labels ▼	Count of Occupation		Row Labels ▼	Count of Occupation
10000	3		10000	3
20000	3		20000	3
30000	4		30000	4
40000	4		40000	4
50000	3		50000	3
60000	3		60000	3

Here's How: Applying Conditional Formatting

It is much easier to read a pivot table if you apply some of the "out of the box" visualisations from standard Excel; for example, compare the pivot table above left with the conditionally formatted version above right. I am sure you agree that it is much easier to read the insights from the table on the right.

Next, I show you how to apply conditional formatting in a pivot table, step by step. If you do it the way I describe here, the formatting will be applied to the entire pivot table, and the formatting will update when the pivot table grows and shrinks. If you just select the cells and apply formatting directly to individual cells or groups of cells, the formatting will not update when the pivot table changes shape.

Follow these steps to apply this type of conditional formatting:

1. Highlight one of the cells that you want to receive the formatting (see #1 below).

2. On the Home tab in Excel, click Conditional Formatting (#2), Data Bars (#3) and select the visualisation effect you want to use (#4).

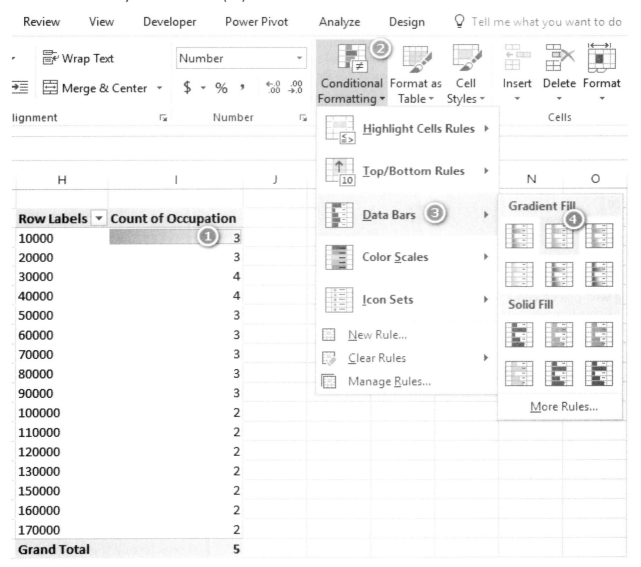

3. Click the formatting popup box that appears.

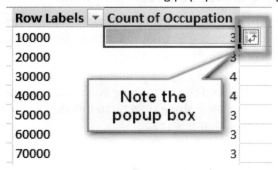

Row Labels ▼	Count of Occupation
10000	3
20000	3
30000	4
40000	4
50000	3
60000	3
70000	3

Note the popup box

4.   You are presented with three options for applying the formatting:

•   The first option is just for the current cell (see #1 below).

•   The second option allows you to apply the formatting to every row in the table *and* the grand total (#2). You should use this option only if the data in the rows *and* the grand total are similar in size and scale. For example, if your grand total has a value of 10,000 and the individual rows in the pivot table have a maximum value of 500, then this second option will not give you very useful results. A good example of when to use this second option is for "percentage change" measures.

•   The third option is the one you should use most often (#3). It applies the formatting to the rows only and *not to the grand total*. Why the third option is the best choice will make more sense when you get to some of the other examples later in the book.

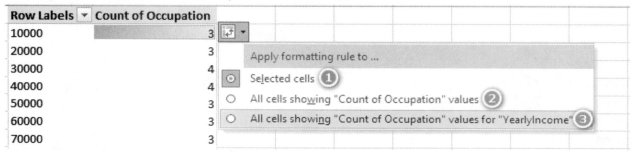

Row Labels ▼	Count of Occupation
10000	3
20000	3
30000	4
40000	4
50000	3
60000	3
70000	3

Apply formatting rule to …
- ⦿ Selected cells ①
- ◯ All cells showing "Count of Occupation" values ②
- ◯ All cells showing "Count of Occupation" values for "YearlyIncome" ③

Using well-placed conditional formatting is a great way to make your pivot tables easier to read and make the insights jump out, as shown below.

Row Labels ▼	Count of Occupation
10000	3
20000	3
30000	4
40000	4
50000	3
60000	3
70000	3
80000	3
90000	3
100000	2
110000	2
120000	2
130000	2
150000	2
160000	2
170000	2
Grand Total	**5**

Practice Exercises: DISTINCTCOUNT(), Cont.

The following exercises give you more practice using `DISTINCTCOUNT()`. Find the solutions to these practice exercises in Appendix A.

14. [Count of Country]

Create a new pivot table and put `Territories[Group]` on Rows. Write a new measure called `[Count of Country]`, using `DISTINCTCOUNT()` over the `Country` column in the `Territories` table. The pivot table below shows you how many countries exist in each sales group.

Row Labels ▼	Count of Country
Europe	3
NA	1
North America	2
Pacific	1
Grand Total	**7**

15. [Customers That Have Purchased]

Create a new pivot table and put `Products[SubCategory]` on Rows. Then, using `DISTINCTCOUNT()` on data from the `Sales` table, create the new measure `[Customers That Have Purchased]`.

If you haven't already done so, apply some conditional formatting to the pivot table, using the technique you learnt in the previous section, and then sort the column from largest to smallest. You can see below that Tires and Tubes has the largest number of customers that have purchased at least once.

Row Labels ↓	Customers That Have Purchased
Tires and Tubes	8,490
Road Bikes	6,397
Helmets	5,960
Bottles and Cages	4,548
Mountain Bikes	4,089
Jerseys	3,192
Touring Bikes	2,143
Caps	2,132
Fenders	2,110
Gloves	1,376
Shorts	1,019
Cleaners	875
Hydration Packs	719
Socks	559
Vests	557
Bike Racks	325
Bike Stands	243
Grand Total	**18,484**

Earlier in the chapter I explained the options to apply conditional formatting to just the rows in the pivot table or the rows and grand total. The conditional formatting in the pivot table above has been applied to the rows only. If I applied the conditional formatting to the grand total as well, the bar in the grand total would be significantly longer than all of the other bars in the pivot table, as you can see in the pivot table below.

Row Labels	↲	Customers That Have Purchased
Tires and Tubes		8,490
Road Bikes		6,397
Helmets		5,960
Bottles and Cages		4,548
Mountain Bikes		4,089
Jerseys		3,192
Touring Bikes		2,143
Caps		2,132
Fenders		2,110
Gloves		1,376
Shorts		1,019
Cleaners		875
Hydration Packs		719
Socks		559
Vests		557
Bike Racks		325
Bike Stands		243
Grand Total		18,484

When you apply this formatting to the grand total, it often makes the conditional formatting harder to read. This is why you normally want to select the third option for applying conditional formatting (see #3 below), particularly in the case where the grand total is an aggregation of the row items above.

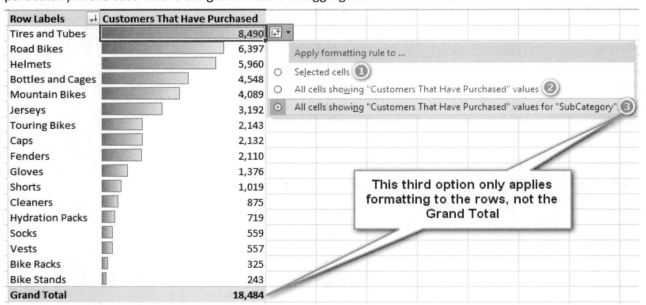

Now put 'Calendar'[CalendarYear] on Columns in your pivot table and notice how the pivot table changes. If you applied the conditional formatting as described in this section, the conditional formatting will "stick" to the pivot table, and it will automatically update as the shape of the pivot table changes.

Customers That Have Purchased	Column Labels ▾				
Row Labels ↓	2001	2002	2003	2004	Grand Total
Tires and Tubes			3,766	5,147	8,490
Road Bikes	840	2,062	2,558	2,369	6,397
Helmets			2,541	3,617	5,960
Bottles and Cages			1,903	2,744	4,548
Mountain Bikes	173	615	1,961	2,094	4,089
Jerseys			1,316	1,922	3,192
Touring Bikes			824	1,332	2,143
Caps			874	1,280	2,132
Fenders			879	1,236	2,110
Gloves			567	829	1,376
Shorts			435	584	1,019
Cleaners			376	509	875
Hydration Packs			300	425	719
Socks			246	317	559
Vests			205	354	557
Bike Racks			136	191	325
Bike Stands			117	129	243
Grand Total	1,013	2,677	9,309	11,377	18,484

Tip: When you wrote this measure, did you remember to select the Sales table as the location to store it? Best practice says to put the measure in the table the data comes from.

Practice Exercises: MAX(), MIN(), and AVERAGE()

MAX(), MIN(), and AVERAGE() are aggregators; that is, they take multiple values as input and return a single value to the pivot table. Create the following new measures. You should use the columns of data in the Sales table for these exercises. There are some additional pricing columns in the Products table, but these prices are only theoretical prices, or "list prices." In this sample data, the actual price information related to the transaction is stored in the Sales table.

Find the solutions to these practice exercises in Appendix A.

16. [Maximum Tax Paid on a Product]

Remember to use a suitable column from the Sales table and use the MAX() function.

17. [Minimum Price Paid for a Product]

Again, use a suitable column from the Sales table but this time use the MIN() function.

18. [Average Price Paid for a Product]

Again, use a suitable column from the Sales table but this time use the AVERAGE() function.

You should end up with a pivot table like the one shown below.

Row Labels ▾	Maximum Tax Paid on a Product	Minimum Price Paid for a Product	Average Price Paid for a Product
Accessories	$12.72	$2.29	$19.42
Bikes	$286.26	$539.99	$1,862.42
Clothing	$5.60	$8.99	$37.33
Grand Total	$286.26	$2.29	$486.09

Note: Notice that when you add these measures straight to a pivot table, you get immediate feedback about whether your measures look correct. This is only a sense check, and you should of course confirm that your formulas return the correct answers as part of the process.

Understanding When Measures Are Added to a Pivot Table Automatically

By now you have probably seen that new measures you write automatically appear in your pivot table. For this to happen, two things must be true. First, you must select the pivot table before you start to write your measure. Second, you must save the measure without creating an error on save. If you forget to click the Check Formula button and save your measure *and* it creates an error, the measure will not be automatically added to your pivot table when you go back and fix the error. If this happens, you need to manually add the measure later, as described next.

Here's How: Manually Adding a Measure to a Pivot Table

Follow these steps to add a measure to a pivot table:

1. Click anywhere inside the pivot table.
2. In the PivotTable Fields list, locate the measure you want to add and then click in the check box next to the measure to add it to the pivot table.

If you can't find the measure, it is most likely that you forgot to select the correct table for storing your measure when you wrote the measure. Check in the other tables in the PivotTable Fields list to see if you can find it. If you have put the measure in the wrong table, you just need to move the measure to the correct table, as described next. You can also use the search box at the top of the PivotTable Fields list to find a measure.

Here's How: Moving an Existing Measure to a Different Table

Follow these steps to move a measure to a different table:

1. In the Excel window, navigate to the Power Pivot menu.
2. Select Measures, Manage Measures.
3. Select the measure in the list and then click Edit.
4. Select the Table Name drop-down at the top of the Measure dialog and then select the correct table from the list.
5. Click OK to save your changes.

Practice Exercises: COUNTBLANK()

In the following exercises, you'll use the COUNTBLANK() function to create a measure to check the completeness of the master data.

Create a new pivot table and put Customers[Occupation] on Rows. Then start to write the new measure. In these exercises, you need to create measures to find out two things:

*   How many customers are missing Address Line 2 from the master data?
*   How many products in the Products table do not have a weight value stored in the master data?

Find the solutions to these practice exercises in Appendix A.

19. [Customers Without Address Line 2]

The Address Line 2 column is in the Customers table. As you write the measure [Customers Without Address Line 2], be sure you do the following:

1. Select the table where you want to store the measure.
2. Give the measure a suitable name.
3. Start typing the measure in the formula box. Pause after you have started to type the formula and read the IntelliSense to see what the formula does (if you don't already know). As shown below, it does exactly what you want it to do: It counts how many blanks are in this column.

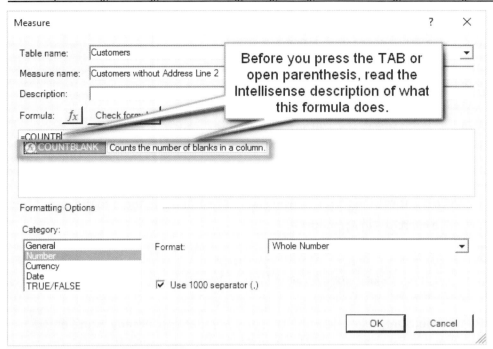

4. Complete the formula, apply the formatting, check the formula, and then save.

20. [Products Without Weight Values]

The column you need to use is in the `Products` table. You should end up with a table like the one shown below.

Row Labels	Customers Without Address Line 2	Products Without Weight Values
Clerical	2,878	122
Management	3,007	122
Manual	2,350	122
Professional	5,440	122
Skilled Manual	4,497	122
Grand Total	**18,172**	**122**

Note that the first measure, [Customers Without Address Line 2], is being filtered by the pivot table (i.e., Customers[Occupation] on Rows), and the values in the pivot table change with each row. But the second measure, [Products Without Weight Values], is not filtered; the values don't change for each row in the pivot table. You have seen this earlier in this book. The technical term for filtering behaviour in Power Pivot is *filter context*. Chapter 5 provides a detailed explanation of what filter context is, and that will help you understand what is happening here and why.

The DIVIDE() Function

DIVIDE() is a simple yet powerful function that is also known as "safe divide." DIVIDE() protects you against divide-by-zero errors in your visuals. A pivot table, by design, hides any rows or columns that have no data. If you get an error in a measure inside a pivot table, it is possible that you will see lots of rows that you would otherwise not see, and you will possibly also see some error messages. The DIVIDE() function is specifically designed to solve this problem. If you use DIVIDE() instead of the slash operator (/) for division, DAX returns a blank where you would otherwise get a divide-by-zero error. Given that a pivot table will filter out blank rows by default, a blank row is a much better option than an error.

The syntax is DIVIDE(*numerator*, *denominator*, *optional-alternate-result*). If you don't specify the alternate result, a blank value is returned when there is a divide-by-zero error.

Practice Exercises: DIVIDE()

In these exercises, you need to create the pivot table shown below.

Row Labels ▼	Total Sales	Total Margin $	Margin %	Markup %	Tax %
Accessories	$700,760	$438,675	62.6%	167.4%	8.0%
Bikes	$28,318,145	$11,505,797	40.6%	68.4%	8.0%
Clothing	$339,773	$136,413	40.1%	67.1%	8.0%
Grand Total	$29,358,677	$12,080,884	41.1%	69.9%	8.0%

Start with a new blank pivot table and put Products[Category] on Rows. Then add [Total Sales] and [Total Margin $] to the pivot table so you have some data to look at. This helps set the context for the new measures you will write next. Write the three measures by using DIVIDE() and add them to the pivot table.

Find the solutions to these practice exercises in Appendix A.

21. [Margin %]

Write a measure that calculates the percentage margin on sales (Total Margin $ divided by Total Sales). Reuse measures that you have already written.

> **Note:** This is a duplicate of a measure, called [Total Margin %], that you already wrote at the start of this chapter (see Practice Exercise 4). This time write the formula using the DIVIDE() function but give it the name [Margin %]. The result will be the same, of course.

22. [Markup %]

Find [Total Margin $] divided by [Total Cost].

23. [Tax %]

Divide the total tax by the total sales.

How Did It Go?

Did you format the results with Category set to Number and Format set to Percentage? These formatting options are a bit hard to find. The dialog below shows how you set these options.

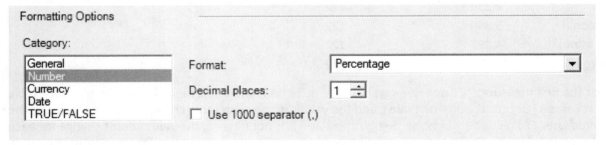

5: Concept: Filter Propagation

Filter propagation is one of the most important things you must learn and understand in order to be skilled at using Power Pivot. Let's start with an example. In Chapter 4 we looked at the COUNT () function and saw some strange behaviour with the [Total Number of Customers] measure. You need to understand the process of filter propagation before you can truly understand what is happening there.

Consider the following pivot table.

Row Labels	Total Number of Customers	Total Number of Products
Accessories ①	18,484	35
Bikes	18,484	125
Clothing	18,484	48
Components	18,484	189
Grand Total	**18,484**	**397**

[Total Number of Products] in this pivot table is displaying a different value for each product category (i.e., each row in the pivot table has a different number of products), but the value for [Total Number of Customers] is the same for each product category in the pivot table. The technical reason this happens is that the row labels in the pivot table (see #1 above) are "filtering" the products in the Products table in the data model *before this measure is evaluated.* But these same rows (product categories) are *not filtering the* Customers *table at all*.

A pivot table "filters" data and then displays subtotals for each row in the pivot table; that's what it's designed to do. The filtering applied to a pivot table is called the *initial filter context—initial* because it is possible to change the filter context later by using the CALCULATE () function. (I cover this in depth in Chapter 9.) So the initial filter context is the standard filtering coming from a pivot table before any possible modifications are applied from DAX formulas using CALCULATE ().

The initial filter context comes from four areas of a pivot table:

- Rows (see #1 below)
- Columns (#2)
- Filters (#3)
- Slicers (#4)

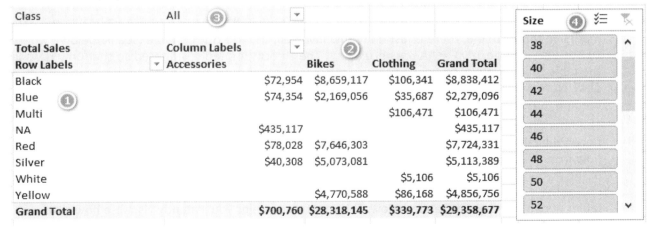

Reading the Initial Filter Context

Let's look again at the sample pivot table, which first appeared in Chapter 4 and is shown again below. It shows [Total Number of Customers] and [Total Number of Products]:

	A	B	C
1	Row Labels ▾	Total Number of Customers	Total Number of Products
2	Accessories	18,484	35
3	Bikes	18,484	125
4	Clothing	18,484	48
5	Components	18,484	189
6	Grand Total	18,484	397

Let's step through the process of reading the initial filter context from this pivot table. Before we do that, though, you should add the [Total Sales] measure to the pivot table so it looks as shown below.

Row Labels ▾	Total Number of Customers	Total Number of Products	Total Sales
Accessories	18,484	35	$700,760
Bikes	18,484	125	$28,318,145
Clothing	18,484	48	$339,773
Components	18,484	189	
Grand Total	18,484	397	$29,358,677

Then point to the cell that's highlighted above and say this out loud (really): *"The initial filter context for this cell is* Products[Category] = "Accessories"*."* Then point to the cell underneath the highlighted cell; this cell has an initial filter context of Products[Category] = "Bikes". You can figure out the rest based on this pattern. It is important that you learn to "read" the initial filter context from your pivot tables because it will help you understand how each value in each cell in a pivot table is calculated. And it is important to refer to the *full table name and column name* because that forces you to look, check, and confirm exactly which tables and columns you are using in your pivots.

Understanding the Flow of the Initial Filter Context

Once you know what the initial filter context is, you can mentally apply the following steps to your data model and track how the filters flow (propagate) through relationships:

- The initial filter context coming from the pivot table is applied to the underlying table(s) in the data model. In this example, there is just one table involved, the Products table (see #1 below), where Products[Category] = "Accessories". The Products table is filtered so that only rows in the table that are equal to Accessories remain; all other rows are filtered so that they are not in play. (Note that the initial filter context can impact more than one table, but in this example, it is just the one table.)

- The filter applied to the Products table automatically propagates through the relationship(s) between the tables, flowing *downhill* to the connected table(s) (see #2 below). The filters automatically flow from the "one" side of the relationship to the "many" side of the relationship, in the direction of the arrow; or you can think of the filters as flowing from the lookup table to the data table. This is one of the reasons it is good to lay out tables using the Collie layout methodology—with the lookup tables above and the data tables below. This mental cue helps you instantly visualise how automatic filter propagation works as you can consider them as flowing *downhill*. (Reread "Shaping Data" in Chapter 2, if necessary.)

- The connected table, the Sales table, is then also filtered (see #3 below). (Remember that there can be more than one connected table.) Only the products that are of the type Products[Category] = "Accessories" remain in play in the Sales table, too, and all the other products are filtered away. This is just temporary—just for this calculation of *this one single cell in the pivot*.

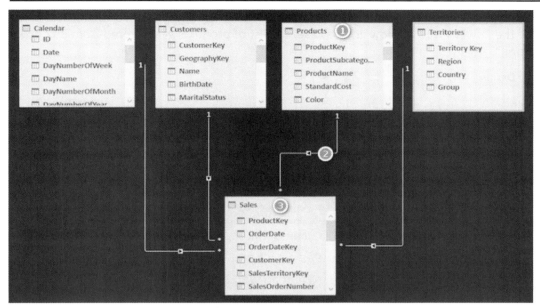

After all the automatic filter propagation has been completed, then and only then does the measure get evaluated. In this case, the measure is [Total Sales] = SUM(Sales[ExtendedAmount]). It returns the value $700,760 to the single pivot table cell we started to look at in this example. This process is repeated for every single cell in the pivot table, including any subtotal and grand total cells.

Simulating What Has Happened Here

I'm going to belabour my point about filter context to ensure that it is clear. A useful simulation is to go to the Power Pivot window, click on the drop-down filter on the Products[Category] column (see #1 below), and select the Accessories filter (#2).

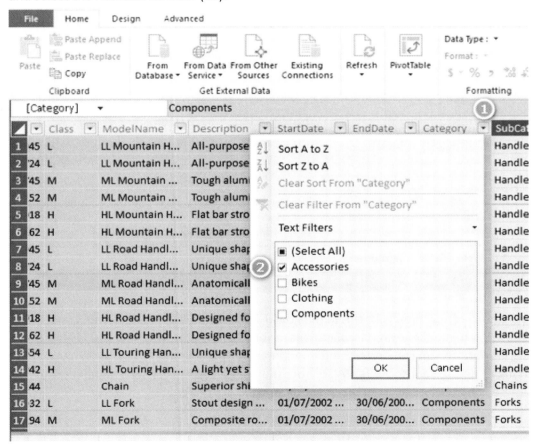

After you do this, you can see how many rows in your table are left after the filter in the record locator in the bottom-left corner of the Power Pivot window. In this case, the list of products gets filtered from 397 down to just the 35 accessories.

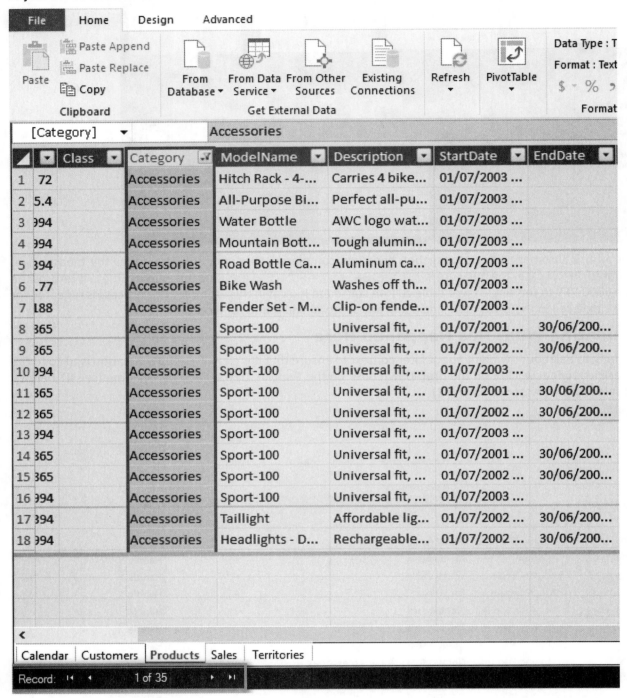

Note: When you manually apply filters like this in the Power Pivot window, *there is no impact at all on your pivot tables*. The manual filtering simulation described here is purely to help you visualise and understand your data so you can understand how the data model works. Use this technique when you are trying to debug your formulas. Also, note that when you apply this manual filter to a lookup table, there is no automatic filter propagation to the data tables.

Understanding Filter Propagation

Let's look at another cell in the pivot table. You always evaluate each cell on its own, without regard for any other cell in the pivot table, even if the cell is a subtotal or grand total cell. All cells are evaluated using the same process, without regard for any other cell in the pivot table.

Look at the pivot table below and read the initial filter context for the highlighted cell out loud: *"The initial filter context for this cell is* `Products[Category] = "Clothing".`*"*

Row Labels ▾	Total Number of Customers	Total Number of Products	Total Sales
Accessories	18,484	35	$700,760
Bikes	18,484	125	$28,318,145
Clothing	18,484	48	$339,773
Components	18,484	189	
Grand Total	**18,484**	**397**	**$29,358,677**

The initial filter context filters the tables in your data model as follows:

- The initial filter context is applied to the table(s)—in this example `Products[Category] = "Cloth-ing"`. The `Products` table (see #1 below) is then filtered so that only rows in the table that are equal to `Clothing` remain.

- This filter automatically propagates through the relationships that exist between the tables, flowing *downhill only* to the connected table(s) (#2).

- The connected table (`Sales` in this example) is then also filtered so that the same products in the `Products` table will remain in the `Sales` table (i.e., only clothing products will be unfiltered in the `Sales` table) (#3).

- The filter applied to the `Sales` table *does not* automatically flow back uphill to the `Customers` table (or to the other two tables, for that matter) (see #4 below). Filters *only* automatically propagate through the relationships *downhill* from the "one" side of the relationship to the "many" side. The arrow (#4) indicates that the filters do not flow from the `Sales` table to the `Customers` table.

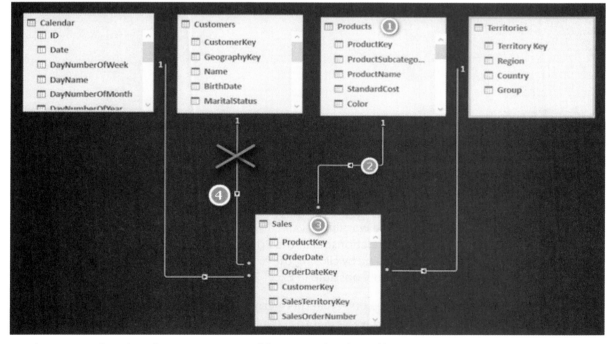

So, the net result is that the `Customers` table is completely *unfiltered* by the initial filter context coming from the pivot table. Because the `Customers` table is unfiltered, the total 18,484 is returned to the pivot table in this cell (and the same is true for every other cell for this measure in the current pivot).

Even if this doesn't seem right to you yet, realise that it is working as designed. Understanding gives you power, so stick with it until you are clear about how it works. Read this section a few times if you need to. You will learn to love the way it is designed and will learn to make it work for you.

Tip: You simply *must* understand how filter propagation works in Power Pivot, or you will never be really good at writing DAX. I suggest that you read this chapter multiple times, if necessary, to make sure you are clear about it.

Adding Relationships Where Needed

It is quite likely that you will now have a warning message from Excel, suggesting that a relationship may be needed. This warning may pop up above the PivotTable Fields list whenever Excel detects that the filter context in your pivot table is not filtering your measures. In the example above, the initial filter context from the `Products` table (`Products[Category]` on Rows) is not filtering the `[Total Number of Customers]` measure. Power Pivot realises that this might be a mistake and sends you a warning message.

If you can't see the message at this point, try removing the `[Total Number of Customers]` measure and then adding it back again, and you should get the warning shown below.

Now sometimes this warning is valid, but in my experience, there are as many false warnings as there are valid warnings, particularly as you write more complex DAX. If you see this message, take a look at your pivot table and data model and decide whether the warning is valid. If you are missing a relationship between tables, then you can go ahead and create that relationship in the Power Pivot window. If you are not missing a relationship, then you can just close this warning by clicking the X. In Excel 2010 you can turn off this warning message prompt, but unfortunately that is only possible in Excel 2010.

Tip: My advice is to never click the Create button in this warning box. If you do click it, Power Pivot tries to work out what is wrong, and it may even automagically fix it. But if that happens, you will have no idea what Power Pivot is doing, and it may or may not be the correct fix for the problem. Either way, it is much better to investigate on your own because doing so will help you improve your understanding of how filter propagation works, and this will make you more confident about ignoring false warnings in the future.

6: Concept: Lookup Tables and Data Tables

All the sample and exercise data in this book so far has been prepared for you; there has been nothing for you to do except follow the instructions. But the simplicity of following my instructions shields you from a deep and important topic: *how* you should structure the tables of data that you load. This chapter covers the various types of tables you can load into Power Pivot.

This topic is easy to skim over and dismiss as trivial, but in my experience, it is one of the easiest things to get wrong, particularly if you don't know why it is important or how to do it properly. If you get the table structure wrong, then everything else becomes orders of magnitude harder.

> **Tip:** Don't brush off this chapter as unimportant. I touched on this topic earlier in the book and revisit it again here; you can't hear this too many times. You need to know this stuff if you want to proceed with speed and confidence, using your own data.

Data Tables vs. Lookup Tables

Two main types of tables can be loaded into Power Pivot: *data tables* (also called *fact tables*, or *transaction tables*) and *lookup tables* (also called *dimension tables*, *reference tables*, or *master data tables*). These two types of tables have some very important differences, as described in the following sections.

Data Tables

Although data tables don't have to be the largest tables loaded into Power Pivot, they typically are. The `Sales` table used in this book is a transactional table that contains details of individual transactions that occurred in AdventureWorks retail outlets around the world. Every row in this table represents a line item on a register receipt for an individual shopping transaction. Data tables can consist of millions (or even billions) of rows of data. Some examples of data tables include `Sales`, `Budget`, `Exchange Rates`, `General Ledger`, `Exam Results`, and `Stock Count`.

There is no limitation on how often similar transactions can occur and be stored in a data table. Consider the AdventureWorks business. There could be literally hundreds of transactions each day that are all but identical because the same bike model can be sold many times on any given day. In this event, there will be many transactions with the same date and the same product code (relating to the bike model that was sold).

Lookup Tables

Lookup tables tend to be smaller than data tables (with fewer rows) and often can be wider (with more columns). Some examples of lookup tables include `Customers`, `Products`, `Calendar`, and `Chart of Accounts`.

Lookup tables have a special feature that makes them different to data tables: A lookup table must have an identifying code of some type to uniquely differentiate each row in the table. This unique code is often called a *key* (or *primary key*, in the database world). Let's consider the `Products` table used in this book. AdventureWorks sells lots of different products—397 to be precise. Each of these products has a unique product code, a three-digit number that is unique for that product. For example, `ProductKey` 212 is a Sports 100 Helmet, Red. No other product in the `Products` table has the same code. If you think about it, this is the way it has to be; there would be chaos if a business used the same product code for different products. The same is true for customers and store ID numbers. In fact, the same is true for the `Calendar` table, given that the date field is a unique ID for each day in the calendar.

Flattened Tables

A good way to help you understand the importance of table structure and the different approaches you can take to loading data is to talk about single large flattened tables. In the early days of Excel pivot tables (before Power Pivot for Excel), you could only create a pivot table on top of a single table of data. If you wanted to do some analysis over a table full of sales data, you could use a pivot table to aggregate the data.

In the image below, the pivot table (see #2 below) has been built on the `Sales` table (see #1 below), and the pivot can easily add up the total sales for each of the products, as identified by the `ProductKey`.

Row Labels	Total Sales		ProductKey	OrderDate	CustomerKey	SalesTerritoryKey	ExtendedAmount
592	$25,425		592	03/06/2004	13035	9	564.99
593	$22,035		592	03/06/2004	16684	9	564.99
594	$28,250		465	03/06/2004	11965	9	24.49
595	$27,120		479	04/06/2004	16730	9	8.99
596	$25,920		482	04/06/2004	13643	9	8.99
597	$26,460		595	06/06/2004	13036	9	564.99
598	$31,319		489	07/06/2004	18715	9	53.99
599	$30,239		491	08/06/2004	19578	9	53.99
600	$22,140		483	08/06/2004	13634	9	120
604	$194,396		484	09/06/2004	13668	9	7.95
605	$196,016		463	09/06/2004	12351	9	24.49
606	$208,436		541	09/06/2004	19623	9	28.99
Grand Total	$837,755		578	09/06/2004	14262	9	1214.85
			489	10/06/2004	17059	9	53.99

That is all well and good until your report needs some extra data that is not part of the `Sales` table. In the image above, what would happen if you wanted to know the total sales by name of product, or the product category, or the subcategory—or anything else for that matter? Well, in the old days, you would find a `Products` table somewhere, and then you would write a `VLOOKUP()` (or `INDEX()`/`MATCH()`) to go and fetch the extra columns of data that you needed for your reporting and bring it into the single `Sales` table. From there you could use the new columns in your pivot tables. This process of bringing in the missing columns is called *de-normalising*. After you have de-normalised, your `Sales` table ends up looking something like the one below (but of course it would be much bigger if you needed more columns).

ProductKey	OrderDate	Category	ProductName	SubCatetory	Color	ExtendedAmount
592	3/06/2004	Bikes	Mountain-500 Silver, 42	Mountain Bikes	Silver	564.99
592	3/06/2004	Bikes	Mountain-500 Silver, 42	Mountain Bikes	Silver	564.99
465	3/06/2004	Clothing	Half-Finger Gloves, M	Gloves	Black	24.49
479	4/06/2004	Accessories	Road Bottle Cage	Bottles and Cages	NA	8.99
482	4/06/2004	Clothing	Racing Socks, L	Socks	White	8.99
595	6/06/2004	Bikes	Mountain-500 Silver, 52	Mountain Bikes	Silver	564.99
489	7/06/2004	Clothing	Short-Sleeve Classic Jersey, M	Jerseys	Yellow	53.99
491	8/06/2004	Clothing	Short-Sleeve Classic Jersey, XL	Jerseys	Yellow	53.99
483	8/06/2004	Accessories	Hitch Rack - 4-Bike	Bike Racks	NA	120
484	9/06/2004	Accessories	Bike Wash - Dissolver	Cleaners	NA	7.95
463	9/06/2004	Clothing	Half-Finger Gloves, S	Gloves	Black	24.49
541	9/06/2004	Accessories	Touring Tire	Tires and Tubes	NA	28.99

Do you spot the issue with the table above? One problem with a table like this is the duplication of data. Note how the different product categories are repeated all the way down the `Category` column. The reality is that for small tables of data (including lookup tables), such repetition doesn't really matter much because the overall file size will be quite small. However, if the table becomes large (millions or billions of rows), then adding all these extra columns of information can become a big problem (literally). In the old days, you had to bring all the relevant columns into the one table by writing one or more `VLOOKUP()` columns to fetch the extra columns needed. Power Pivot is built differently, though. It doesn't require you to bring all the columns into the one table, and this makes everything easier and more efficient. A second problem is that a single table can become very wide as you add more and more columns of data. In Power Pivot, a table that is large (lots of rows) and wide (lots of columns) is very troublesome indeed.

Note: The Power Pivot data modelling engine is a columnar database that compresses the data it loads. The details behind this are quite technical and beyond the scope of this book. However, there are a couple of key points you should be aware of. The more unique values in a column, the less the data will be compressed. In addition, the number of columns you have in your data tables is much more important than the number of rows; that is, fewer columns and more rows is better than more columns and fewer rows. This is particularly true for large tables.

Joining Tables by Using Relationships

A better approach to solving the problem of repetitive data is to keep the repeating data in separate tables. In the case of products, there is only one column of information that is needed in the `Sales` table to uniquely identify every single product, and that is the product code (`ProductKey`). If the `Sales` table contains the unique product key, it is possible to fetch any extra information needed from a product master table when it is needed. So rather than require you to write a `VLOOKUP()` to go and bring the product information into the `Sales` table, Power Pivot allows you to load both tables into the data model and create a single relationship between them. Once the relationship has been created, the tables work together as if they were a single unit, without requiring you to inefficiently create duplicate data in the `Sales` table or unnecessarily add additional columns to the `Sales` table.

As mentioned briefly in Chapter 2, the structure of the tables and any relationships between them in a data model is sometimes referred to as a *schema*. There are a few different classes of schemas, and the following sections cover the most common types.

Star Schema

The image below shows the star schema structure used in this book. The `Sales` table (see #1 below) is a data table and is located at the centre of the star. The other tables (#2, #3, #4, and #5) are lookup tables and are shown as points on the star. This structure is called a *star schema* due to its shape.

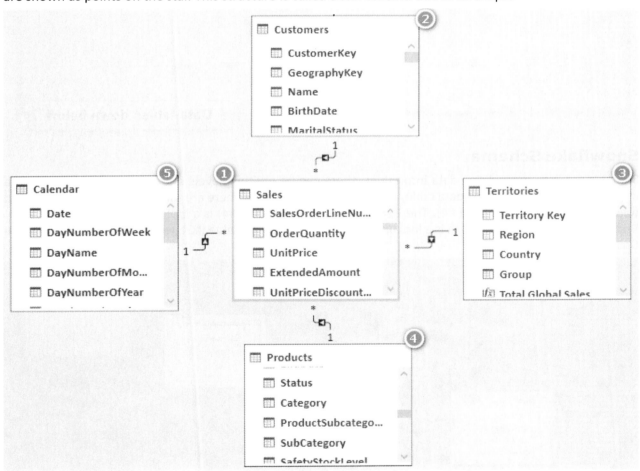

However, as you learnt in Chapter 2, you can reposition the tables any way you choose, and I recommend using the Collie layout methodology, as shown below. You can see that the tables here are the same as in the image above, but the layout is different. The layout has no impact at all on the way Power Pivot operates, but it does give you a visual clue as to which are the lookup tables and which are the data tables because you have to "look up" to see the lookup tables. Also, in the old days, you would write a VLOOKUP() to go and fetch those extra columns, so there is another link to the past between the words VLOOKUP() and *lookup* table.

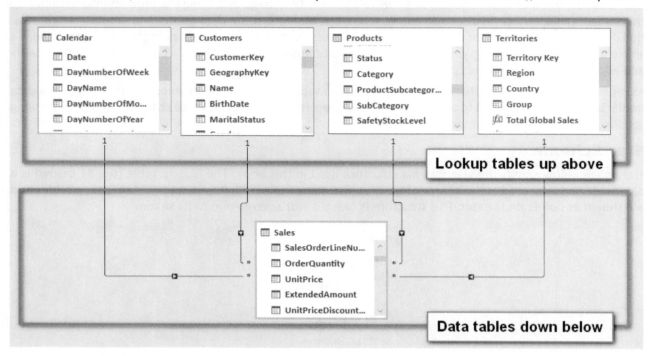

Snowflake Schema

Sometimes when normalising data into tables, there can be multiple levels of lookup tables. Consider the image below. There is a single data table, Sales (see #1 below), and there are three lookup tables all chained together in a row (#2, #3, and #4). The ProductCategory table (#4) is a lookup table of the Product-SubCategory table (#3), which is a lookup table of the Products table (#2), which is a lookup table of the Sales table (#1).

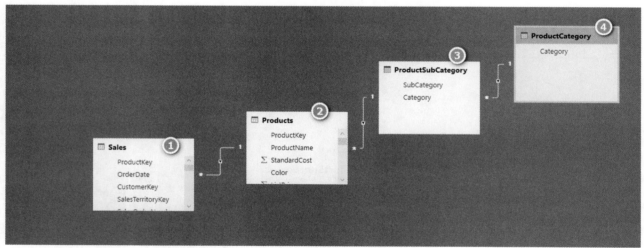

This data structure is common in traditional transactional databases as it is the most efficient way to store the data *in those systems*. However, this is not the best way to structure data *in Power Pivot*. This approach is not the best for Power Pivot for a few reasons:

- Every relationship comes at a cost. Extra relationships will potentially have negative performance impacts on the database (in terms of size and speed).

- Business users will be building reports using your database design, and they will see all the tables in the data model. The structure above is confusing to and onerous on an end user who is trying to understand.

- Power Pivot was built from the ground up to be very efficient in the way it stores repetitive data in columns, particularly in the smaller lookup tables, so there is simply no reason to do it as shown in the image above.

Advice on Loading Your Own Data

There are a few things you can do to get off on the right track when it is time to build your own data models:

- Where possible, keep your *data tables* long and skinny. If necessary, get rid of extra columns of "data" by unpivoting your data, particularly if a data table is very wide (i.e., has a lot of columns). Each additional column of data compresses less well than the last one, which means long, wide data tables can be a real issue.

- Move repeating attribute columns from your data tables and create lookup tables instead. But be careful that you don't overdo it. If a lookup table has only two columns (e.g., `Key` and `Description`), then it may be better to drop the `Key` column and just load the description directly into the data table.

- If you have lookup tables joined to other lookup tables, consider flattening them out into a single wider lookup table. This is generally a better design for Power Pivot.

Definitely do not just accept the table shape and structure coming from your transactional system.

Note: Transactional databases and reporting databases are not the same, so don't try to use the table structure from your transactional system in Power Pivot.

7: DAX Topic: The Basic Iterators SUMX() and AVERAGEX()

The functions covered in Chapter 4 are all aggregation functions. Each of those aggregation functions acts on an entire column or table and uses a specific aggregating technique to return a single value to a cell in the pivot table.

Another class of functions can possibly return the same answers as the aggregation functions—but using a different approach. These "X-functions" (i.e., any functions that have an X at the end of the name) are part of the family called *iterators*.

Iterators and Row Context

The main difference between iterators and the other functions we have looked at so far is that iterators have what is called "row context." *Row context* means that a function is "aware" of *which row* it is referencing at any point in time. Rather than getting into a theoretical explanation, let's move on to working with the iterator SUMX() and talk about row context as we use this function.

Using SUMX(*table, expression*)

SUMX() takes two parameters: a table name and an expression to evaluate. SUMX() creates a row context in the specified table and then iterates through each row of the table, one row at a time, and evaluates the expression for each row as it gets to it before finally adding together the interim results for each row. Row context is a concept in DAX that involves creating "awareness" of the existence of the rows in the table so a function can iterate through them one at a time until it has touched every single row once and only once. You can think of row context as a *checklist* of all rows that SUMX() uses to keep track of where it is. SUMX() can work through the rows one at a time, metaphorically "checking off" each row to make sure none has been missed. This row context exists only in certain DAX formulas, including the X-functions (discussed in this chapter), calculated columns (see Chapter 8), and with Filter() (see Chapter 14).

To demonstrate the point, let's look at how to write a new version of the [Total Sales Including Tax] measure. First, create a new pivot table, put Products[Category] on Rows, and then write out this measure:

```
Total Sales Including Tax SUMX Version
    = SUMX(Sales, Sales[ExtendedAmount] + Sales[TaxAmt])
```

Notice that in this measure, you are not wrapping the columns in an aggregation function. In this case, you are referring to "naked columns," and that is perfectly okay inside an iterator such as SUMX(). There is no need to wrap the columns in an aggregation function when using an X-function (or any other function that creates a row context). The way an X-function works is that it goes to the table specified in the first parameter (in this case, Sales), creates a row context for it to use as a reference, and then takes each single row in the table, one at a time, and evaluates the expression for that single row. Once it has created an interim result for each row in the table, it adds together all the interim results.

As you can see illustrated with the box in the image below, when there is only one single row from the table in play, DAX is able to refer to the exact intersection of each column referred to in the formula and the specific row it is currently iterating over. Therefore, during each step of the iteration process, the column names in the expression are actually only referring to a single value—the value that is the intersection of the single column and the current row in the row context.

ExtendedAmount	TaxAmt
564.99	45.1992
564.99	45.1992
24.49	1.9592
8.99	0.7192
8.99	0.7192
564.99	45.1992

One row at a time, the single value in the `Sales[ExtendedAmount]` column is added to the single value of the `Sales[TaxAmt]` column. After the first row is evaluated (and the result is stored temporarily in memory for later), `SUMX()` selects the second row and does the same thing, then the third row and does the same thing, and so on until it has iterated through every single row in the table, missing none. It iterates through every single row once and only once (not necessarily in the order you see on the screen). When it has completed this calculation for every single row in the specified table (specified by the first parameter), it sums all the results together and returns a single value to the pivot table cell.

> **Note:** I refer above to iterators working "one row at a time." It is convenient to think of iterators working in this way, and indeed that is the logical execution approach. In reality, though, the Power Pivot engine has been built and optimised to work very efficiently under the hood. In many circumstances, the actual physical execution is much more efficient than is implied by "one row at a time" logical execution. This is a very deep technical topic and is beyond the scope of this book. The key thing to note is that you should not think that iterators are inherently inefficient because the Power Pivot engine optimisations can make the physical execution very efficient indeed.

Practice Exercises: SUMX()

Write the following measures for practice. Find the solutions to these practice exercises in Appendix A.

24. [Total Sales SUMX Version]

Multiply quantity by unit price from the appropriate columns in the `Sales` table.

25. [Total Sales Including Tax SUMX Version]

Add the `ExtendedAmount` column together with the appropriate tax column in the `Sales` table.

26. [Total Sales Including Freight]

Add the `ExtendedAmount` column to the `Freight` cost.

How Did It Go?

Did you get the following pivot table?

Row Labels	Total Sales SUMX version	Total Sales Including Tax SUMX Version	Total Sales Including Freight
Accessories	$700,760	$756,821	$718,281
Bikes	$28,318,145	$30,583,596	$29,026,099
Clothing	$339,773	$366,954	$348,267
Grand Total	**$29,358,677**	**$31,707,371**	**$30,092,647**

Make sure you are following these steps to minimise rework:

1. Put the measures in the correct tables.
2. Give each measure a meaningful name and include spaces in the name.
3. Write the formula and check it to ensure that there are no syntax errors.
4. Apply suitable formatting immediately after writing the measure.
5. Ensure that the measure was written correctly by adding it to a pivot table to check your results.

27. [Dealer Margin]

Create a new pivot table. Put `Products[Category]` on Filters and select Accessories from this filter. Then put `Products[ProductName]` on Rows. You should have something like the table below (though what is shown here is truncated).

Category	Accessories ⊤
Row Labels ▼	
All-Purpose Bike Stand	
Bike Wash - Dissolver	
Cable Lock	
Fender Set - Mountain	
Headlights - Dual-Beam	

Write a measure that shows the theoretical margin the dealer gets (i.e., the difference between the product list price and the product dealer price). Both columns you need for this measure are in the `Products` table.

Did you get the answers shown below? (Once again, the pivot table in the image below is truncated; it shows only the first nine rows when, in reality, it is longer.)

Category	Accessories ⊤
Row Labels ▼	**Dealer Margin**
All-Purpose Bike Stand	$63.60
Bike Wash - Dissolver	$3.18
Cable Lock	$10.00
Fender Set - Mountain	$8.79
Headlights - Dual-Beam	$14.00
Headlights - Weatherproof	$18.00
Hitch Rack - 4-Bike	$48.00
HL Mountain Tire	$14.00
HL Road Tire	$13.04

When to Use X-Functions vs. Aggregators

Now you know that you can use X-functions such as `SUMX()`, and you can also use aggregators such as `SUM()`, and they do similar things but using different approaches. Which should you use? The following examples will help you figure this out. The samples below are simplistic tiny tables for illustration purposes only. In real life, tables of data are, of course, much larger.

Example 1: When the Data Doesn't Contain the Line Total

If your `Sales` table contains a column for quantity (`Qty` in the image below) and another column for price per unit, you need to multiply the quantity by the price per unit to calculate total sales (because the actual total doesn't exist at the line level in the table).

Date ▼	Product ▼	Qty ▼	Price Per Unit ▼
01/01/2003	A	3	2.5
01/01/2003	B	1	6.8
02/01/2003	A	5	2.5
02/01/2003	B	3	3.5

If this is the structure of your data, then you simply must use SUMX(), like this:

```
Total Sales 1 = SUMX(Sales, Sales[Qty] * Sales[Price Per Unit])
```

In this example, you have to calculate the total for each row first, one row at a time. This is what the iterator functions are designed to do.

Example 2: When the Data Contains a Line Total

If your data contains a single column with the extended total sales for that line item, you can use SUM() to add up the values:

```
Total Sales 2 = SUM(Sales[Total Sales])
```

Date	Product	Total Sales
01/01/2003	A	7.5
01/01/2003	B	6.8
02/01/2003	A	12.5
02/01/2003	B	10.5

There is no need for an iterator in this example. Note, however, that you *could* still use SUMX(), like this, to get the same answer:

```
Total Sales 2 alternate = SUMX(Sales, Sales[Total Sales])
```

> **Note:** In the formula above, there is only a single column for the expression parameter: Sales[Total Sales]. This is a valid DAX expression, and it will work just fine. For each row in the iteration of SUMX, the formula just takes the line-level total for this column. At the end, it simply adds up all the values.

So Which Should You Use, SUM() or SUMX()?

Whether you use SUM() or SUMX() comes down to personal preference and the structure of your data. For most data models, which one you use makes little or no difference, so you can choose the one that suits you the best. However, let's take another look at the two approaches by looking at the examples from above. First, let's take another look at the table of data from Example 2 (see the previous image).

Every value in the column Sales[Total Sales] is unique (i.e., there are no duplicates). In real life, if the real table is very large and has lots of unique values, this column would not compress well. The more unique values in a column, the less well the column will compress.

Now look again at the table from Example 1 (see the image repeated below).

Date	Product	Qty	Price Per Unit
01/01/2003	A	3	2.5
01/01/2003	B	1	6.8
02/01/2003	A	5	2.5
02/01/2003	B	3	3.5

In this table, there are duplicate values in the Qty column and also duplicates in the Price Per Unit column. In real life, if the real table is very large, it is likely that loading the data in this table (as in Example 1) will result in better compression than with the data in Example 2 because of these duplicate values in each column. In real life, data that compresses the best in columns often is the most efficient. This may seem counterintuitive if you think about "iteration" as being a slow, row-by-row evaluation—and it is understandable that you may think of it that way. However, the underlying Power Pivot engine is optimised to work just as efficiently with SUMX() as it does with SUM(). (There are exceptions to this rule, but that is quite a complex topic and beyond the scope of this book.)

Avoiding Data You Don't Need

One important point to note before moving on is that you *should not* have all three columns as shown in the previous two examples. It should be obvious that if you have quantity and price per unit in a table, you can "calculate" the value of total sales any time you need it. Similarly, if you have total sales and quantity in a table, you can calculate price per unit any time you like.

Generally speaking, you should not include in your data model columns of redundant data that can be calculated on-the-fly. Including those extra columns increases file size and makes everything refresh more slowly. The general rule is to bring in the minimum number of columns you need to do the job, and it is best to bring in the columns with the lowest numbers of unique values, where possible.

When Totals Don't Add Up

This use case requires you to use SUMX() or some other iterator to make the totals add up as you would expect to see them. I have created a small table of sample data (shown below) to explain the problem and show the solution.

Customer	Spend per Visit	Number of Visits
A	50	7
B	40	3
C	100	12
D	15	4

The table above shows four customers, with the average amount of money they have spent each time they have shopped as well as the number of times they have shopped. If you load this data into Power Pivot and then use aggregating functions to find the average amount spent across all customers as well as the total amount spent, you get the wrong answers, as shown below.

Row Labels	Avg Spent per visit Wrong	Total Number of Visits	Total Spent Wrong
A	$50	7	$350
B	$40	3	$120
C	$100	12	$1,200
D	$15	4	$60
Grand Total	$51	26	$1,333

The following measures are used above:

```
Total Number of Visits = sum(VisitData[Number of Visits])
Avg Spent per visit Wrong = AVERAGE(VisitData[Spend per Visit])
Total Spent Wrong = [Avg Spent per visit Wrong] * [Total Number of Visits]
```

The first measure, [Total Number of Visits], is correct because the data is additive, but the other two measures give the wrong results. This is a classic situation where you can't perform multiplication on the averages at the grand total level. Given the original sample data, the only way to calculate the correct answer is to complete a row-by-row evaluation for each customer in the table, as shown below.

Row Labels	Total Number of Visits	Total Spent SUMX	Avg Spent per visit Correct
A	7	$350	$50
B	3	$120	$40
C	12	$1,200	$100
D	4	$60	$15
Grand Total	26	$1,730	$67

The pivot table above includes a SUMX() to find the total spent, row by row. Only then does the pivot table calculate the average spent per visit. Here is the complete set of correct formulas:

```
Total Number of Visits = SUM(VisitData[Number of Visits])
Total Spent SUMX = SUMX(VisitData,VisitData[Spend per Visit] * Visit-
Data[Number of Visits])
Avg Spent per visit Correct = DIVIDE([Total Spent SUMX] , [Total Number of
Visits])
```

Whenever you see that the totals in your visuals don't add up, you should try to figure out what is happening row by row in the visual that is not happening in the total row. Such a problem is always caused by some sort of filter context provided by the rows in the visual that is not replicated in the total rows. You should look at the visual and ask, "How can I simulate the row-by-row filtering that I see in the visual in the total row?" When you answer this question, you will know how to solve the problem of totals not adding up—normally using an iterating function like SUMX().

Avoiding Too Many Calculated Columns

Now is a good time to talk about another common mistake I see Excel users make when learning Power Pivot. The formulas we have been writing using SUMX() can also be written directly into a custom calculated column in a table. But that *normally* is the *wrong* way to do it. Let me explain why.

To write a calculated column, go to the Power Pivot tab in Excel and click the Manage button, as shown below.

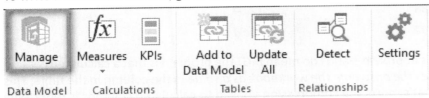

Once you are in the Power Pivot window, you can select Design (see #1 below), Add Columns (#2).

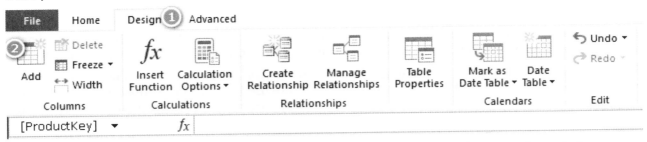

You could rewrite the [Total Sales Plus Tax] measure as a calculated column, as shown below.

fx =Sales[ExtendedAmount]+Sales[TaxAmt]

Before we move on, let me point out something with regard to the syntax of the above calculated column and the measure [Total Sales Including Tax SUMX Version]. Here are the two formulas:

```
Total Sales Plus Tax Column
    = Sales[ExtendedAmount] + Sales[TaxAmt]
Total Sales Including Tax SUMX Version
    = SUMX(Sales,Sales[ExtendedAmount] + Sales[TaxAmt])
```

Take a look at the part of the two formulas highlighted in bold. This section is identical in the two formulas; it adds together the values in these two columns while iterating in a row context. What is different with the SUMX() function is that there is an additional parameter that specifies *which* table SUMX() should iterate over. This extra parameter is not required in a calculated column because the column is physically placed in the table itself. In other words, a calculated column is an iterator that iterates over the table in which it is placed.

A calculated column has a row context—just like SUMX()—and as a result, it is fine to refer to naked columns. Just as with SUMX(), the calculated column has a row context and iterates over the rows in the calculated column, one at a time. At each step in the process, there is only one row in play, and hence each column has only one possible value for each row in each iteration step. So, you end up with a column of data like the one below, with the calculated total for each row stored in the column.

ExtendedAmount ▼	TaxAmt ▼	Sales Plus Tax Column ▼
564.99	45.1992	$610.19
564.99	45.1992	$610.19
24.49	1.9592	$26.45
8.99	0.7192	$9.71
8.99	0.7192	$9.71
564.99	45.1992	$610.19
53.99	4.3192	$58.31
53.99	4.3192	$58.31
120	9.6	$129.60
7.95	0.636	$8.59
24.49	1.9592	$26.45
28.99	2.3192	$31.31
1214.85	97.188	$1,312.04
53.99	4.3192	$58.31

But there is one *big* problem with this approach—and I do mean *BIG*. The problem is that a calculated column always evaluates every row *and stores the answer in the workbook as a value* in the column in the table. This takes up space in the workbook. What's more, the compression applied to calculated columns is reportedly not as good as for imported columns, and hence the data could be stored less efficiently in the workbook. Now compare this to the SUMX() measure created earlier. The measure [Total Sales Including Tax SUMX Version] uses the same core formula, but it does not store any values in your workbook other than values needed to display in any pivot tables in your workbooks. If your Sales table has 60,000 rows of data, it probably doesn't matter. But if your Sales table has 50 million rows of data, it definitely does matter.

People with an Excel background tend to gravitate toward writing calculated columns rather than writing measures because that's what they're used to doing. They are used to living in a spreadsheet world, where they have lots of rows and columns and can refer to them in calculations. Writing measures in DAX is a different experience because you don't get to "see" the data table in front of you when you're writing the code. Instead, you have to visualise in your mind what you are doing. This is why I recommend creating a pivot table to get immediate feedback after you write your formulas; it helps you visualise the result.

My number-one piece of advice for now (while you are learning) is that *you shouldn't write calculated columns unless you have no other option and you know why you need them*. You'll learn more about calculated columns and when to use them in Chapter 8. Until then, you should assume that using a calculated column is not a good approach unless you know from experience what the exceptions are—and you will learn that with time and experience.

Are You Writing Your Measures Correctly?

It's time to practice using some new functions. Before you get into the following practice exercises, here is a refresher on the process you should use to write all your measures:

This is the process used so far to write X-function formulas:

1. Create a new pivot table on a new sheet.
2. Put Products[Category] on Rows.
3. Click in the pivot table and create a new measure.
4. Select the table where the measure will be stored.
5. Give the measure a descriptive name.

6. Start typing the formula and stop once the formula is highlighted in IntelliSense—before you press Tab or type **(**—so you can read the description of the formula, as shown below.

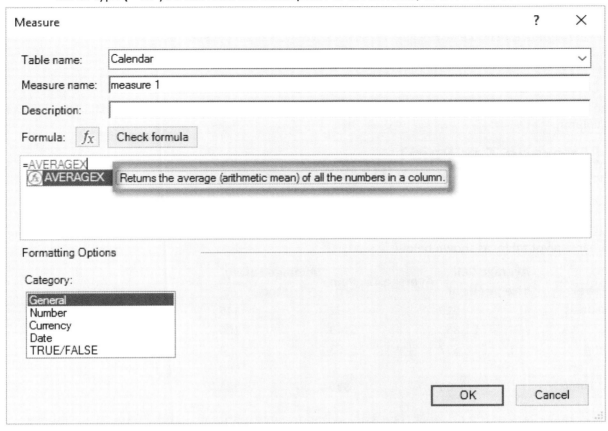

7. Pause after you press Tab or type **(** to get the syntax, as shown below.

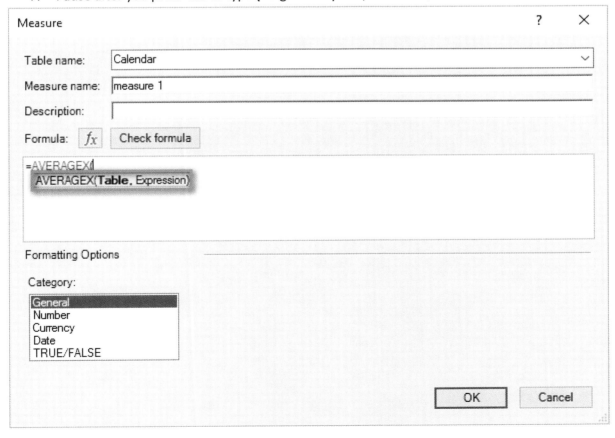

Practice Exercises: AVERAGEX()

Set up a new pivot table and put Products[Category] on Rows. Then write the following measures using AVERAGEX(). Don't worry about the logic of weighted averages in these exercises. These exercises are designed for simple practice, and you should ignore any real-world business logic.

Find the solutions to these practice exercises in Appendix A.

28. [Average Sell Price per Item]

Find the column in the Sales table that gives the sell price per unit and use AVERAGEX() to find the average of this column.

29. [Average Tax Paid]

Find the tax column in the Sales table and find the average of this column.

30. [Average Safety Stock]

There is an Average Safety Stock column in the Products table. You should put the results of this measure in a pivot table, as shown below.

Row Labels ▼	Average Sell Price per Item	Average Tax Paid	Average Safety Stock
Accessories	$19	$2	146
Bikes	$1,862	$149	100
Clothing	$37	$3	4
Components			500
Grand Total	$486	$39	283

Note: There are other X-functions that are not discussed in this book, such as MAXX(), MINX(), COUNTAX(), and COUNTX(). You can find out how these are used by typing a formula into the Measure Wizard and reading the IntelliSense.

8: DAX Topic: Calculated Columns

It's time for a change of pace. I have deliberately left the main discussion of calculated columns until now to allow you to get accustomed to the power of measures. As mentioned in Chapter 7, a common mistake I see Excel users make is to use too many calculated columns. And when you think about it, a calculated column is a very comfortable place for an Excel user to hang out because a table in the Power Pivot window looks and feels a lot like Excel. But as I warned previously, you should avoid using calculated columns until you know when and why to use them. Consciously avoiding calculated columns and trying to find a measure solution will make you a stronger DAX user. Trust me.

In general, you should not use a calculated column if:

- You can use a measure instead.
- You can bring the data into a table directly from the source data.
- You can create the column during data load by using Power Query.
- Be careful with the last two options above: These alternate methods are no substitute for writing a measure. Always prefer writing measures as you are learning because doing so will help you minimise mistakes until you learn more about how to use calculated columns correctly. I always recommend that you prefer the following order to source a missing column (only when a measure will not do the job):

1. Get it added to the source and import it from there.
2. Create it in Power Query on data load.
3. Use a calculated column.

By pushing a required column as far back to the source as possible, you increase the possibility of reuse down the track. But the truth is that this is a purist view, and it doesn't really matter very much. If you know how to do it in a calculated column and you don't know how to do it in Power Query, then there is no harm in using the calculated column. Indeed, you can and should use calculated columns when you need them. You should definitely use a calculated column when both of the following two conditions are satisfied at the same time:

- You need to filter/slice a visual based on the results of a column (i.e., you want to use the column on Filter, Slicer, Rows, or Columns). Measures don't work in this case.
- You can't bring in the column of data you need from your source data or by using Power Query (for whatever reason).

These are the most common reasons you can't get a column you need from your source data:

- It doesn't exist.
- You can't arrange to get it added (e.g., you don't have access to the source system).
- You can't get it added in a timely manner.
- You want to reuse measures that exist in your data model as part of the formula needed to create the new column.

As mentioned earlier, if possible, you should try to get the column you need added to the source data. When you do this, you get the full benefit of compression on data import; in addition, the column is available for reuse in all your future workbooks. But sometimes this simply isn't possible, and other times it is possible, but you can't wait two weeks (or two years!) to get it done. Calculated columns are useful in such cases. And if a new column becomes available in the future, you can simply delete your calculated column and replace it with the new column coming in from the source.

Here's How: Creating a Day Type Calculated Column

Let's look at an example of where you should use calculated columns. Let's say that you extract the `Calendar` table from your enterprise database, and you want a new column that shows whether each date is a weekend or a weekday, but you can't arrange to have that column added for now. Of course, you could use Power Query, but this book is about DAX, so this section discusses how to create a calculated column to solve this problem.

Follow these steps to create a `Day Type` calculated column in the `Calendar` table:

1. In the Power Pivot window, navigate to the `Calendar` table and make sure you have the Data view selected.

2. Scroll all the way to the right side of the table, and you see Add Column at the top of the next available column in the table (as shown below).

3. Click anywhere in the column to select a blank row (see #1 below).

4. Click in the formula bar at the top of the window (#2).

5. Type the following calculated column formula:

    ```
    = IF('Calendar'[DayNumberOfWeek] = 1 ||
    'Calendar'[DayNumberOfWeek]=7,"Weekend","Weekday")
    ```

> **Note:** Note the use of the two pipe symbols (| |) in the formula above. The pipe can be found on your keyboard above the backslash key (which is right above the Enter/Return key). The two pipe symbols are the inline text version of a logical OR function.

6. You can also write an OR function in DAX as follows:

    ```
    OR('Calendar'[DayNumberOfWeek] = 1, 'Calendar'[DayNumberOfWeek] = 7)
    ```

7. Personally, I prefer to use the two pipes because you can have as many of them as you like in a single formula. The `OR()` function above accepts only two parameters as inputs; if you have more than two logical OR inputs, you need to use multiple nested `OR()` functions to make it work.

> **Note:** The inline version of the logical AND is the double ampersand (`&&`), which equates to the `AND()` function.

8. Note that the formula you just created, as shown below, is a single formula for the entire column. Just as with Excel tables, with Power Pivot, it is not possible to have more than one formula in a calculated column. You therefore have to write the one formula so that it evaluates and handles all the possible scenarios you need.

9. To rename the column, double-click the column name and change it to `Day Type`.

`[Day Type]` ▾   *fx* `=IF('Calendar'[DayNumberOfWeek] = 1 || 'Calendar'[DayNumberOfWeek]=7,"Weekend","Weekday")`

	Cale...	Calend...	FiscalQuarter	FiscalYear	FiscalSemester	Period	DayName	Day Type	
1	7	3	2001	1	2002	1	200107	Sunday	Weekend	
2	7	3	2001	1	2002	1	200107	Monday	Weekday	
3	7	3	2001	1	2002	1	200107	Tuesday	Weekday	
4	7	3	2001	1	2002	1	200107	Wednesday	Weekday	
5	7	3	2001	1	2002	1	200107	Thursday	Weekday	
6	7	3	2001	1	2002	1	200107	Friday	Weekday	
7	7	3	2001	1	2002	1	200107	Saturday	Weekend	
8	7	3	2001	1	2002	1	200107	Sunday	Weekend	
9	7	3	2001	1	2002	1	200107	Monday	Weekday	
10	7	3	2001	1	2002	1	200107	Tuesday	Weekday	
11	7	3	2001	1	2002	1	200107	Wednesday	Weekday	
12	7	3	2001	1	2002	1	200107	Thursday	Weekday	
13	7	3	2001	1	2002	1	200107	Friday	Weekday	
14	7	3	2001	1	2002	1	200107	Saturday	Weekend	
15	7	3	2001	1	2002	1	200107	Sunday	Weekend	
16	7	3	2001	1	2002	1	200107	Monday	Weekday	

10. Now that you have the new calculated column, it is time to use it in your pivot table. Go to a new worksheet in your workbook and create a new pivot table. Place `Products[Category]` on Rows, place your new column `'Calendar'[Day Type]` on Columns, and then add `[Total Sales]` to the Values section. You end up with the pivot table shown below.

Total Sales	Column Labels ▾		
Row Labels ▾	Weekday	Weekend	Grand Total
Accessories	$495,995	$204,764	$700,760
Bikes	$20,047,702	$8,270,442	$28,318,145
Clothing	$240,664	$99,109	$339,773
Grand Total	**$20,784,362**	**$8,574,316**	**$29,358,677**

With the calculated column placed in the pivot table, you can successfully glean some new insights from the data that weren't evident before. You have used data modelling techniques to enhance the data for weekday/weekend analysis. Sweet!

Practice Exercise: Calculated Columns

Write the following calculated column in the `Calendar` table. Find the solution to this practice exercise in Appendix A.

31. Creating a Half Year Column

In the `Calendar` table write a calculated column that returns the value `H1` for the first half of each year (January through June) and `H2` for the second half of each year (July through December). *Hint:* You might want to use an `IF` statement to do this.

9: DAX Topic: CALCULATE()

CALCULATE() is the most important and powerful function in DAX. It is the only function that has the ability to modify the filter context coming from your visuals.

Note: Actually, there is another function that can modify filter context: CALCULATETABLE(). This function is typically used inside DAX queries, though discussing it is beyond the scope of this book.

I am going to provide you with a solid understanding of how CALCULATE() works in this book, but you will need to continue to learn in the future—and there is a lot to learn. If you want to be an expert, you need to read lots of other books and blogs to build on the foundation you get from this book.

Note: You can find a link to an up-to-date curated list of the best (in my view) Power BI, Power Pivot, and Power Query books in Chapter 22.

CALCULATE() Explained: Altering the Standard Offering

Have you ever gone into a restaurant and looked at the menu, only to discover that the standard offering is not quite what you are after? Lots of people love Caesar salad, for example, but many people do not like anchovies. Say that you're one of them, and you read the following on the menu:

Caesar Salad: Romaine lettuce, croutons, parmesan cheese, anchovies, and egg tossed in a creamy Caesar dressing.

When you order the salad, you alter the standard menu option and instead say, "I'll have the Caesar salad, no anchovies." CALCULATE() is a lot like that: It allows you to alter the standard offering (that you get from a pivot table rather than a menu, of course) so you can get some variation that ends up being exactly what you want.

Technically speaking, CALCULATE() alters filter context. It modifies an expression (which can be a measure or another DAX formula) by modifying filters. The syntax of CALCULATE() is:

```
= CALCULATE(expression, filter 1, filter 2, filter n...)
```

CALCULATE() alters the filter context coming from the pivot table by applying none, one, or more filters prior to evaluating the expression. CALCULATE() "reruns" the built-in filter engine in Power Pivot—the one that makes the filters automatically propagate from the lookup tables and flow downhill to the data tables. When the filter engine is rerun by CALCULATE(), if there are any filters inside the CALCULATE() function, these filters become part of the filter context before the filter engine kicks in. (You'll learn more about how this works in Chapter 10.)

Note: I mentioned earlier that you can use none, one, or more filters inside CALCULATE(). It may seem strange that you can use none at all. Why would you want to do this? Using no filters at all is a special use case that is covered in Chapter 10.

Simple Filters

CALCULATE() can use two types of filters: simple and advanced. A simple filter (or raw filter) has a column name on the left and a value on the right, as in these examples:

```
Customers[Gender] = "F"
Products[Color] = "Blue"
'Calendar'[Date] = "1/1/2002"
'Calendar'[CalendarYear] = 2003
```

You can use these simple filters as the second and subsequent parameters to CALCULATE() to alter the original meaning of an expression (which is the first parameter). Simple filters are really important in Power Pivot because they were designed to be easy to use and understand. Taking a filter from a lookup table and propagating it to the data tables is what Power Pivot was built and optimised to do.

Note: Under the hood, Power Pivot converts a simple filter into a much more complex formula that is harder for beginners to learn and understand. Consider the following measure, using a simple filter:

```
Total Sales to Females
    = CALCULATE([Total Sales], Customers[Gender] = "F")
```

Under the hood, Power Pivot converts this into the following formula prior to execution:

```
Total Sales to Females
    = CALCULATE([Total Sales],
            FILTER(ALL(Customers[Gender]),
                Customers[Gender] = "F"
            )
        )
```

I am sure you will agree that the first formula is easier to read and understand. The Microsoft developers call this type of simple syntax "syntax sugar." The simple syntax is provided to allow beginners to use Power Pivot without having to first become DAX experts.

I cover the `ALL()` function in Chapter 13 and the `FILTER()` function in Chapter 14.

To see `CALCULATE()` in action (using the simple syntax), set up a new pivot table like the one below, with `Products[Category]` on Rows and `[Total Sales]` on Values. (You should be getting used to this by now!)

Row Labels ▾	Total Sales
Accessories	$700,760
Bikes	$28,318,145
Clothing	$339,773
Grand Total	**$29,358,677**

Then write the following measure:

```
Total Sales of Blue Products
    = CALCULATE([Total Sales], Products[Color]="Blue")
```

In the image below, can you see how the simple filter used here, `Products[Color]="Blue"`, has altered the initial filter context coming from the pivot table and given a variation to the regular measure `[Total Sales]`. It is as if you have changed the recipe for the standard product on the menu and instead received a variation of that regular menu item. Think Caesar salad without anchovies.

Row Labels ▾	Total Sales	Total Sales of Blue Products
Accessories	$700,760	$74,354
Bikes	$28,318,145	$2,169,056
Clothing	$339,773	$35,687
Grand Total	**$29,358,677**	**$2,279,096**

Practice Exercises: CALCULATE() with a Single Table

It's time for you to write some simple CALCULATE() examples that filter a single table. Set up a new pivot table with Customers[Occupation] on Rows and [Total Number of Customers] on Values. You should have the pivot table shown below as your starting point.

Row Labels ▼	Total Number of Customers
Clerical	2,928
Management	3,075
Manual	2,384
Professional	5,520
Skilled Manual	4,577
Grand Total	18,484

Then write the following measures, using CALCULATE(). Find the solutions to these practice exercises in Appendix A.

32. [Total Male Customers]

Write a new measure that modifies the [Total Number of Customers] measure you wrote previously (see Practice Exercise 9) to come up with a total for male customers only. You need to look for a suitable column from the Customers table to use in your filter.

33. [Total Customers Born Before 1950]

In this case, you need to enter the date < January 1, 1950, into the formula as the filter parameter. You need to use the DATE() function to be able to refer to a date. Remember that you can get help from the tooltips that IntelliSense provides when writing the measure. Just start typing =DATE inside the formula bar, and a tooltip pops up, explaining the purpose and syntax of the function, as shown below.

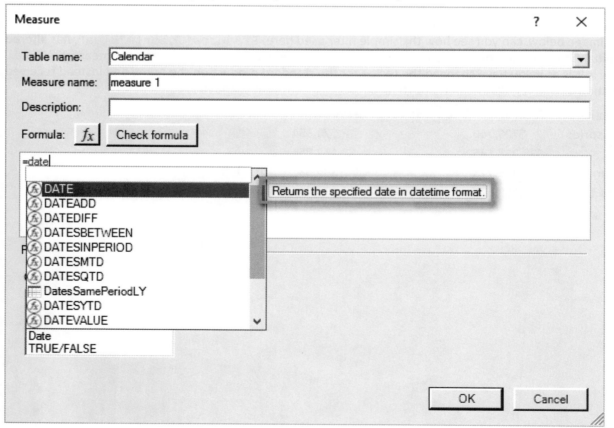

```
Formula:  fx  | Check formula |

=date(
   DATE(Year, Month, Day)
```

As soon as you type **(**, the tooltip changes and gives you the syntax you need to use the function. Now that you know how to write a date inside a formula, you can go ahead and write the measure [Total Customers Born Before 1950].

34. [Total Customers Born in January]

This exercise is similar to Practice Exercise 33, but this time you need to use the MONTH() function to turn the information in the Customers[BirthDate] column into a month.

35. [Customer Earning at Least $100,000 per Year]

Write a measure that counts the number of customers who earn more than $100,000 per year. The following pivot table shows what you should end up with. Look for a suitable column to use for the filter in the Customers table.

Row Labels	Total Number of Customers	Total Male Customers	Total Customers Born Before 1950	Total Customers Born in January	Customers Earning at least $100,000 per year
Clerical	2,928	1,488	433	132	
Management	3,075	1,592	1,543	136	1,406
Manual	2,384	1,251	134	128	
Professional	5,520	2,727	609	254	792
Skilled Manual	4,577	2,293	234	192	
Grand Total	18,484	9,351	2,953	842	2,198

Using CALCULATE() over Multiple Tables

In Practice Exercises 32–35 above, the CALCULATE() function operates over a single table; the filtering is applied to a table, and the expression is evaluated on the same table. However, CALCULATE() can work over multiple tables, too. When you use the CALCULATE() function, it first applies the filters to the relevant tables, and then it reruns the filter propagation engine and makes sure that any new filters inside your CALCULATE() function automatically propagate from the "one" side of the relationship to the "many" side (i.e., the filters flow downhill) before the expression is evaluated. So you can apply a filter to one or more of the lookup tables, and these filters will propagate to the data tables, and any expression that evaluates over the connected data tables will reflect the filters from the lookup tables. Are you feeling supercharged now? You should be!

Practice Exercises: CALCULATE() with Multiple Tables

Set up a new pivot table. Put Territories[Region] on Rows and [Total Sales] on Values. Note that there are now two tables involved. The initial filter context is coming from the Territories table (see #1 below), and the calculation [Total Sales] is operating over the Sales table (#2).

Row Labels	Total Sales
Australia ① ②	$9,061,001
Canada	$1,977,845
Central	$3,001
France	$2,644,018
Germany	$2,894,312
Northeast	$6,532
Northwest	$3,649,867
Southeast	$12,239
Southwest	$5,718,151
United Kingdom	$3,391,712
Grand Total	$29,358,677

With your pivot table set up as described above, write the following new measures. Find the solutions to these practice exercises in Appendix A.

36. [Total Sales of Clothing]

Use the `Products[Category]` column in your simple filter. The filter gets applied to the lookup table, but then the measure `[Total Sales]` is modified by the filter.

37. [Sales to Female Customers]

As the name of this measure suggests, you use `CALCULATE()` to modify the standard measure `[Total Sales]` and create a new measure that is for sales to female customers.

38. [Sales of Bikes to Married Men]

You need to use multiple filters on two tables for this one. `CALCULATE()` can accept as many filters as you pass to it. Just separate the filters with commas.

How Did It Go?

When you have finished these three practice exercises, you should have a pivot table something like the one shown below.

Row Labels	Total Sales	Total Sales of Clothing	Sales to Female Customers	Sales of Bikes to Married Men
Australia	$9,061,001	$70,260	$4,634,993	$2,205,159
Canada	$1,977,845	$53,165	$1,011,320	$517,808
Central	$3,001	$157	$124	
France	$2,644,018	$27,035	$1,271,964	$726,649
Germany	$2,894,312	$23,565	$1,539,713	$694,776
Northeast	$6,532	$106	$3,836	$2,295
Northwest	$3,649,867	$58,230	$1,843,586	$982,266
Southeast	$12,239	$301	$11,938	
Southwest	$5,718,151	$74,714	$2,881,098	$1,451,036
United Kingdom	$3,391,712	$32,240	$1,615,046	$1,031,765
Grand Total	$29,358,677	$339,773	$14,813,619	$7,611,754

Advanced Filters

So far you have used only simple filters inside `CALCULATE()`, in this format:

```
TableName[ColumnName] = some value
```

You can also use a more advanced filter that is passed in the form of a table containing the values required for the filter. This table can be either of the following:

- A physical table
- A function that returns a table (e.g., `ALL()`, `VALUES()`, `FILTER()`)

Importantly, both physical tables and functions that return tables, when used as advanced filter parameters, *retain all relationships that exist in the data model*. Advanced filters and the way tables retain their relationships in the data model is a complex topic that is covered in more detail in upcoming chapters. For now, it is enough to know that so far you have only learnt about simple filters for `CALCULATE()`, and the advanced table filters are coming later.

Making DAX Easy to Read

Now is a good time to pause and talk about how to lay out your DAX so it is easy to read. Consider this example:

```
Total Sales Value of Bikes Sold to Single Males in
Australia= CALCULATE([Total Sales], Customers[MaritalStatus]=
"S" ,Products[Category]="Bikes",Customers[Gender]=
"M",Territories[Country]="Australia")
```

When you get formulas that are very long like this, they can be very hard to read. The generally accepted approach is to lay out a formula using line breaks and spaces so it is easier to see which parts of the formula belong together. There is no single right way to do this. Here is one way that I find useful:

```
Total Sales Value of Bikes Sold to Single Males in Australia
= CALCULATE([Total Sales],
    Customers[MaritalStatus] = "S",
    Products[Category]= "Bikes"
    Customers[Gender] = "M",
    Territories[Country] = "Australia"
  )
```

To create a new line in the Measure dialog box, you need to press Shift+Enter on the keyboard.

In the example above, I put the first parameter in `CALCULATE()` (which is the expression) on the first line, followed by a comma. Then I placed each filter on a new line and indented them so it is easy to see that they belong to the `CALCULATE()` function.

The final closing parenthesis for the `CALCULATE()` function is on a new line of its own, aligned with the C in `CALCULATE()` so that I know that this bracket closes the `CALCULATE()` function.

> **Note:** To create indents from the left, simply press the spacebar four or five times for each line. It is fine to use as many spaces as you like in your DAX formulas: Spaces and line breaks have no impact on the evaluation of the formulas.

Using DAX Formatter

DAX Formatter is a very useful (and free) tool that you can use to help format your DAX. Marco Russo and Alberto Ferrari from SQLBI developed the free http://daxformatter.com website. You simply paste your DAX code into the website, and DAX Formatter formats the code for you. You can then cut and paste it back into the formula bar in Power Pivot. But be sure to read the following warning before you try it for yourself.

> **Warning: Switching Windows with the Measure Dialog Open:** Remember that the Measure dialog box (shown below) is a modal window. When you cut and paste a formula from this window, and then switch to a browser so you can use DAX Formatter, you may experience a problem when you try to switch back to Excel. If this Measure dialog box is open, it can sometimes "hide" behind the regular Excel window when you switch back to Excel from another window. When this happens, you can see the regular Excel window, but when you try to click in Excel, you get an annoying "bing, bing" sound that tells you something is wrong. The likely issue is that the Measure dialog box is open and hiding behind the Excel window. To fix this, press and hold the Alt key and then press Tab. Task Manager shows all the windows that are currently open in the background. Look

for the Measure dialog and, while still holding down Alt, select it by pressing Tab multiple times until it is in focus. When you release the Alt key, Windows brings the modal window into focus and allows you to finish the task.

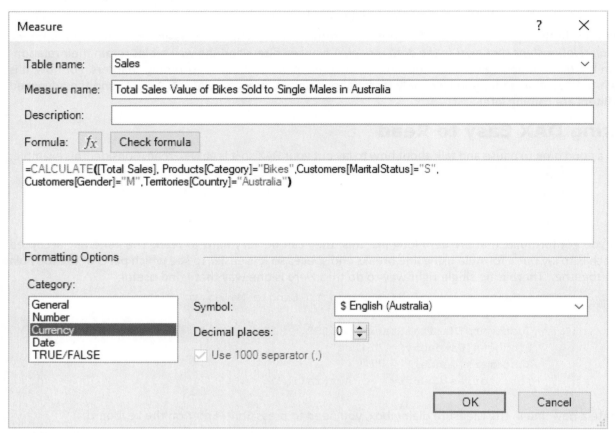

When you use DAX Formatter, you have a choice about whether to include the measure name. In Excel, when you cut and paste a measure from the Measure dialog box, the measure name is not copied. The example below therefore excludes the measure name. (If you were to do this in Power BI Desktop, the measure name would be copied as well.)

Here is the measure from above without the measure name:

```
1    =
2    CALCULATE (
3        [Total Sales],
4        Customers[MaritalStatus] = "S",
5        Products[Category] = "Bikes",
6        Customers[Gender] = "M",
7        Territories[Country] = "Australia"
8    )
```

Error Checking

DAX Formatter does another important job for you: It checks whether your DAX formula is valid and written correctly. If it is not, DAX Formatter does its best to show you where any errors are located. To see this in action, try removing one of the commas from the DAX code above (such as the one after Gender = M, so it looks like this):

```
Total Sales Value of Bikes Sold to Single Males in Australia
= CALCULATE( [Total Sales],
    Customers[MaritalStatus] = "S",
    Products[Category]= "Bikes",
    Customers[Gender] = "M"
    Territories[Country] = "Australia"
  )
```

When you put this erroneous code into DAX Formatter, a triangle points to the part of the code where an unexpected value is found, as shown below.

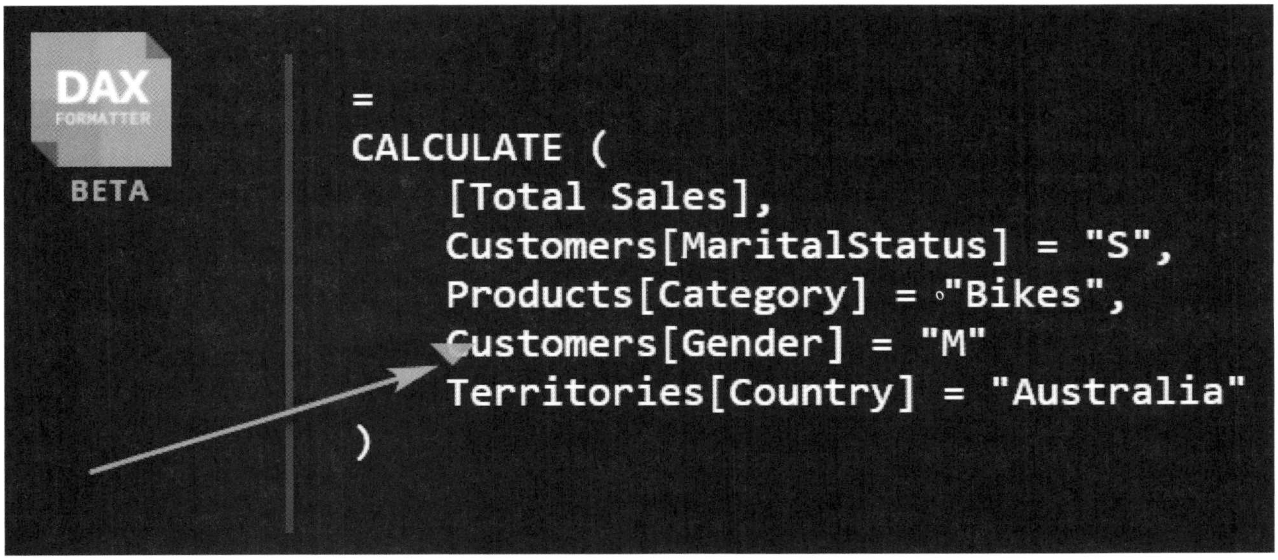

In this case, DAX Formatter is expecting a comma but instead finds the letter T—the start of the next column name. DAX Formatter is a great tool for helping you debug your DAX code when you can't work out what is wrong (although it was not strictly designed to do this). I use DAX Formatter all the time to help me with my DAX. I suggest you do, too.

> **Note:** Marco Russo told me that DAX Formatter was never designed to be an official error-checking tool, as I describe using it above. As a result, the error checking is not perfect, but in my view, it is still worth trying this approach if you are stuck.

10: Concept: Evaluation Context and Context Transition

This chapter covers one of the most difficult topics to understand and master in DAX. It is not essential that you understand this topic as you start using DAX. But if you want to be a DAX superhero, you will have to learn it at some time. If you find it hard to understand, don't worry. Simply come back later, when you have more experience, and read this chapter again. Do this as many times as needed.

As you saw in Chapter 5, DAX has a concept of a *filter context*. As you saw in Chapter 7, DAX also has a concept of a *row context*. Filter context and row context are the two different types of *evaluation context*, the topic of this chapter.

A Refresher on Filter Context

In Chapter 5 I introduced a number of concepts, including *filter context* and *initial filter context*. Here is a quick refresher.

Filter context refers to any filtering that is applied to the data model in DAX. Filter context is created by a pivot table and also by the CALCULATE() function. The *initial filter context* is the natural filtering that is applied by a pivot table. The initial filter context can come from the following four areas of a pivot table:

- Rows (see #1 below)
- Columns (#2)
- Filters (#3)
- Slicers (#4)

Don't confuse the filter context coming from Rows in a pivot table with row context. These are two completely different things. Filter context is the natural "slicing" that comes from the coordinates of a pivot table. The Rows section in a pivot table is one of the four locations that can slice your data, and all four locations are part of the initial filter context.

The filter context coming from a report *filters* the underlying tables in the data model. If the tables are joined, the filters propagate from the "one" side of the relationship to the "many" side of the relationship. But the filter does not propagate from the "many" side of the relationship to the "one" side. This is why I recommend (for Excel users anyway) setting up the data model using the Collie layout methodology, described in Chapter 2 and shown again below. When you use this layout, you have less to get your head around, and you can simply visualise filter propagation flowing downhill like water.

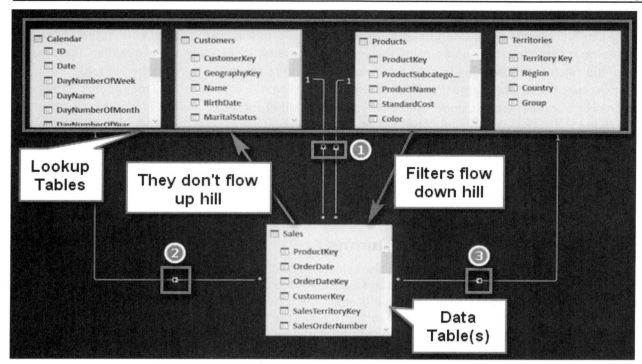

This setup provides a visual clue that the filters flow downhill through the relationships but do not flow uphill through the relationships.

> **Note:** It is possible to filter a lookup table (sitting above) based on the results in a data table (sitting below) using DAX instead of filter propagation. But filters only ever automatically propagate through the relationships downhill in the direction of the arrows.

A Refresher on Row Context

Row context refers to the ability of a special iterating function or calculated column to be "aware" of which row it is acting on at each stage of formula evaluation. Some functions (e.g., the X-functions, FILTER()) and all calculated columns have a row context. When you think about row context, think of the function (or calculated column) iterating through the table one row at a time and *selecting* the single value (the intersection between the column and row) and then acting on that single value. Regular measures can't do this; only formulas that have a row context and calculated columns can perform this trick.

Let's look again at the SUMX() measure from Chapter 7, shown below.

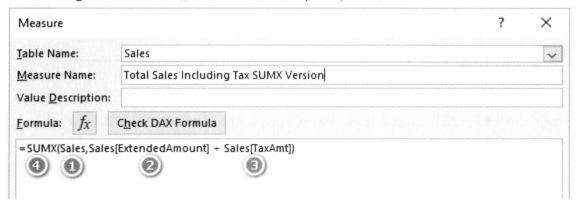

SUMX() first creates a row context over the Sales table (see #1 above). It then iterates through this table one row at a time. At each row, it takes the single value that is the intersection of the Sales[ExtendedAmount] column (#2) and the current row and adds it to the single value that is the intersection of the Sales[TaxAmt] (#3) column and the current row. It does this for each row in the table specified in the first parameter (#1) and then adds up all the values (#4).

Note: One thing I often get asked at this point is "Why does the formula refer to the table name twice—once in the first parameter and again inside the second and subsequent parameters?" The reason is that the table names inside the second parameter are actually a fully qualified address of the column. It is possible to have two columns with the same name in two different tables. You must specify the table name first (*TableName* [*ColumnName*]); otherwise, you may get the wrong answer from the wrong column (same column name, different table). Also, it is possible that the table in the first parameter could be (and often is) different to the tables where the columns come from in the second and subsequent parameters.

In short, think of the first parameter as the name of the table to iterate over and think of the references to the table name in the second parameter, *TableName* [*ColumnName*], as being the fully qualified address of the column you are operating on.

Row Context in Calculated Columns

You already know that iterator functions and also calculated columns have a row context. The main difference between an iterator function (e.g., SUMX()) and a calculated column is that the calculated column stores the value calculated at each row of the iteration process in the column itself. Measures that have a row context do not do this. In the SUMX() example, the function returns the final result to the pivot table without storing all the intermediate values (beyond the need to temporarily keep track of them in memory during the calculation process). This is the main reason you should avoid using calculated columns, if possible: They take up storage space in your data model and hence make your files larger and generally slower.

Understanding That a Row Context Does Not Automatically Create a Filter Context

This is a very important point that you must understand clearly: A row context does not automatically create a filter context. Also, a row context does not follow relationships. To understand this better, go to the Power Pivot data model and jump to the Products table. Then go all the way to the right and insert a new calculated column, as shown below.

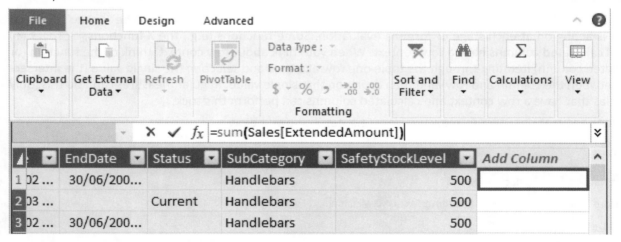

You should recognise this formula because it is exactly the same as the first formula in this book ([Total Sales]):

        =SUM(Sales[ExtendedAmount])

What value do you think will appear in every row of this new column? Do you expect it to be the total for the product in each row? Do you expect it to be the total for all products? Well, the answer may surprise you, and it is directly related to the point that a row context does not automatically create a filter context.

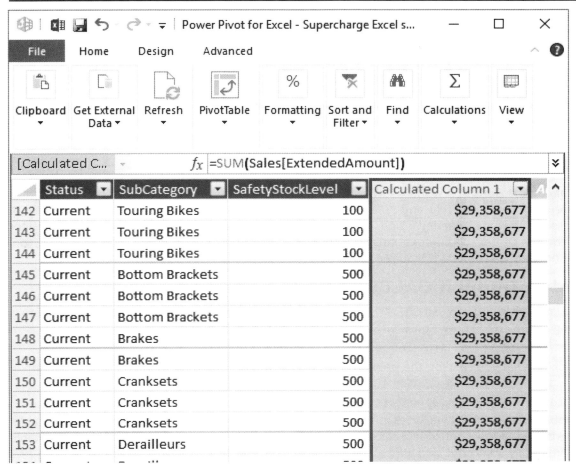

As you can see in the figure above, the value is the same for every single row in the table. There is no filtering on the Sales table (or any other table, for that matter) as a result of this formula, and hence the answer is always the same for every row. There is a row context in this formula: The rows are evaluated one at a time. But that row context does not create a filter context. Given that there is no filter context, the Sales table is completely unfiltered, and hence SUM(Sales[ExtendedAmount]) must return the result of the unfiltered Sales table.

It is, however, possible to turn the row context from this calculated column into a filter context through a process called *context transition*. To do this, simply wrap the above formula in a CALCULATE() function, as shown below.

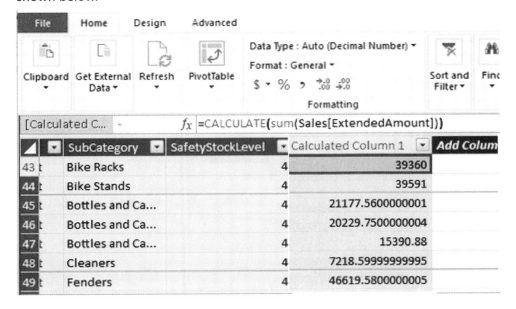

When you do this, the row context that exists in the calculated column is transformed into an equivalent filter context. The `CALCULATE()` function then "runs" the filter propagation engine so the filter on the `Products` table propagates through the relationship to the `Sales` table *before* the calculation is completed (for each row in the table). You therefore potentially end up with a different value in each row of the column. The value is actually the total sales for the product in each row (and some rows are blank because there are no sales).

You can think of the formula working like this:

```
= CALCULATE(SUM(Sales[ExtendedAmount]),
    Products[ProductKey] = the product represented
   by this row in the table
   )
```

The concept of context transition works anywhere that a row context exists—that is, in calculated columns as well as in iterators like `FILTER()` and `SUMX()`. This is the special use case first mentioned in Chapter 9, where there are no filters at all needed inside `CALCULATE()`, but instead `CALCULATE()` creates a new filter context from the row context via context transition. You can add additional filters inside `CALCULATE()`, too, if you want or need to, but none are required.

The Hidden Implicit CALCULATE()

Now that you know that you can use `CALCULATE()` to convert a row context into a filter context, there is one more thing you need to know. Consider this formula from earlier in the book:

```
Total Sales = SUM(Sales[ExtendedAmount])
```

Now think back to what you read on the previous page. What happened when we added a new column in the `Products` table, as follows?

```
Total Sales Column =SUM(Sales[ExtendedAmount])
```

Do you remember? We got the value $29.3 million all the way down the new column in the `Products` table. Why? Because there is a row context in a calculated column, but there is no filter context. The `Sales` table is therefore completely unfiltered, and hence `SUM(Sales[ExtendedAmount])` simply must return $29.3 million for every row.

Now back to this measure:

```
Total Sales = SUM(Sales[ExtendedAmount])
```

Notice that the formula for this measure is identical to the calculated column (the first example above but with a different name, of course). So if the formula inside the measure is identical to the formula in the calculated column, you can be excused for thinking that you could substitute the formula in the calculated column with the actual measure, as follows:

```
Total Sales Column Alternate = [Total Sales]
```

If the measure `[Total Sales]` has the same formula, won't we get the same result? Well, actually no. We get a different result from before, as shown below.

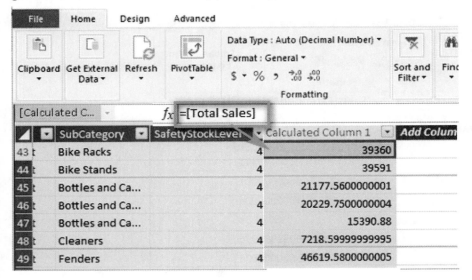

Go back and look again. Here is a summary of what you will find:

```
Total Sales Column 1 = SUM(Sales[ExtendedAmount])
```

This calculated column will return $29.3 million all the way down the column. There is a row context but no filter context, so the formula must return $29.3 million for each row in the table.

This next calculated column will return the total sales for each product in the products table (a different number for each product):

```
Total Sales Column 2 = CALCULATE(SUM(Sales[ExtendedAmount]))
```

There is a row context, and because of the CALCULATE() function, the row context is converted to an equivalent filter context through the process of context transition. CALCULATE() converts the row context from the Products table into an equivalent filter context, and this new filter context propagates to the Sales table for each row of the calculated column.

The following calculated column also returns the total sales for each product in the Products table:

```
Total Sales Column 3 = [Total Sales]
```

This calculated column returns exactly the same result as Total Sales Column 2. If you take a look inside the measure [Total Sales], you can't actually see a CALCULATE() function; you didn't include CALCU-LATE() in the measure. But there is an implicit CALCULATE() there that you can't see. Every measure has an implicit CALCULATE(), and that is why this calculated column behaves like column 2 and not like column 1.

> **Note:** There is a lot to learn about context transition that is more advanced and beyond the scope of this book. Any book by Marco Russo and Alberto Ferrari that covers context transition would be a great learning resource (but not for the fainthearted). There are also some great videos available at http://sqlbi.com and several articles on my blog, http://xbi.com.au/blog, on the topic. I provide links to these and many other resources in Chapter 22.

If you've arrived at this point and don't fully understand context transition, don't worry: You are not alone. This is one of the hardest topics to learn and understand well. Sleep on it for a few nights, do some practice, and then come back and reread this chapter again (along with Chapter 9, on CALCULATE()). You may need to reread this content many times before it completely sinks in.

11: DAX Topic: IF(), SWITCH(), and FIND()

DAX has a number of useful functions that allow you to apply a test and then branch the formula based on the results from that test. You will most likely be familiar with this concept from the IF() function in Excel.

The IF() Function

The IF() function in DAX is almost identical to IF() in Excel:

> IF(*Logical Test*, *Result if True*, [*Result if False*])

Note that the last parameter, [*Result if False*], is optional. If you omit this parameter and the result is FALSE, the IF() formula returns BLANK().

The SWITCH() Function

The SWITCH() function is a lot like Select Case in VBA programming. The structure of a SWITCH() formula is as follows:

> SWITCH(*expression*, *value*, *result*[, *value*, *result*]...[, *else*])

This syntax is a little confusing, so let's go through a simple example with another calculated column.

Navigate to the Power Pivot window, go to the Customers table Data view, and move to the right, ready to add this new calculated column:

> = SWITCH(Customers[HouseOwnerFlag],1,"Owns their house",0,"Doesn't own their house","Unknown")

It is much easier to understand SWITCH() if you use http://daxformatter.com to improve the layout, as shown below.

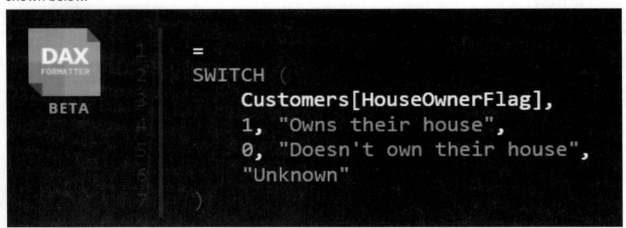

You can see in this figure above that line 3 is the branching point. The possible values in the HouseOwnerFlag column are 0 and 1 in this instance. Lines 4 and 5 offer up pairs of input and output values. So, if the value of HouseOwnerFlag is 1, the result "Owns their house" is returned. If the value of HouseOwnerFlag is 0, the result "Doesn't own their house" is returned.

Line 6 is a single value, and it applies to all other possible values of HouseOwnerFlag (although there are none in this example).

The FIND() Function

The FIND() function in DAX is almost identical to the FIND() function in Excel. In DAX it has this format:

> =FIND (*FindText*, *WithinText*,[*StartPos*],[*NotFoundValue*])

Even though this syntax suggests that *StartPos* and *NotFoundValue* are optional, in my experience (as of this writing), you actually do need to provide values for these parameters.

An Example Using IF() and FIND()

This example shows how to create a calculated column on a lookup table. As I have said previously, it is perfectly valid to create calculated columns in lookup tables, but wherever possible, it is better practice to create these columns in your source data or using Power Query. Remember why this is important:

- Calculated columns may take up more space than imported columns (but this is generally not a major issue for lookup tables).
- If you are manually creating a calculated column, it exists only in that single workbook, and you need to re-create it over and over for every other workbook where you need the column.

If it is not possible to create a column in your source data for some reason, then creating a calculated column instead is a great solution, particularly for lookup tables.

In this example, you are going to create a column for mountain products that doesn't exist in your lookup table. Any product with the word *mountain* in the description will be flagged as a mountain product.

In Power Pivot, switch to Data view if needed and navigate to the `Products` table. Scroll all the way to the right of the table until you see the Add Column heading. Click just below Add Column (see #1 below) and then click in the formula bar (#2).

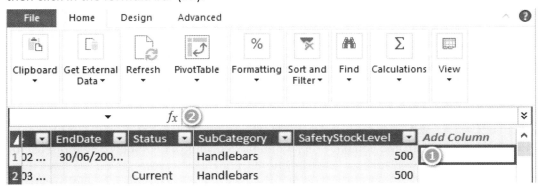

Then type the following formula:

```
=FIND("Mountain", Products[ModelName],1,0)
```

This formula searches for the word *mountain* in the `ModelName` column. Remember that because a calculated column has a row context, it is possible to refer to the column in this way, and it will calculate a result for every row in the `Products` table and store the answer in the column.

The result is an integer representing the starting position where the word *mountain* is found. If the word *mountain* is not found, then the value `0` (the last parameter in the formula) will be returned. So, you get something like the table shown below.

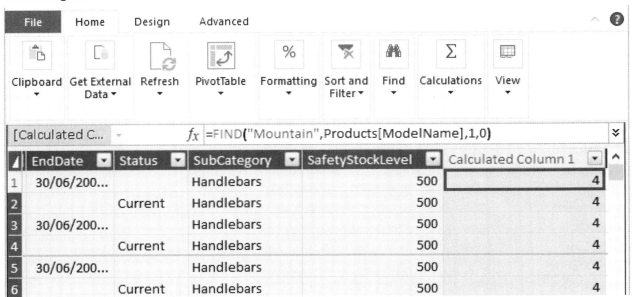

This table is not overly useful as is, but you can wrap an `IF()` statement around this formula to make it more useful. As shown below, you can use the `IF()` statement to return TRUE if the number is greater than zero (i.e., if it is a mountain product) and return FALSE if it is equal to zero (i.e., it is not a mountain product). You should also rename the column heading `Is Mountain Product` (by double-clicking the heading and typing the new name).

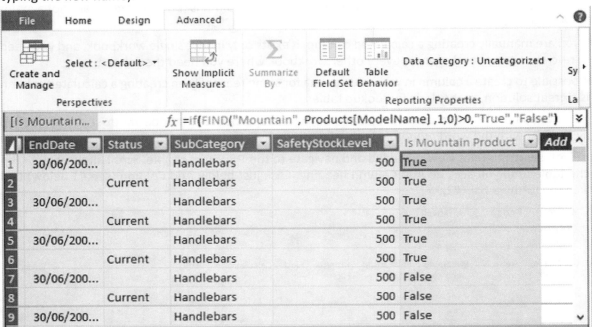

Now you have a new calculated column, and you have further enhanced your data model to be more useful. Remember that this calculated column will take up space in your file and disk. However, given the small number of unique values (only `True` and `False` in this case) and the fact that this column is in a lookup table, this column won't take up much space. The greater the number of unique values in a column, the more disk space and memory the column consumes.

You can now use this new column anywhere in a pivot table to produce new insights that weren't previously visible in the data. Because this formula is a column in the data model, it can be used to filter the pivot table.

In the example below, this new column is placed on Columns in a pivot table.

Total Sales	Column Labels		
Row Labels	False	True	Grand Total
Clerical	$3,283,754	$1,401,033	$4,684,787
Management	$3,431,066	$2,036,795	$5,467,862
Manual	$1,964,880	$893,091	$2,857,971
Professional	$6,088,790	$3,819,187	$9,907,977
Skilled Manual	$4,378,594	$2,061,487	$6,440,081
Grand Total	$19,147,085	$10,211,593	$29,358,677

12: DAX Topic: VALUES() and HASONEVALUE()

In Chapter 9 I introduced the idea that CALCULATE() can use two types of filters: simple filters and advanced filters. Simple filters are in this form:

TableName[ColumnName] = some value

On the other hand, an advanced filter takes a table as a filter input. In other words, you use an existing table (or create a virtual table on-the-fly) that contains the rows you want included in the filter, and CALCULATE() applies that filter to the data model before completing the evaluation of the main expression.

Creating Virtual Tables

The tables you create using functions can be thought of as being "virtual" because they are not physically stored as part of the data model. They are created on-the-fly inside your DAX formulas and can be used during the evaluation of just the specific formulas containing the virtual table. Importantly, when you create a virtual table using a formula, the new virtual table will have a virtual relationship to the data model, and that virtual relationship will propagate the filter context in exactly the same way that the permanent relationships do. (You'll learn more about this later in the chapter.) Virtual tables are said to *retain lineage* with their source tables.

The VALUES() Function

VALUES() is the first function you have come to in this book that returns a (virtual) table. If you type the word **values** into the Measure dialog and read the tooltip before typing **(**, you can see that this function returns a table, as shown below.

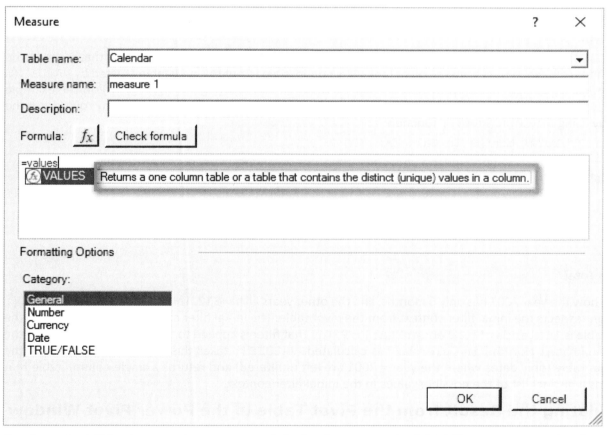

One important thing to note about VALUES() is that it respects the initial filter context coming from your pivot table. So if you combine this fact that VALUES() respects the initial filter context with the information provided by IntelliSense in the image above, you will see that VALUES() returns a single-column table that contains the list of all possible values in the initial filter context.

It's time to work through some examples that demonstrate the point.

A Calendar Example

Set up a new pivot table like the one shown below and put 'Calendar'[CalendarYear] on Rows.

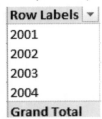

Then write the following measure in the Measure dialog box:

```
Total Months in Calendar
    = COUNTROWS(VALUES('Calendar'[MonthName]))
```

> **Note:** The following formula will not work here:
> ```
>         Total Months in Calendar wrong
>             = COUNTROWS('Calendar'[MonthName])
> ```
> This formula doesn't work because COUNTROWS() expects a table as the input, but 'Calendar'[MonthName] is not a table; rather, it is a column that is part of a bigger table (the Calendar table, in this case).

When you wrap 'Calendar'[MonthName] inside the VALUES() function, this single column that is part of the Calendar table is converted into a table in its own right, and it retains a relationship (lineage) to the original Calendar table. This new table returned by VALUES() is still a single column, but now it technically is a table *with the* column instead of simply being a column that is part of some other table (Calendar, in this case).

So VALUES('Calendar'[MonthName]) returns a single-column table of possible values that respects the initial filter context coming from the pivot table. It is not possible to put this new table created by VALUES() into a regular measure unless you wrap it inside some other formula (e.g., an aggregator). In the example above, you first create the table (the VALUES part of the formula) and then count how many rows are in the table by using the COUNTROWS() function:

```
Total Months in Calendar
    = COUNTROWS(VALUES('Calendar'[MonthName]))
```

Row Labels ▾	Total Months in Calendar
2001	6
2002	12
2003	12
2004	12
Grand Total	**12**

Notice how the year 2001 has only 6 months, and the other years all have 12. This is proof that the VALUES() function respects the initial filter context from the pivot table. The initial filter context for the first row in the pivot table is 'Calendar'[CalendarYear] = 2001. That filter is applied to the calendar table before the formula [Total Months in Calendar] is calculated. VALUES() takes this "prefiltered" version of the calendar table (only dates where the year = 2001 are left unfiltered) and returns a single-column table that contains a distinct list of the possible values in the initial filter context.

Simulating the Result from the Pivot Table in the Power Pivot Window

You can simulate what is happening here by going into the Power Pivot window, browsing to the Calendar table, and applying a filter on the Calendar table to show only calendar year = 2001 (see below).

If you then go to the MonthName column and select the filter, you see that only months in the second half of the calendar year exist.

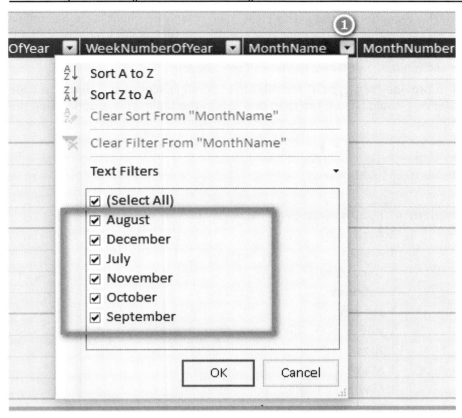

Returning a Single Value

VALUES() returns a single-column table of unique values from any column in any table, and this new table of values respects the initial filter context coming from the pivot table. There is another very cool feature of VALUES() that is very powerful: In the special case where VALUES() returns just a single row in the single-column table (i.e., one value), you can refer to this value directly in your formulas.

If you take the example created above, remove CalendarYear from Rows, and put MonthName on Rows instead, you should get the following.

Row Labels	Total Months in Calendar
April	1
August	1
December	1
February	1
January	1
July	1
June	1
March	1
May	1
November	1
October	1
September	1
Grand Total	**12**

Now you can see above that with the exception of the grand total, each row in the pivot table has only a single value for `[Total Months in Calendar]`. So as long as you write the formula in such a way that it operates over only a single row of the table, you can create a measure that *returns the name of the month* into the actual pivot table Values section (i.e., not Rows, as you can see above).

To write this formula, you need to provide "protection" for the other possible scenarios where the code `VALUES('Calendar'[MonthName])` could have more than one row in the table. This is done using the formula `HASONEVALUE()`, like so:

```
Month Name (Values)
    = IF(HASONEVALUE('Calendar'[MonthName]),
      VALUES('Calendar'[MonthName])
    )
```

Row Labels ▾	Total Months in Calendar	Month Name (Values)
April	1	April
August	1	August
December	1	December
February	1	February
January	1	January
July	1	July
June	1	June
March	1	March
May	1	May
November	1	November
October	1	October
September	1	September
Grand Total	**12**	

Remember that the structure of an `IF()` statement is as follows:

```
= IF(Logical Test, Result if True, [Result if False])
```

The last parameter is optional. If you leave it out, then you are accepting the default value of `BLANK()`.

If you write the above formula without the `HASONEVALUE()` function, it will throw an error. Even if you remove the grand total from the pivot table, it will still throw an error. DAX allows you to use the single value returned in a single row of the single-column table (created by `Values`) only if you protect the formula with `HASONEVALUE()`.

> **Note:** The DAX function called `CONCATENATEX()`, first released in Excel 2016, iterates over a list of values in a table and concatenates them together into a single value. Using this new function therefore allows you to write a formula that returns the single value when there is just one value and then concatenate all the values into a single value when there are multiple values. Such a formula might look like this:
>
> ```
> Month Name (Values)
>     = CONCATENATEX(VALUES('Calendar'[MonthName]),
>       'Calendar'[MonthName],", ")
>     )
> ```
>
> There is no need to use the `IF HASONEVALUE()` test in this example because `CONCATENATEX()` correctly manages the scenario where there is more than one row in the `Values` virtual table.

Here's How: Changing the MonthName Sort Order

In the example above, you can see that the month names in the pivot table are sorting in alphabetical order rather than in the logical month order of a calendar year. By default, all columns in all tables sort in alphanumeric order. It is, however, possible to change the sort order.

Follow these steps to change the sort order in a table:

1. Go to the Power Pivot window and navigate to the `Calendar` table in the Data view.

2. Click in the `MonthName` column (see #1 below) and then click the Sort by Column button (#2) and select Sort by Column (#3).

3. In the Sort by Column dialog box that appears, set the By Column value to `MonthNumberOfYear`.

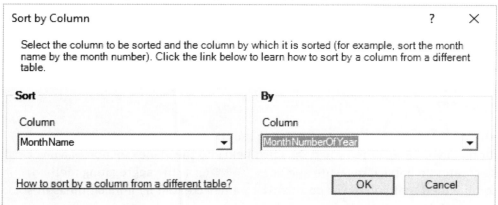

4. When you return to your pivot table, the rows are sorted in logical month order, as shown below.

Row Labels ▼	Total Months in Calendar	Month Name (Values)
January	1	January
February	1	February
March	1	March
April	1	April
May	1	May
June	1	June
July	1	July
August	1	August
September	1	September
October	1	October
November	1	November
December	1	December
Grand Total	**12**	

It is best practice to always load a numeric column in your lookup table for every alphabetical column that needs to be sorted in a different order. You should therefore always include a numeric column in your `Cal-endar` table for days of week as well as months of year.

> **Note:** When you create a numeric sort column in a table, there must be a one-to-one match between the values in the numeric sort order and the values in the column to be sorted.

Practice Exercises: VALUES()

Create a new pivot table and put Products[Category] on Rows and the measure [Total Number of Products] on Values. Then write the following measures by first creating a VALUES() table and then wrapping this table inside a COUNTROWS() function, as in the example shown earlier in this chapter. Find the solutions to these practice exercises in Appendix A.

39. [Number of Color Variants]

40. [Number of Sub Categories]

41. [Number of Size Ranges]

Use the column Products[SizeRange] for this one.

You should end up with a pivot table that looks like the one below.

Row Labels	Total Number of Products	Number of Color Variants	Number of Sub Categories	Number of Size Ranges
Accessories	35	6	12	2
Bikes	125	5	3	5
Clothing	48	5	8	5
Components	189	7	14	6
Grand Total	**397**	**10**	**37**	**11**

> **Note:** Each of these measures is the equivalent of dragging the column name and dropping it into the Values section for the pivot table. When you drop a text field into the Values section of a pivot table, the pivot table creates an implicit measure and uses COUNT() as the aggregating method. But recall that I recommended that you never do this. The names created by implicit measures are ugly, and you need the DAX practice, so you should always write explicit DAX measures.

Next, you should use the same pivot table from above but remove the measure [Number of Size Ranges] from the pivot table. Then write the following measures that each return a single value (the text name) into a cell in the pivot table. Each formula has the word (Values) in the name so it is clear that the formulas are returning the actual value to the pivot; this is just a "note to self." In each example, make sure you wrap your VALUES() function in an IF(HASONEVALUE()) function, as in the example earlier in the chapter.

42. [Product Category (Values)]

43. [Product Subcategory (Values)]

44. [Product Color (Values)]

When you have finished, your pivot table should look as shown below. Notice that two of these measures are blank. This is because the VALUES formula has more than one value, and hence the IF HASONEVALUE part of the formula returns a BLANK(); this is the default if you omit the last parameter.

Row Labels	Total Number of Products	Number of Color Variants	Number of Sub Categories	Number of Size Ranges	Product Category (Values)	Product Subcategory (Values)	Product Color (Values)
Accessories	35	6	12	2	Accessories		
Bikes	125	5	3	5	Bikes		
Clothing	48	5	8	5	Clothing		
Components	189	7	14	6	Components		
Grand Total	**397**	**10**	**37**	**11**			

45. Modifying Practice Exercise 43

Try editing the IF() statement for [Product Sub Category (Values)] so that it returns the value More than 1 Sub Category instead of BLANK(). The syntax for IF is IF (Logical Test, Result if True, Result if False).

46. Modifying Practice Exercise 44

Now try editing the IF() statement for [Product Color (Values)] so that it returns More than 1 Color instead of BLANK(). You should end up with something like the following (which shows answers for Practice Exercises 45 and 46).

Row Labels	Total Number of Products	Number of Color Variants	Number of Sub Categories	Number of Size Ranges	Product Category (Values)	Product Subcategory (Values)	Product Color (Values)
Accessories	35	6	12	2 Accessories	More than 1 Sub Category	More than 1 Color
Bikes	125	5	3	5 Bikes	More than 1 Sub Category	More than 1 Color
Clothing	48	5	8	5 Clothing	More than 1 Sub Category	More than 1 Color
Components	189	7	14	6 Components	More than 1 Sub Category	More than 1 Color
Grand Total	397	10	37	11		More than 1 Sub Category	More than 1 Color

Finally, add a couple slicers to your pivot table and watch what happens when you use them. Click inside your pivot table and then select Insert, Slicer from the main ribbon. From the Products table, add slicers for colour and subcategory. When you click on these slicers, the values in the pivot table update to reflect the filtering in the slicers.

Row Labels	Total Number of Products	Number of Color Variants	Number of Sub Categories	Number of Size Ranges	Product Category (Values)	Product Subcategory (Values)	Product Color (Values)
Accessories	3	1	1	1 Accessories	Helmets	Blue
Bikes	13	1	1	4 Bikes	Touring Bikes	Blue
Clothing	3	1	1	3 Clothing	Vests	Blue
Components	9	1	1	4 Components	Touring Frames	Blue
Grand Total	28	1	4	8		More than 1 Sub Category	Blue

SubCategory		Color	
Helmets	^	Black	^
Touring Bikes		Blue	
Touring Frames		Grey	
Vests	v	Multi	v

13: DAX Topic: ALL(), ALLEXCEPT(), and ALLSELECTED()

The DAX functions ALL(), ALLEXCEPT(), and ALLSELECTED() are all very similar in what they do. Let's start with ALL() and then look at the other two variants.

The ALL() Function

The ALL() function removes all current filters from the initial filter context (or any other filter context that exists, for that matter). For this reason, ALL() can be considered the "remove filters" function. The easiest way to understand this is with an example.

Create a new pivot table and put Products[Category] on Rows and put the [Total Number of Products] measure you created earlier on Values. You get the pivot table shown below.

Row Labels ▾	Total Number of Products
Accessories	35
Bikes	125
Clothing	48
Components	189
Grand Total	397

Technically what is happening above is that the first row in the pivot table (which is highlighted in the figure) is filtering the Products table so that only products that are of type Products[Category]="Accessories" are visible (unfiltered) in the underlying table; the other products are all filtered out. They are not really visible, but you can imagine what the underlying table in your data model would look like with a filter applied to Accessories behind the scenes. You can simulate this in the Power Pivot window as shown below.

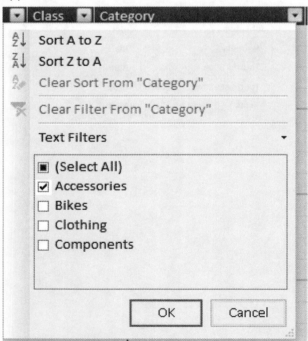

Back to the pivot table. After the pivot table applies a filter to the underlying tables, the measure [Total Number of Products] counts the rows that survive the filter. It does this for every cell in the pivot table, one at a time, including the grand total cell. In the case of the grand total cell, there is no filter applied at all, so the measure counts all rows in the table—completely unfiltered.

Now create the following new measure that uses the ALL() function:

```
Total All Products = COUNTROWS(ALL(Products))
```

The ALL() function returns a table. You can't see the table, but you can wrap COUNTROWS() around it so you can see how many rows are in the table.

As you type this formula, if you pause while typing, IntelliSense displays the syntax for ALL(), as shown below.

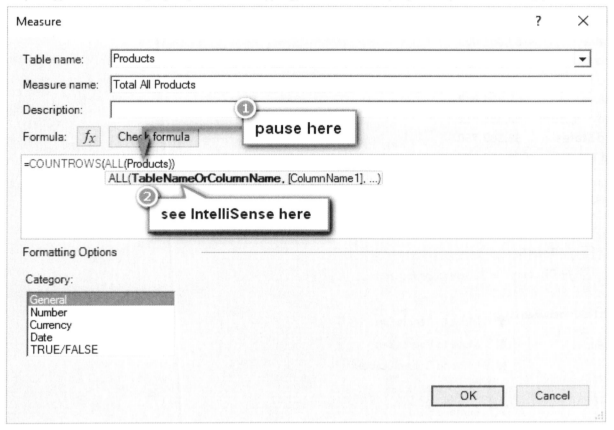

In this case, IntelliSense is saying that you can pass either a table or a single column as the first parameter for ALL(). In this example, you are passing the entire table. When you have finished typing this formula, add the measure to your pivot table, and you should get the results shown below.

Row Labels ▾	Total Number of Products	Total All Products
Accessories	35	397
Bikes	125	397
Clothing	48	397
Components	189	397
Grand Total	397	397

You can see from this pivot table that the new measure (the one on the right) is ignoring the initial filter context coming from the rows in the pivot table. What is happening here is that, first of all, the initial filter context is set by the row Products[Category], but the ALL() function always returns an unfiltered copy of the table, and hence it returns the entire Products table instead of the filtered Products table. So COUNTROWS() returns 397 for every row in the pivot table—including the grand total, as before.

Using ALL() as an Advanced Filter Input

The most common use of ALL() is as an advanced filter table input to a CALCULATE() function. Let's look at an example using ALL() as a table input to CALCULATE().

A good use for ALL() inside CALCULATE() is to remove the filters that are naturally applied to a pivot table so that you can access the number that is normally in the grand total line of the pivot table. Once you can access the equivalent grand total from any row in the pivot table, you can easily create a measure that finds the percentage of the total, which would be very useful indeed. The concept will make more sense as you work through the following example.

Calculating the Country Percentage of Total Sales

Say that you want to calculate the country percentage of global sales. First of all, set up a pivot table with Territories[Country] on Rows and [Total Sales] on Values, as shown below.

Row Labels	Total Sales
Australia	$9,061,001
Canada	$1,977,845
France	$2,644,018
Germany	$2,894,312
United Kingdom	$3,391,712
United States	$9,389,790
Grand Total	**$29,358,677**

It is then possible to go to the Values area, click on the measure [Total Sales], and select Value Field Settings.

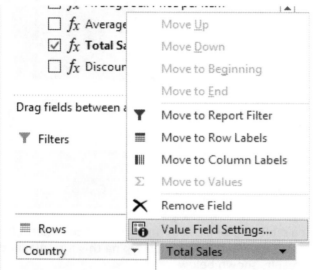

Then you can change the values and force them to display as % of Grand Total.

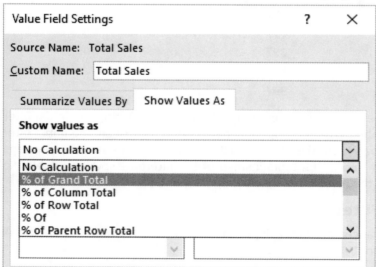

But if you do this, you are only changing the display format of the result and not actually calculating the percentage as part of your data model. This means you can't use these percentages inside other measures, and you also can't reference the percentages from cube formulas (discussed in Chapter 20).

Writing Your Own DAX Measures

As illustrated in the preceding section, it is a good practice to create a new measure that will return the actual value as a reusable asset in your data model. You can do this in two steps.

Tip: It is good practice to break the problem you are solving into pieces and solve one piece of the puzzle at a time.

Step 1: Create a Grand Total Measure

Click inside your pivot table and create the following new measure:

```
Total Global Sales
    = CALCULATE([Total Sales], All(Territories))
```

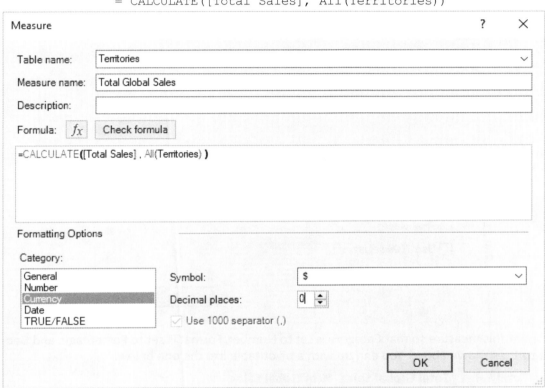

As you know, the first parameter of CALCULATE() is an expression, and the subsequent parameters are filters that modify the filter context. In this case, you are passing a table as the filter context. This table is ALL(Territories), which is actually an unfiltered copy of the entire Territories table.

After you add the new measure to the pivot table, it looks as shown below. Do you see that the new measure is ignoring the initial filter context coming from the pivot table? CALCULATE() is the only function that can modify the filter context (along with CALCULATETABLE()). In this case, CALCULATE() is replacing the initial filter context on Territories[Country] with a new filter context (an unfiltered copy of the Territories table).

Row Labels	Total Sales	Total Global Sales
Australia	$9,061,001	$29,358,677
Canada	$1,977,845	$29,358,677
France	$2,644,018	$29,358,677
Germany	$2,894,312	$29,358,677
NA		$29,358,677
United Kingdom	$3,391,712	$29,358,677
United States	$9,389,790	$29,358,677
Grand Total	**$29,358,677**	**$29,358,677**

Step 2: Create the Percentage of Total

After you have created the measure [Total Global Sales], it is easy to create a new calculated field to calculate the country percentage of global sales, as follows:

```
% of Global Sales
    = DIVIDE([Total Sales] , [Total Global Sales])
```

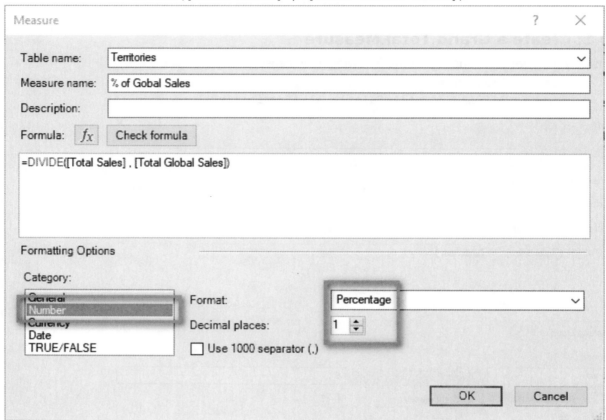

Make sure you format this measure so that Category is set to Number, Format is set to Percentage, and Decimal Places is set to 1, as shown above. You end up with a pivot table like the one below.

Row Labels	Total Sales	Total Global Sales	% of Gobal Sales
Australia	$9,061,001	$29,358,677	30.9%
Canada	$1,977,845	$29,358,677	6.7%
France	$2,644,018	$29,358,677	9.0%
Germany	$2,894,312	$29,358,677	9.9%
NA		$29,358,677	
United Kingdom	$3,391,712	$29,358,677	11.6%
United States	$9,389,790	$29,358,677	32.0%
Grand Total	$29,358,677	$29,358,677	100.0%

The final step is to remove the [Total Global Sales] measure from the pivot table.

> **Note:** You don't actually need the interim measures you write to be placed in the pivot table in order for the [% of Global Sales] measure to work. But you should notice how much easier it is to visualise what is happening when you write these measures in the context of a pivot table. When you do it this way, you can easily see how the [Total Global Sales] value is the same, regardless of the country in the pivot table, and hence you can immediately see that you just need to divide the country sales by this total global sales amount, and it is going to work.

The final pivot table is shown below, with some conditional formatting applied to make it easier to read.

Row Labels	Total Sales	% of Gobal Sales	
Australia	$9,061,001		30.9%
Canada	$1,977,845		6.7%
France	$2,644,018		9.0%
Germany	$2,894,312		9.9%
United Kingdom	$3,391,712		11.6%
United States	$9,389,790		32.0%
Grand Total	**$29,358,677**		100.0%

Passing a Table or a Column to ALL()

Before we finish with `ALL()`, it is worth pointing out that this next measure would return exactly the same result as [Total Global Sales] in the pivot table example in the section "Step 1: Create a Grand Total Measure," above:

```
Total All Country Sales
    = CALCULATE([Total Sales] , ALL( Territories[Country] ) )
```

Notice that this measure passes a single *column* instead of the entire *table* to the `ALL()` function. So in this specific pivot table, the values for [Total Global Sales] and [Total All Country Sales] are identical (see below).

Row Labels	Total Sales	Total Global Sales	Total All Country Sales
Australia	$9,061,001	$29,358,677	$29,358,677
Canada	$1,977,845	$29,358,677	$29,358,677
France	$2,644,018	$29,358,677	$29,358,677
Germany	$2,894,312	$29,358,677	$29,358,677
NA		$29,358,677	$29,358,677
United Kingdom	$3,391,712	$29,358,677	$29,358,677
United States	$9,389,790	$29,358,677	$29,358,677
Grand Total	**$29,358,677**	**$29,358,677**	**$29,358,677**

However, the measure [Total All Country Sales] would not work (i.e., it would not remove the filter) if there were some other column on Rows in the pivot table (something other than `Country`).

To test this, remove `Territories[Country]` from Rows in the pivot table and replace it with `Territories[Region]`. You get the result shown below.

Row Labels	Total Sales	Total Global Sales	Total All Country Sales
Australia	$9,061,001	$29,358,677	$9,061,001
Canada	$1,977,845	$29,358,677	$1,977,845
Central	$3,001	$29,358,677	$3,001
France	$2,644,018	$29,358,677	$2,644,018
Germany	$2,894,312	$29,358,677	$2,894,312
NA		$29,358,677	
Northeast	$6,532	$29,358,677	$6,532
Northwest	$3,649,867	$29,358,677	$3,649,867
Southeast	$12,239	$29,358,677	$12,239
Southwest	$5,718,151	$29,358,677	$5,718,151
United Kingdom	$3,391,712	$29,358,677	$3,391,712
Grand Total	**$29,358,677**	**$29,358,677**	**$29,358,677**

Notice the difference between passing the entire table name to the `ALL()` function and passing a single column. [Total Global Sales] removes the filter from the entire `Territories` table, but [Total All Country Sales] removes filters only from the `Territories[Country]` column of the table. In the image above, there is no filter on the `Territories[Country]` column of the table, and hence `ALL()` has no effect on the visual.

Remove [Total All Country Sales] from the pivot table before proceeding.

The ALLEXCEPT() Function

ALLEXCEPT() allows you to remove filters from all columns in a table except the ones that you explicitly specify. Consider the following example:

```
Total Sales to Region or Country
    = CALCULATE([Total Sales], All(Territories[Region]), All(Territories[Country])
    )
```

ALLEXCEPT() solves the problem implied above where you need to specify many columns individually in the case that you want most (but not all) columns in your formula. The above formula works when you have Territories[Country] on Rows and also when you have Territories[Region] on Rows, but it does not work with Territories[Group] on Rows. If you have a lot of columns in your table, you have to write a lot of DAX code to make such a formula work *for all but a few of the columns*.

This is where ALLEXCEPT() comes into play. The above formula can be rewritten as follows:

```
Total Sales to Region or Country 2
    = CALCULATE([Total Sales],
      ALLEXCEPT(Territories, Territories[Group])
    )
```

Note: You must first specify the table that is to be included and then specify the exception columns. The above formula removes all the filters from all columns in the Territories table, except for any filters applied to the Territories[Group] column. If there were 20 columns in the table and you wanted to remove filters on 19 of them, this function would be very useful indeed.

The ALLSELECTED() Function

The ALLSELECTED() function is useful when you want to calculate percentages as shown above and you have a filter applied (say, via a slicer), but you want the total in your pivot table to add up to 100%.

Say that you're working with the same pivot table used earlier in this chapter but now with a slicer that filters on Territories[Group]. Notice below that [% of Global Sales] adds up to 38.7%; this is correct because the other countries that make up the remaining 61.3% have been filtered out by the Group slicer.

Group	Row Labels	Total Sales	% of Gobal Sales
Europe	Canada	$1,977,845	6.7%
North America	Central	$3,001	0.0%
Pacific	Northeast	$6,532	0.0%
NA	Northwest	$3,649,867	12.4%
	Southeast	$12,239	0.0%
	Southwest	$5,718,151	19.5%
	Grand Total	**$11,367,634**	38.7%

But say that you want to see the percentage of each region out of all the values in the pivot (in this example, just the regions in the group North America as selected in the slicer). This is where ALLSELECTED() comes in. ALLSELECTED() removes the filters from the pivot table but respects the filters in the slicer.

Add the following measure to the above pivot:

```
Total Selected Groups
    = CALCULATE([Total Sales], ALLSELECTED(Territories))
```

Group	Row Labels	Total Sales	% of Gobal Sales	Total Selected Groups
Europe	Canada	$1,977,845	6.7%	$11,367,634
NA	Central	$3,001	0.0%	$11,367,634
North America	Northeast	$6,532	0.0%	$11,367,634
Pacific	Northwest	$3,649,867	12.4%	$11,367,634
	Southeast	$12,239	0.0%	$11,367,634
	Southwest	$5,718,151	19.5%	$11,367,634
	Grand Total	**$11,367,634**	38.7%	**$11,367,634**

Notice how the interim measure [Total Selected Groups] is returning the same value as the grand total of the items in the pivot table. Using the same steps as before, you can now write a new measure [% of Selected Groups] and then remove the interim measure [Total Selected Groups] from the pivot table.

Now write the following measure:

```
% of Selected Groups
    = DIVIDE([Total Sales] , [Total Selected Groups])
```

Group ⋮≡ ▼ₓ	Row Labels ▼	Total Sales	% of Global Sales	% of Selected Groups
Europe	Canada	$1,977,845	6.7%	17.4%
North America	Central	$3,001	0.0%	0.0%
Pacific	Northeast	$6,532	0.0%	0.1%
NA	Northwest	$3,649,867	12.4%	32.1%
	Southeast	$12,239	0.0%	0.1%
	Southwest	$5,718,151	19.5%	50.3%
	Grand Total	**$11,367,634**	**38.7%**	**100.0%**

Remember to format this new measure with Category set to Number, Format set to Percentage, and Decimal Places set to 1.

Using Interim Measures

Remember that it is good practice to split a problem into pieces and solve one piece of the problem at a time. My advice is to get used to creating interim measures first and then writing the final measure that you actually need. Doing this helps you visualise each step of the process and makes it easier to get each part of the end-state formula correct before you proceed to the next step.

It is, of course, possible to write one single measure that does all the steps you just went through. This is what it would look like:

```
% of Selected Groups ONE STEP
    = DIVIDE (
        [Total Sales] ,
        CALCULATE([Total Sales], ALLSELECTED(Territories))
    )
```

But this all-in-one formula is much harder to write, read, and debug—particularly when you are learning to write DAX. It's not wrong; it's just harder, and life is too short to do things that are harder than they need to be.

Practice Exercises: ALL(), ALLEXCEPT(), and ALLSELECTED()

It's time for some practice. Create a new pivot table and put Customers[Occupation] on Rows and the measure [Total Sales] on Values. You get the pivot table shown below.

Row Labels ▼	Total Sales
Clerical	$4,684,787
Management	$5,467,862
Manual	$2,857,971
Professional	$9,907,977
Skilled Manual	$6,440,081
Grand Total	**$29,358,677**

Then, using the principles covered in this chapter, create the following measures by first creating the interim measure you need and then creating the final measure. Find the solutions to these practice exercises in Appendix A.

47. [Total Sales to All Customers]

48. [% of All Customer Sales]

Now add a slicer for `Customers[Gender]` to the pivot table you just created and filter by Gender = M, as shown below.

Gender	Row Labels ▾	Total Sales	Total Sales to All Customers	% of All Customer Sales
F	Clerical	$2,421,327	$29,358,677	8.2%
M	Management	$2,793,527	$29,358,677	9.5%
	Manual	$1,463,060	$29,358,677	5.0%
	Professional	$4,773,493	$29,358,677	16.3%
	Skilled Manual	$3,093,651	$29,358,677	10.5%
	Grand Total	$14,545,059	$29,358,677	49.5%

Note that `[% of All Customer Sales]` doesn't add to 100%. This is correct because the other 50.5% of customers are filtered out with the slicer.

Set up another pivot table with `Customers[NumberCarsOwned]` on Rows, `Customers[Occupation]` on Slicer, and `[Total Sales]` on Values. Your job is to create the other measure in the pivot table below: `[% of Sales to Selected Customers]`. When you are done, your pivot table should look like the one below, with the last column showing the percentage of sales to customers based on the number of cars they own, and that still adds to 100% even after you select different values in the slicer.

Occupation	Row Labels ▾	Total Sales	% of Sales to Selected Customers
Clerical	0	$2,660,886	56.8%
Management	1	$1,204,496	25.7%
Manual	2	$790,154	16.9%
Professional	3	$28,141	0.6%
Skilled Manual	4	$1,109	0.0%
	Grand Total	$4,684,787	100.0%

Remember that in this case, you want to create an interim measure first, so you actually need to create the following two measures and then remove the first one from the pivot table.

49. [Total Sales to Selected Customers]

50. [% of Sales to Selected Customers]

Inserting Slicers

It's time to revisit slicers. Create a new pivot table and place `DayName` on Rows and place `CalendarYear` and `MonthName` on Slicer (by clicking in the pivot table, navigating to the Insert tab, and selecting Slicer). Create the pivot table shown below now and then read on to learn about the slicers.

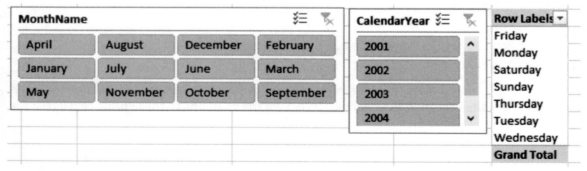

There are two things to notice here. First, the day names and month names are not sorted correctly in the slicer (as discussed in Chapter 12), and also the month name is set up to display in a grid four wide by three high instead of the default one column wide.

> **Note:** Chapter 12 provides instruction on how to change column sort order. The sort order of the table columns affects the sort order in pivot tables and also in slicers. You only need to set the sort order once in your data model (for each column), and the new sort order will change the sorting of both pivot tables and slicers. You should have already changed the sort order for the MonthName column in Chapter 12. If you haven't done that already, though, do it now.

There are two ways to insert a slicer with Excel 2013+. First, you can click in the pivot table and then click Insert, Slicer and select the column you need (in this case, MonthName). But there is an easier way, as described next.

Here's How: Inserting a Slicer

Follow these steps to insert a slicer:

1. Click inside the pivot table.
2. Go to the PivotTable Fields list and right-click the column you need (see #1 below).
3. Select Add as Slicer (#2).

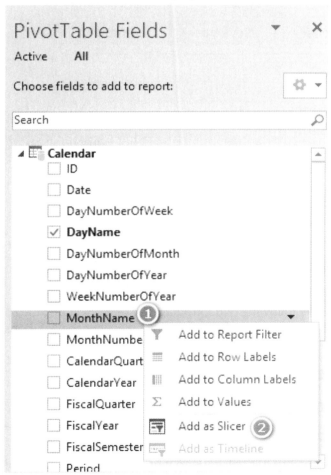

4. You can then optionally change the slicer layout. Select the slicer, click Slicer Tools, Options (see #1 below), and then change the number of columns to 4 (#2).

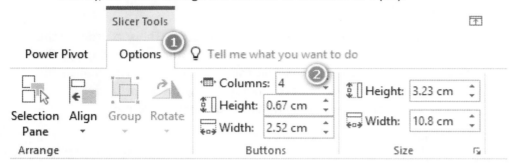

Now is a good time to add [Total Sales] to the pivot table as it will help you visualise the interim steps in producing this measure.

MonthName			
January	February	March	April
May	June	July	August
September	October	November	December

CalendarYear
2001
2002
2003
2004

Row Labels	Total Sales
Sunday	$2,321,342
Monday	$2,279,220
Tuesday	$2,315,978
Wednesday	$2,391,460
Thursday	$2,349,082
Friday	$2,307,355
Saturday	$2,356,967
Grand Total	**$16,321,404**

Practice Exercises: ALL(), ALLEXCEPT(), and ALLSELECTED(), Cont.

Okay, it's time for some more practice exercises. Write the following two formulas. The first one is an interim formula and can be removed from the pivot once you have finished the second formula. Find the solutions to these practice exercises in Appendix A.

51. [Total Sales for All Days Selected Dates]

52. [% Sales for All Days Selected Dates]

Here's How: Using ALLEXCEPT()

I don't use ALLEXCEPT() much, and you may not either, but it is still good to work through an example of how it can be used. This section will give you some practice while also demonstrating one possible use case.

Say that you want to compare the percentage of sales across all occupations and see how it changes depending on the other customer filters. Follow these steps:

1. Set up a new pivot table and place Customers[Occupation] on Rows.

2. Add slicers for Gender and NumberCarsOwned.

3. Put [Total Order Quantity] on Values. You should have the pivot table shown below. Note that the total order quantity will change as you click on the slicers.

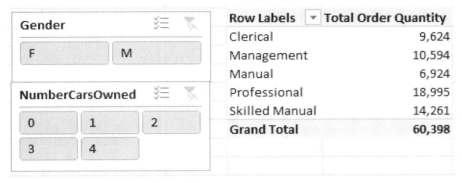

Row Labels ▼	Total Order Quantity
Clerical	9,624
Management	10,594
Manual	6,924
Professional	18,995
Skilled Manual	14,261
Grand Total	**60,398**

A number of steps are required to get to the end state (which is shown below). The following practice exercises show the measures you need to create, in the proper order, to get to the end state. As you create each measure, check that the results you see in your pivot table make sense. Once again, this is the reason to write DAX in the context of a pivot table: It makes it easier to get your head around what you are doing.

The following pivot table shows all the measures you need to write (just so you have an overview of what you'll accomplish with the following steps).

Row Labels ▼	Total Order Quantity	Total Orders All Customers	Baseline Orders for All customers with this Occupation	Baseline % this Occupation is of All Customer Orders	Total Orders Selected Customers	Occupation % of Selected Customers	Percentage Point variation to baseline
Clerical	7	60,398	9,624	15.9%	2,199	0.3%	-15.6%
Management	872	60,398	10,594	17.5%	2,199	39.7%	22.1%
Manual	1	60,398	6,924	11.5%	2,199	0.0%	-11.4%
Professional	1,263	60,398	18,995	31.4%	2,199	57.4%	26.0%
Skilled Manual	56	60,398	14,261	23.6%	2,199	2.5%	-21.1%
Grand Total	**2,199**	**60,398**	**60,398**	**100.0%**	**2,199**	**100.0%**	**0.0%**

The image below shows the end state you are working toward, with just the final measures included.

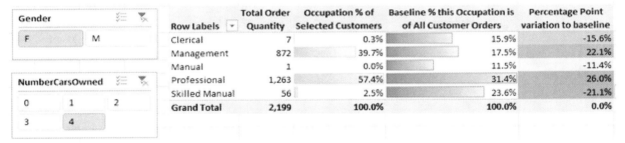

Row Labels ▼	Total Order Quantity	Occupation % of Selected Customers	Baseline % this Occupation is of All Customer Orders	Percentage Point variation to baseline
Clerical	7	0.3%	15.9%	-15.6%
Management	872	39.7%	17.5%	22.1%
Manual	1	0.0%	11.5%	-11.4%
Professional	1,263	57.4%	31.4%	26.0%
Skilled Manual	56	2.5%	23.6%	-21.1%
Grand Total	**2,199**	**100.0%**	**100.0%**	**0.0%**

As you can imagine, with this pivot table, it is possible to select different combinations of gender and number of cars and then compare the variation between the baseline order quantity and the order quantities for the selected filter.

Practice Exercises: ALL(), ALLEXCEPT(), and ALLSELECTED(), Cont.

Write the following DAX formulas one at a time, checking to make sure each one looks correct before moving to the next one. Find the solutions to these practice exercises in Appendix A.

53. [Total Orders All Customers]

To check this measure, click on the slicers and note that [Total Order Quantity] should change but [Total Orders All Customers] should not change based on the slicers.

54. [Baseline Orders for All Customers with This Occupation]

This measure should also not change when you make changes to the slicers. However, note that you should get a different value for each occupation—unlike with [Total Orders All Customers] above. This will be the baseline for comparison.

55. [Baseline % This Occupation of All Customer Orders]

This measure converts the baseline measure above into a percentage of the baseline for all orders. The description of this measure should help you work out how to write the DAX. Test the slicers again and make sure this new baseline percentage doesn't change with the slicers.

56. [Total Orders Selected Customers]

This measure should adjust depending on the selections you have in the slicers. *Hint:* Use ALLSELECTED().

57. [Occupation % of Selected Customers]

You can use the interim measures above to create this one. Click the slicers a few times and see which values change. This new measure should change based on the values you select in the slicers.

58. [Percentage Point Variation to Baseline]

This measure is the percentage of selected customers (Practice Exercise 57) minus the baseline (Practice Exercise 55).

Now you should have an interactive pivot table where you can drill into customer attributes (gender and number of cars owned) and see the impact on the mix of business vs. the baseline of all customers.

It is also worth pointing out here that sometimes it may be useful to change the descriptions of the final measures as they appear in a pivot table. For example, while [Baseline % This Occupation of All Customer Orders] is a good name for your measure because you know what it means, when you use this measure in a specific pivot table, it may be a good idea to rename it. You can do this by just clicking on the heading in the pivot table and giving it a new name.

After giving your measures new names, you might end up with something like the pivot table shown below.

Gender ⊟ ▼	Row Labels ▼	Total Orders	Share of Selected Filter	Baseline Share All Customers	Variation to baseline
F M	Clerical	7	0.3%	15.9%	-15.6%
	Management	872	39.7%	17.5%	22.1%
NumberCarsOwned ⊟ ▼	Manual	1	0.0%	11.5%	-11.4%
0 1 2	Professional	1,263	57.4%	31.4%	26.0%
3 4	Skilled Manual	56	2.5%	23.6%	-21.1%
	Grand Total	2,199	100.0%	100.0%	0.0%

Note: If you change the description in the pivot table, the easiest way to change it back is to right-click the heading name in the pivot, select Value Field Settings, and then change the Custom Name setting in the Value Field Settings dialog box, as shown below.

Row Labels ▼	Total Orders	Share of Selected Filter	Baseline Share All Customers	Variation to baseline
Clerical	7	0.3%	15.9%	-15.6%
Management	872	39.7%	17.5%	22.1%
Manual	1	0.0%	11.5%	-11.4%
Professional	1,263	57.4%	31.4%	26.0%
Skilled Manual	56	2.5%	23.6%	-21.1%
Grand Total	2,199	100.0%	100.0%	0.0%

Value Field Settings   ?   ✕

Source Name: Baseline % this Occupation is of All Custome...

Custom Name: Baseline Share All Customers

Summarize Values By   Show Values As

Show values as

No Calculation   ⌄

14: DAX Topic: FILTER()

FILTER() is a very powerful function in DAX. When FILTER() and CALCULATE() are combined, these two functions allow you to alter the filter context in your pivot tables any way you want. However, before we move on to using FILTER() with CALCULATE(), I think it is worth looking at FILTER() on its own with a couple of simple examples.

These examples demonstrate how the FILTER() function works, but you probably would not actually write such formulas in real DAX. These formulas are created here just for demonstration purposes.

The syntax of FILTER() is as follows:

```
= FILTER(Table, myFilter)
```

Table is any table (or function that returns a table, such as ALL()), and *myFilter* is any expression that evaluates to a TRUE/FALSE answer.

The FILTER() function returns a table that contains zero or more rows from the original table. Said another way, the table returned by FILTER() can contain zero rows, one row, two rows, or any other number of rows up to and including the total number of rows in the original table. The purpose of FILTER(), therefore, is to determine which rows will be returned to the final table result after you use the myFilter test.

FILTER() is an iterator, and it can therefore complete granular analysis to determine which rows will be included in the final table. Generally, it is fine to use FILTER() over lookup tables, but it is somewhat more risky to use it over data tables, particularly if they are very large (millions of rows). Whether you should use FILTER() depends on your data, on the quality of your DAX formulas inside FILTER(), and on what you need to achieve.

Let's work through an example. Set up a new pivot table with Customers[Occupation] on Rows and the measure [Total Number of Customers] on Values. The pivot table, as shown below, indicates how many customers there are in the entire Customers database for each occupation type.

Row Labels ▼	Total Number of Customers
Clerical	2,928
Management	3,075
Manual	2,384
Professional	5,520
Skilled Manual	4,577
Grand Total	**18,484**

But what if you want to know how many customers in the database have an income of more than $80,000 per year? Consider the following formula:

```
=FILTER(Customers, Customers[YearlyIncome] >= 80000)
```

The result of this formula is a table of customers, and this new virtual table of customers includes all the customers that have an income greater than or equal to $80,000 per year. But note that it is a table, and you can't put a table of values into a pivot table. So if you want to "see" the result (in this case, the total count of rows) inside a pivot table, you have to wrap this table that was returned by FILTER() inside a function that returns a value instead of a table of values (such as an aggregator).

It is possible to count the number of rows in this table by wrapping the formula above inside another formula, like this:

```
Total Customers with Income of $80,000 or above
    = COUNTROWS ( FILTER(
        Customers, Customers[YearlyIncome]>=80000
        )
      )
```

If you write this formula and put it in the pivot table, it looks as shown below. You should do this now for practice.

Row Labels	Total Number of Customers	Total Customers with Income of $80,000 or above
Clerical	2,928	
Management	3,075	1,963
Manual	2,384	
Professional	5,520	1,976
Skilled Manual	4,577	443
Grand Total	18,484	4,382

You can see from the pivot table that not all occupations have customers that earn this amount of money.

These are the key points to take away from this example:

- FILTER() returns a table. It is a virtual table, and hence you can't "see" it.

- The virtual copy of the table that is used inside the measure above retains a link to the original table (lineage) and can have an effect on the other tables in the data model. (You'll learn more about this later in this chapter.)

- You can't put the table returned by Filter() into a pivot table as is because you simply can't put a table into a pivot table; it has too many rows and columns for a single cell in a pivot table. But you can count how many rows there are in the table and put that answer into the pivot table. This is exactly what happens with this measure.

So How Does FILTER() Actually Work?

It is essential that you understand how the FILTER() function works before moving on. Let's look just at the FILTER() portion of the formula above:

```
FILTER(Customers, Customers[YearlyIncome]>=80000)
```

FILTER() is an iterator just like SUMX(), covered in Chapter 7. As such, FILTER() first creates a row context on the specified table (the first parameter) and then iterates through each row in the table to check whether the row passes the test. If an individual row passes the test, it is retained in the final table result. If an individual row fails the test, it is omitted from the final table result.

> **Note:** As mentioned in Chapter 7 about SUMX(), it is convenient to think of iterators working one row at a time, and indeed that is the logical execution approach. In reality, though, the Power Pivot engine has been built and optimised to work very efficiently under the hood. You should not assume that iterators are inherently inefficient because the Power Pivot engine can make the physical execution very efficient indeed.

Let's look at a simple example. Assume that the Customers table has five rows, as shown below.

Row	CustomerKey	YearlyIncome
1	11003	$ 70,000
2	11004	$ 80,000
3	11005	$ 70,000
4	11007	$ 60,000
5	11058	$ 80,000

> **Note:** The column with the name Row has been added here to assist in the explanation of how filter works; it does not actually exist in the Customers table. Here again is the FILTER() portion of the formula from above:
>
> ```
> FILTER(Customers, Customers[YearlyIncome]>=80000)
> ```

This is what the FILTER() function does (logically speaking):

- It first creates a new row context over the Customers table. The row context allows FILTER() to keep track of which row it is looking at, and it also provides the capability to isolate a single row (one at a time) and refer to the single value that is the intersection between the single row and any column(s) in the table.

- Now that there is a row context, FILTER() goes to row 1 and asks the question (from the myFilter portion of the formula) "Is the value in the column Customers[YearlyIncome] for the customer in this row greater than or equal to $80,000?" If the answer is yes, row 1 survives the filter test, and the row is kept in the final table result. If the answer is no, row 1 is discarded from the final table result. So in this case (row 1), the yearly income is $70,000, so it fails the test, and row 1 is discarded from the final table result.

- FILTER() then moves to the second row (using the row context to keep track of where it is) and asks the same question again for this new row: "Is the value in the column Customers[Yearly-Income] for the customer in this row greater than or equal to $80,000?" If the answer is yes, the row survives the filter test, and the row is kept in the final table result. If the answer is no, it fails the test, and the row is discarded from the final table result. In the case of row 2, it passes the test, and hence row 2 is retained.

- FILTER() works down the table one row at a time and tests each row against the filter test. It decides which rows to keep and which rows to discard by checking each row, one at a time, against the filter test.

- When the last row has been evaluated, FILTER() returns a table that contains just the rows that passed the test, as shown below. All rows that failed the test are discarded.

Rows that pass the test				Rows that fail the test		
Row	CustomerKey	YearlyIncome		Row	CustomerKey	YearlyIncome
2	11004	$ 80,000	Final result	1	11003	$ 70,000
5	11058	$ 80,000		3	11005	$ 70,000
				4	11007	$ 60,000

Remember that, in reality, under the hood, FILTER() may use a more efficient process than checking the rows one at a time. It may seem that FILTER() completes its task row by row, but in reality, it may use an optimised algorithm to perform the task. The most important thing to know is that you shouldn't use complex, multicolumn comparison tests inside a filter with functions like IF(). Here is a good "bad" example:

```
Count of Customers Earning > 80,000 and Own a House =
COUNTROWS (
    FILTER (
        Customers,
        IF ( Customers[YearlyIncome] > 80000 &&
            Customers[HouseOwnerFlag] = 1, TRUE )
    )
)
```

If you avoid such IF() tests inside FILTER(), you should be fine.

So, it is clear from the image above that if you now count the rows of the table on the left (which is the result of FILTER()), you get the answer 2 (i.e., there are two rows in this filtered table).

If you now refer back to the earlier example, it is clear how the formula gave you the results. Here is the formula, shown again for convenience:

```
Total Customers with Income of $80,000 or above
= COUNTROWS (
    FILTER (
        Customers, Customers[YearlyIncome]>=80000
    )
)
```

The measure [Total Customers with Income of $80,000 or Above] iterates through the Customers table using the FILTER() function, checking the value in the Customers[YearlyIncome] column of each individual customer to see if the value is greater than or equal to $80,000. FILTER() returns a table of all customers that passed this test, and then COUNTROWS () counts them. As shown below, the formula finds that 1,963 customers with the occupation Management pass this test, and 4,382 customers in total pass the test.

Row Labels	Total Number of Customers	Total Customers with Income of $80,000 or above
Clerical	2,928	
Management	3,075	1,963
Manual	2,384	
Professional	5,520	1,976
Skilled Manual	4,577	443
Grand Total	18,484	4,382

Using FILTER() Inside CALCULATE()

As mentioned earlier, FILTER () is most commonly used as an advanced filter inside CALCULATE (). FILTER () is an iterator, and it therefore allows a very granular level of evaluation of a table and is a very powerful tool for altering the filter context of a pivot table any way you want and at a level of detail that is not possible by using a *simple filter* inside CALCULATE ().

Consider the following formula:

```
Total Customers with Income of $80,000 or above 2
= CALCULATE(COUNTROWS(Customers),
Customers[YearlyIncome]>=80000)
```

This formula returns exactly the same result as the FILTER () version above. In this version, the filter portion of the formula uses a simple filter. A simple filter has a column name on one side of the formula (in this case, Customers[YearlyIncome]) and a value on the right side (in this case, 80000).

CALCULATE () is designed to accept this type of calculation on its own, without the use of the FILTER () function. But in reality, as mentioned earlier, this is just "syntax sugar" created by the developers to make it easier for you to write measures. Under the hood, the formula above is converted to the following formula:

```
Total Customers with Income of $80,000 Under the Hood
    = CALCULATE(COUNTROWS(Customers),
        FILTER(
            ALL(Customers[YearlyIncome]),
            Customers[YearlyIncome]>=80000
        )
    )
```

There is a limit to what CALCULATE () can do with one of these simple filters. It works only if you have a column name compared to a value. But what if you want to do something more complex, like check whether a measure is greater than a value? Let's look at another example.

Example: Calculating Lifetime Customer Purchases

Say that you want to know how many customers have purchased more than $5,000 of goods from you over the course of all time. You can't use a simple CALCULATE () filter in this case because customers may have purchased from you on many occasions, and you don't have a column that contains a single value that tells the total sales for each customer. If you tried to write this formula using a simple filter, it would look like this:

```
Customers with Sales Greater Than $5,000 Doesn't Work
= CALCULATE(COUNTROWS (Customers),[Total Sales] > 5000)
```

This formula includes a measure (in bold)—and that is not allowed with a simple filter! A simple filter *must* have a column compared to a value, so a simple filter doesn't work in this scenario.

This is where you have to write your own FILTER () functions. Now take a look at the following formula:

```
Customers with Sales Greater Than $5,000
= CALCULATE(
    COUNTROWS(Customers),
        FILTER(Customers,
        [Total Sales] >= 5000
```

```
        )
    )
```

It is worth stepping through how FILTER() works in this example because there is a significant difference from the earlier example.

> **Note:** The FILTER() portion of the formula is *evaluated first*. This is always the case with CAL-CULATE(). The filter portion is *always* evaluated first (for both simple filters and advanced filters).

Let's start by looking at just the FILTER() portion of this formula:

```
FILTER(Customers, [Total Sales] >= 5000)
```

Here's what's happening in this portion of the formula:

- FILTER() creates a row context for the Customers table. FILTER() then goes to row 1 in the Customers table and applies a filter to that single customer.

- **This is very important:** Because of the implicit CALCULATE() inside the measure [Total Sales], context transition occurs, and the row context is converted to an equivalent filter context. Because of the context transition, the filter then propagates down through the relationship from the Customers table to the Sales table and, hence, filters the Sales table so that only sales for this one customer are unfiltered. Do you remember this from the end of Chapter 10, on context transition?

- The measure [Total Sales] is evaluated after the Sales table is filtered for this one single customer.

- FILTER() then asks the question "Is the value of [Total Sales] for this one customer in this first row of the Customers table greater than or equal to $5,000?" If the answer is yes, then this customer survives the filter test, and the row is kept in the final table result. If the answer is no, the customer is discarded from the final table result.

- FILTER() then moves to the second row in the row context of the Customers table. Because of the implicit CALCULATE() inside the measure [Total Sales], the row context is converted to a filter context (context transition), and the filter propagates the filter for the second customer from the Customers table through to the Sales table, evaluates the measure [Total Sales] against the rows in the Sales table that remain, and then checks whether [Total Sales] for this second customer is greater than $5,000. Once again, if the answer is yes, the customer survives the filter and remains in the final table results. Any customer that fails the test is discarded.

- FILTER() proceeds through every customer in the Customers table, testing each one to see if the total sales of all the records for that specific customer in the Sales table is greater than $5,000. All customers that pass the test are retained in the final table, and the ones that fail the test are discarded from the final table.

When the FILTER() portion finishes its work, FILTER() returns a table of customers that passed the test. You can imagine the myFilter portion of the original formula looking like this:

```
Customers with Sales Greater Than $5,000
= CALCULATE(
    COUNTROWS(Customers),
    Only_Use_The_Table_of_Customers_Provided_By_FILTER
)
```

The FILTER() formula above determines which customers passed the test and returns this filtered table of customers to CALCULATE(). The resulting filtered table of customers is then accepted and applied as a filter by CALCULATE(). Finally, CALCULATE() evaluates the COUNTROWS(Customers) portion of the formula. There are actually 1,732 customers out of a total of 18,484 customers that passed the FILTER() test. By the time COUNTROWS() is executed, just the 1,732 customers that passed the FILTER() test remain, so COUNTROWS() returns 1,732.

Practice Exercises: FILTER()

Set up a new pivot table with Products[Category] on Rows and [Total Sales] on Values and then write the following two formulas. Find the solutions to these practice exercises in Appendix A.

59. [Total Sales of Products That Have Some Sales but Less Than $10,000]

What you need to do here is get FILTER() to iterate over the Products table to determine whether each product has some sales and also whether the total of those sales is less than $10,000.

Note that you can use the double ampersand operator (&&) if you need more than one condition in your filter expression:

```
Condition1 && Condition2
```

Alternatively, you can use two separate FILTER() functions.

60. [Count of Products That Have Some Sales but Less Than $10,000]

You should end up with a pivot table like the one below.

Row Labels ▾	Total Sales	Total Sales of Products That Have Some Sales but Less Than $10,000	Count of Products That Have Some Sales but Less Than $10,000
Accessories	$700,760	$31,431	4
Bikes	$28,318,145		
Clothing	$339,773	$5,106	2
Grand Total	$29,358,677	$36,538	6

A good exercise now is to remove [Total Sales] from the pivot table and add ProductName on Rows, keeping Category, too. If you don't remove [Total Sales] first, you will get every single product that has sold at least once in your pivot table.

You should end up with a pivot table like the one below.

Row Labels ▾	Total Sales of Products That Have Some Sales but Less Than $10,000	Count of Products That Have Some Sales but Less Than $10,000
⊟ Accessories		
Bike Wash - Dissolver	$7,219	1
Patch Kit/8 Patches	$7,307	1
Road Tire Tube	$9,480	1
Touring Tire Tube	$7,425	1
⊟ Clothing		
Racing Socks, L	$2,427	1
Racing Socks, M	$2,679	1
Grand Total	$36,538	6

Revisiting Filter Propagation

Earlier in this chapter, we looked at a FILTER() example with a measure on the left side of the filter test and a value on the right side:

```
Customers with Sales Greater Than $5,000
= CALCULATE(COUNTROWS(Customers),
        FILTER(Customers,
        [Total Sales] >= 5000
        )
    )
```

Let's revisit how FILTER() operates in the formula above. (You can't hear this too many times.) The FILTER() portion is evaluated first:

- FILTER() creates a row context for the Customers table. FILTER() then goes to row 1 in the Customers table, and because of the implicit CALCULATE() inside the measure [Total Sales], context transition occurs, converting the row context from FILTER() into an equivalent filter context.

- Because of the context transition, the filter on the first row of the Customers table propagates down through the relationship with the Customers table and filters the Sales table so that only sales for this customer are unfiltered.

- The measure [Total Sales] is evaluated after the Sales table is first filtered for this one single customer (returning the value $8,249 in this case).

Context Transition Revisited

Let me go over context transition again as it is very important.

Do you remember what the formula for [Total Sales] is? The formula is as follows:

```
[Total Sales] = SUM(Sales[ExtendedAmount])
```

Given that [Total Sales] evaluates to exactly the same result as SUM(Sales[ExtendedAmount]), what do you expect will happen if you substitute SUM(Sales[ExtendedAmount]) into the formula above, like this:

```
Customers with Sales Greater Than $5,000 Version2
= CALCULATE(COUNTROWS(Customers),
        FILTER(Customers,
            SUM(Sales[ExtendedAmount]) >= 5000
        )
    )
```

You should go ahead and create this formula and see what happens. When you do this, you create a pivot table like the one below.

Row Labels	Total Sales	Customers That Have Purchased	Customers with Sales Greater Than $5,000	Customers with Sales Greater Than $5,000 Version2
Australia	$9,061,001	3,591	719	18,484
Canada	$1,977,845	1,571	42	18,484
France	$2,644,018	1,810	163	18,484
Germany	$2,894,312	1,780	158	18,484
United Kingdom	$3,391,712	1,913	280	18,484
United States	$9,389,790	7,819	370	18,484
Grand Total	$29,358,677	18,484	1,732	18,484

The new formula returns the entire table of customers instead of the value you are looking for. Why is this? There is a very important difference between a measure and the formula inside a measure. Technically speaking, when you write the following measure:

```
Total Sales = SUM(Sales[ExtendedAmount])
```

what is actually happening under the hood is the following:

```
Total Sales = CALCULATE(SUM(Sales[ExtendedAmount]))
```

Power Pivot adds a CALCULATE() function (shown in bold above) and wraps it around your formula for you. You can't see this CALCULATE(), but it is there. We call this "invisible" CALCULATE() an "implicit CALCULATE()."

Okay, let's get back to the problem at hand. Go back into the new measure you just created and wrap the SUM() function in CALCULATE() as follows:

```
Customers with Sales Greater Than $5,000 Version2
= CALCULATE(COUNTROWS(Customers),
        FILTER(Customers,
            CALCULATE(SUM(Sales[ExtendedAmount])) >= 5000
        )
    )
```

When you manually place CALCULATE() like this, it is called an "explicit CALCULATE()." Once you make this change, you get the expected result, as shown below.

Row Labels ▼	Total Sales	Customers That Have Purchased	Customers with Sales Greater Than $5,000	Customers with Sales Greater Than $5,000 Version2
Australia	$9,061,001	3,591	719	719
Canada	$1,977,845	1,571	42	42
France	$2,644,018	1,810	163	163
Germany	$2,894,312	1,780	158	158
United Kingdom	$3,391,712	1,913	280	280
United States	$9,389,790	7,819	370	370
Grand Total	$29,358,677	18,484	1,732	1,732

Note: I have swapped the column Products[Category] with Territories[Country] above to show an alternate view of the data. These measures work regardless of which column you have on Rows on the pivot table.

The point is that without the CALCULATE() function wrapped around SUM(Sales[ExtendedAmount]), something stops working. It doesn't matter if there is an implicit CALCULATE() that you can't see (inside another measure) or if there's an explicit CALCULATE() that you add yourself. You simply must have a CALCULATE() if you want this formula to work. Why is this?

Remember that Chapter 10 said that a row context does not automatically create a filter context. Chapter 10 was talking about the row context in a calculated column, but it is exactly the same in a function that has a row context—in this case, the FILTER() function. The CALCULATE() function tells Power Pivot to run the filter engine again. If you don't have this extra CALCULATE(), the filter that is first applied to the Customers table *will not* propagate to the Sales table as described above. It is the second CALCULATE() (either implicit or explicit) that causes the filter on the Customers table to propagate through the relationship to the Sales table *before* the rest of the FILTER() expression is evaluated for each row in the table.

So let's step through what happens without the extra CALCULATE() by going back to this version, which didn't work:

```
Customers with Sales Greater Than $5,000 Version2
= CALCULATE(COUNTROWS(Customers),
        FILTER(Customers,
            SUM(Sales[ExtendedAmount]) >= 5000
        )
    )
```

Of course, the FILTER() portion is evaluated first, just as before. And then the following happens:

- FILTER() creates a row context on the Customers table. FILTER() then goes to the first row in the table. No filter context currently exists because a row context doesn't automatically create a filter context.

- SUM(Sales[ExtendedAmount]) is then evaluated over the entire Sales table for *all customers* and returns the value $29,358,677. There is no filter context, and hence the Sales table is completely unfiltered. Since $29 million is greater than $5,000, this customer survives the filter test.

- FILTER() then goes to the next customer, and exactly the same thing happens again. It doesn't matter what customer is selected in the row context in the Customers table; there is no filtering through to the Sales table, and therefore the result of every iteration step is that every customer passes the test. Because they all pass the test, all customers are returned in the answer.

Note: The only way to create a filter context in this example is if you use a second CALCULATE() function (implicit or explicit) wrapped around SUM(Sales[ExtendedAmount]) to tell Power Pivot to convert the row context into a filter context; then you need to propagate the filter down through the existing relationships before completing the evaluation. If this `CALCULATE()` (implicit or explicit) is omitted, then *no filtering happens*, and, as a result, the `Sales` table is completely unfiltered.

This topic can take some time to get your head around. If it is not crystal clear, I recommend that you go back through this chapter (and also Chapter 10) and work through the examples again until it is clear in your mind. If you can't get it now, leave it for a few weeks (or even months) and come back again when you have more real-life experience under your belt.

Virtual Table Lineage

Let's jump back to the version of the measure we've been working on that works:

```
Customers with Sales Greater Than $5,000
= CALCULATE(COUNTROWS(Customers),
        FILTER(Customers,
            [Total Sales] >= 5000
        )
    )
```

When you think about the new table returned by `FILTER()` in the above formula, your first inclination may be to think about it as a standalone table, but that's not the case. Any virtual table object returned by a table function in DAX always retains a link to the data model for the life of the evaluation of the measure or calculated column; this is called *lineage*. I find it useful to visualise an imaginary temporary table being created above the real table in the data model, as shown below.

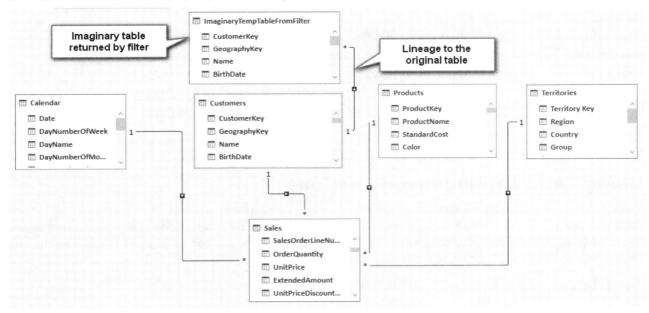

This new temporary table contains a subset of rows as determined by `FILTER()`, but, importantly, it has the link back to the original table. Therefore, when this new temporary table is used inside `CALCULATE()` (as is the case here), `CALCULATE()` tells Power Pivot to run the filter propagation again, and this new table therefore filters the original table and any other tables that are connected downstream to the original table.

> **Note:** The preceding is just an illustration and a useful way for you to think about what is happening under the hood.

15: DAX Topic: Time Intelligence

Time intelligence is a very important and powerful feature in DAX. *Time intelligence* refers to the ability to write formulas that refer to other time periods within a pivot table without needing to change the time filters.

Consider the following pivot table, which shows sales for the year 2003.

CalendarYear	2003	⊤

Row Labels ▼	Total Sales
Accessories	$293,710
Bikes	$9,359,103
Clothing	$138,248
Grand Total	**$9,791,060**

Now what if you wanted to see the sales for the preceding year as well as the change in sales compared to the preceding year? Well, one thing you could do is to toggle the filter between the calendar years 2003 and 2002 to see the results for the preceding year, or you could bring `CalendarYear` and place it on Columns and then filter out the years that you are not interested in, as shown below.

> **Bring CalendarYear into columns and then hide the years you don't need**

Total Sales	Column Labels ▼				
Row Labels ▼	2001	2002	2003	2004	Grand Total
Accessories			$293,710	$407,050	$700,760
Bikes	$3,266,374	$6,530,344	$9,359,103	$9,162,325	$28,318,145
Clothing			$138,248	$201,525	$339,773
Grand Total	**$3,266,374**	**$6,530,344**	**$9,791,060**	**$9,770,900**	**$29,358,677**

But doing it this way is a bit of a hack, and it isn't reusable in other pivot tables without doing further hacks. And besides, you can't calculate the change compared to the preceding year.

Using Time Intelligence Functions

You can use time intelligence functions to create new relative measures, such as `[Total Sales LY]` (total sales last year), as discussed above, without having to change the date selections in the pivot table to see the prior year. This makes everything easier to do, and it also means you can build pivot tables, like the one shown below, that would not be possible any other way.

Row Labels ▼	Total Sales	Change in Sales vs LY
2001	$3,266,374	$3,266,374
2002	$6,530,344	$3,263,970
2003	$9,791,060	$3,260,717
2004	$9,770,900	-$20,161
Grand Total	**$29,358,677**	**$9,770,900**

DAX comes bundled with a number of inbuilt time intelligence functions, and you can also write custom time intelligence functions yourself when needed. There are some limitations to the inbuilt time intelligence functions, and they work only under certain circumstances. These are a couple of the rules for using inbuilt time intelligence functions:

- You must have a `Calendar` table that contains a contiguous range of dates that covers every day in the period you are analysing. Every date must exist once and only once in the `Calendar` table. You can't skip any dates (e.g., you can't skip weekend dates just because you don't work weekends).

- Inbuilt time intelligence works only on a standard calendar—that is, a calendar like one that you might hang on a wall, where the start of the year is January 1, the end of the year is December 31, the last day of May is May 31, etc. A standard calendar can also be customised for different financial years (e.g., you can set the end date for a calendar to be June 30 instead of December 31, or any other date for that matter).

If for some reason these rules can't be met, then you can't use the inbuilt time intelligence functions. In such a case, you can write your own custom time intelligence functions from scratch, using `FILTER()`. The DAX for this tends to be a bit complex, but don't worry, you can learn it, and I explain it later in this chapter.

Nonstandard Calendars

In some cases, you may need to use a nonstandard calendar for reports. These are some examples of when you could not use a standard calendar:

- When you are building a data model using weekly or monthly time periods and using a weekly or monthly calendar instead of a daily calendar. (Note that you could load your data weekly or monthly and still use a daily calendar—and this would still work with inbuilt time intelligence, as long as all the other criteria were still met. I would consider this a hack as well, though.)

- If you use an ISO or 445 calendar for your accounting periods. This is very common in the retail industry, where businesses want to have regular trading periods. In the case of a 445 calendar, there are 2 months that consist of 4 calendar weeks followed by 1 month with 5 calendar weeks. This helps smooth the months so they all start on a Monday and finish on a Sunday (for example) while also having 91 days in the quarter (91 × 4 quarters = 364 days).

- With 13 4-week periods instead of calendar months.

- If you had a calendar that uses time as well as date (e.g., an hourly calendar).

There are so many variations that it is impossible to mention them all here, and it is also impossible for Power Pivot to cater for them all with inbuilt functions. So the rule is, if you have a standard day calendar, you can use the inbuilt functions. If you don't have a standard day calendar, then you need to write your own custom time intelligence using `FILTER()`.

Inbuilt Time Intelligence

Before using the inbuilt time intelligence functions, you need to validate that certain requirements, described next, are covered.

Using a Contiguous Date Range

In the sample data that you have been working with, the `Calendar` table already contains all the days of the year for the period that covers the `Sales` table. It is easy to check this. Just create a new pivot table, put `'Calendar'[CalendarYear]` on Rows, and drop any string-based column (such as `MonthName`) into the Values area.

Row Labels ▾	Count of MonthName
2001	184
2002	365
2003	365
2004	366
Grand Total	**1280**

I did tell you never to create implicit measures unless you are just doing a quick test. This is one of those cases where it is fine to use them, though. These are not wrong; it is just that you can't reuse implicit measures inside other formulas. In this case, we don't need to reuse this measure, so it is fine. As you can see above, the `Calendar` table has half a year for 2001 plus a full year for each of the following three years (including a leap year for 2004). Now that we have confirmed the data in the `Calendar` table, we can just remove this implicit measure from the visual as we don't need it anymore.

Here's How: Marking a Table as a Date Table

Technically, you need to mark a table as a date table only if you are joining your data table (`Sales` in this example) to your `Calendar` table by using a surrogate key. A *surrogate key* is a column of data that looks like a date but is not really a date at all. An example is a column of data in the format YYYYMMDD (e.g., 20180317). This is not really the date 17 March 2018 but a surrogate for that date. If you use surrogate keys in your data model, you must mark your date tables as such by using the approach described below. If you are using real dates formatted as dates, then strictly speaking you don't need to do this; even so, it won't hurt.

To mark a table as a data table, do the following:

1. Go to the Power Pivot window, navigate to the `Calendar` table (see #1 below), and go to the Data view.

2. In the Design tab (#2), click on Mark as Date Table (#3).

3. Power Pivot automatically detects the date column in your table and offers this column to you in the Mark as Date Table dialog box. Just click OK to confirm.

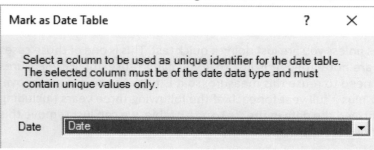

Now you'll write some measures using some inbuilt time intelligence functions.

The SAMEPERIODLASTYEAR() Function

Let's look at an inbuilt time intelligence function you can use to easily write the [Total Sales LY] measure discussed earlier.

First, set up your pivot table like the one below, with 'Calendar'[CalendarYear] on Rows and [Total Sales] on Values.

Row Labels	Total Sales
2001	$3,266,374
2002	$6,530,344
2003	$9,791,060
2004	$9,770,900
Grand Total	**$29,358,677**

Click in the pivot table and write the following new measure:

```
Total Sales LY
= CALCULATE([Total Sales], SAMEPERIODLASTYEAR('Calendar'[Date]))
```

As shown below, if you pause after typing **SAMEPERIODLASTYEAR** and before you type **(**, IntelliSense says that this function will return a list of dates from the initial filter context but time shifted back by a year.

You should recognise that SAMEPERIODLASTYEAR() returns a table of values and that the table is being used inside CALCULATE() as an advanced filter.

> **Note:** The word Calendar is a reserved word in Power Pivot. Calendar is actually a function that will return a calendar table. Personally, I never use this function as I think there are better ways to create calendar tables. It is still okay to call a calendar table Calendar, but you must always add single quotes when referencing the table inside your formulas, as shown in the formula above.

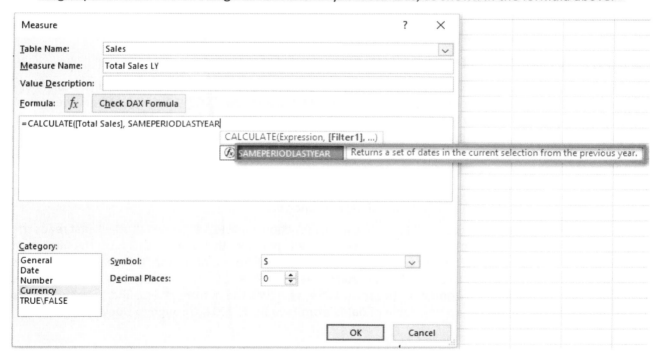

Also notice in the IntelliSense below that SAMEPERIODLASTYEAR() takes a single *Dates* parameter as its only input.

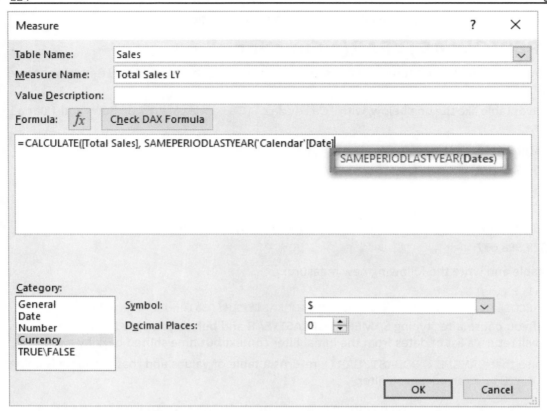

All inbuilt time intelligence functions ask for this *Dates* parameter, and it always refers to the date column in the `Calendar` table. This is the same column you indicated in the Power Pivot Mark as Date Table dialog box. Frankly, I think this is a duplication of effort, given that you have already told Power Pivot where the date column is, but this is just the way it works. You have to tell Power Pivot twice where your date column is—once inside the Power Pivot window in the Mark as Date Table dialog box and again inside every inbuilt time intelligence formula you write.

How Does SAMEPERIODLASTYEAR() Work?

In Chapter 14 I explained that `CALCULATE()` can take a table as an advanced filter input, and you can imagine the new table being connected to the data model. The table inside `CALCULATE` then filters the rest of the tables in the data model (in this case, the `Calendar` table and the `Sales` table) before `CALCULATE()` completes the calculation. It is exactly the same with `SAMEPERIODLASTYEAR()`, as shown here:

```
Total Sales LY =
        CALCULATE([Total Sales], SAMEPERIODLASTYEAR('Calendar'[Date]))
```

In this instance, `SAMEPERIODLASTYEAR()` returns a table of dates that are the same dates coming from the pivot table for the selected year but shifted back by one year.

Consider the cell highlighted in the pivot table below. The function `SAMEPERIODLASTYEAR()` first reads the filter context from the current pivot table to see which dates apply for "this year." In this case, the filter is on `CalendarYear`, and the filter for this cell is 2003 (see #1 below). So the dates for "this year" are all dates from January 1, 2003, through to December 31, 2003. The `SAMEPERIODLASTYEAR()` function then takes the dates from the initial filter context in the pivot table, removes the current filters, and then time shifts them back one year before returning a table of dates from January 1, 2002, through to December 31, 2002.

Row Labels	Total Sales	Total Sales LY
2001	$3,266,374	
2002	$6,530,344	$3,266,374
2003 ①	$9,791,060	$6,530,344
2004	$9,770,900	$9,791,060
Grand Total	**$29,358,677**	**$19,587,777**

You can imagine the new table created by SAMEPERIODLASTYEAR() as a temporary table sitting above the Calendar table and retaining a relationship to the original Calendar table, as shown below.

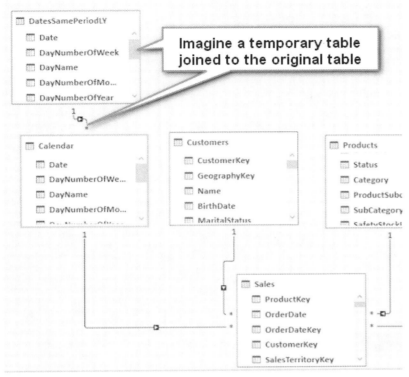

Remember that this is logically how it works; you can't actually see this table, and it doesn't actually exist.

This table is then passed to CALCULATE(), and CALCULATE() uses this temporary table to rerun the filter propagation. The temporary table (the table of dates from SAMEPERIODLASTYEAR()) filters the Calendar table, which then filters the Sales table before the calculation for [Total Sales LY] is evaluated.

Tip: Read the paragraph above a couple of times if you need to until you have it clearly in your head.

Calculating Sales Year to Date

A very common business need is to calculate figures on a year-to-date (YTD) basis. Fortunately, there is an inbuilt function for this.

Before you write any YTD formula, it is a good idea to set up a pivot table that will give you immediate feedback if your formula is performing as expected. It is also important to set up your pivot table so that you only have a continuous date range. Set up a new pivot table like the one shown below before proceeding. Note the filter on CalendarYear = 2003.

Note how the periods in the pivot are contiguous (i.e., the months of the year 2003). If you didn't have a filter on CalendarYear = 2003 but instead had CalendarYear = ALL, the pivot table would show the total sales for January across all years, for February across all years, etc. This would not be a contiguous range, and hence the formula would not work.

Now click in the pivot table and write the following measure:

CalendarYear	2003 ▼	
Row Labels ▼	**Total Sales**	
January	$438,865	
February	$489,090	
March	$485,575	
April	$506,399	
May	$562,773	
June	$554,799	
July	$886,669	
August	$847,414	
September	$1,010,258	
October	$1,080,450	
November	$1,196,981	
December	$1,731,788	
Grand Total	**$9,791,060**	

```
Total Sales YTD =
     TOTALYTD([Total Sales], 'Calendar'[Date])
```

Apply appropriate formatting to the measure. When you are done, it is very easy to check whether the formula is working correctly. You can select a contiguous range of cells starting from January in the Total Sales column and then check the running total against the result in the Total Sales YTD column.

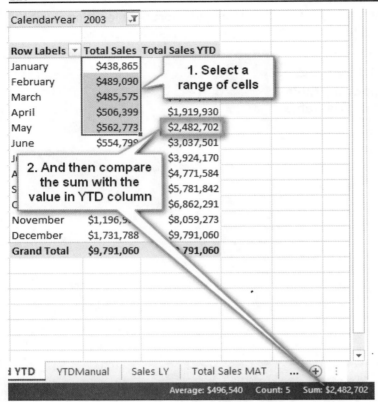

CalendarYear	2003	
Row Labels ▾	**Total Sales**	**Total Sales YTD**
January	$438,865	
February	$489,090	
March	$485,575	
April	$506,399	$1,919,930
May	$562,773	$2,482,702
June	$554,799	$3,037,501
July		$3,924,170
August		$4,771,584
September		$5,781,842
October		$6,862,291
November	$1,196,9..	$8,059,273
December	$1,731,788	$9,791,060
Grand Total	**$9,791,060**	**.791,060**

1. Select a range of cells

2. And then compare the sum with the value in YTD column

..YTD	YTDManual	Sales LY	Total Sales MAT	...	⊕	

Average: $496,540   Count: 5   Sum: $2,482,702

Note: It is very important that you test your measures after you write them. You are a data modeller now! Along with this title comes the responsibility to check that the measures you write are returning the expected results.

This is a really good example of the benefit of writing measures in the context of a pivot table. The immediate feedback you get allows you to check whether your formula is correct and is well worth the effort. As mentioned before, this is not the only way to do it, but it is the best way for Excel users to learn how to write DAX. At some time in the future, when you are a DAX superhero, you may choose to write some of your formulas in the Power Pivot window. Until then, stick with writing them in the context of a suitably configured pivot table.

Once you have written a formula, you can apply some conditional formatting to your pivot table, as shown below, to get another visual clue about whether all is working well.

CalendarYear	2003	
Row Labels ▾	**Total Sales**	**Total Sales YTD**
January	$438,865	$438,865
February	$489,090	$927,956
March	$485,575	$1,413,530
April	$506,399	$1,919,930
May	$562,773	$2,482,702
June	$554,799	$3,037,501
July	$886,669	$3,924,170
August	$847,414	$4,771,584
September	$1,010,258	$5,781,842
October	$1,080,450	$6,862,291
November	$1,196,981	$8,059,273
December	$1,731,788	$9,791,060
Grand Total	**$9,791,060**	**$9,791,060**

Practice Exercises: Time Intelligence

When writing the previous formula, you may have noticed from the IntelliSense tooltip that there are two other functions that are very similar: TOTALMTD() and TOTALQTD(). In this section you'll get some practice using these two functions. Before you do these two exercises, make sure you set up a pivot table like the one below that will give you feedback if your formula is correct. Set up the pivot table like this:

1. Place 'Calendar'[CalendarYear] and 'Calendar'[MonthName] on Filters.

2. Filter for Calendar Year = 2003 and Month Name = January.

3. Put 'Calendar'[DayNumberOfMonth] on Rows.

4. Place the [Total Sales] measure on Values.

CalendarYear	2003	
MonthName	January	

Row Labels	Total Sales
1	$12,445
2	$19,703
3	$13,520
4	$18,629
5	$13,497
6	$4,363
7	$14,623

Write formulas for the following measures. Find the solutions to these practice exercises in Appendix A.

61. [Total Sales Month to Date]

> **Tip:** Do you remember the pivot table I showed with [Total Sales YTD] earlier in this chapter? Placing MonthName on rows will not work for Practice Exercise 61. Instead, you need to put a column such as DayNumberOfMonth in the pivot table if you want to be able to "see" that the formula is working correctly.

62. [Total Sales Quarter to Date]

Changing Financial Year-Ending Dates

Many of the inbuilt time intelligence functions allow you to specify a different end-of-year date. In such a case, there will be an optional parameter where you specify the year-end date:

```
Total Sales FYTD
    = TOTALYTD([Total Sales], 'Calendar'[Date],"YearEndDateHere")
```

Here's an example for a financial year ending April 30:

```
Total Sales FYTD
    = TOTALYTD([Total Sales], 'Calendar'[Date],"30/4")
```

Note that this example uses a non-U.S. date format. If you are using the U.S. date format, then it would be as follows:

```
Total Sales FYTD USA
    = TOTALYTD([Total Sales], 'Calendar'[Date],"4/30")
```

Notice that there is no need to specify a year when referring to the year-end date. It is simply day and month.

Practice Exercises: Time Intelligence, Cont.

Write formulas for the following measures. Find the solutions to these practice exercises in Appendix A.

63. [Total Sales FYTD 30 June]

64. [Total Sales FYTD 31 March]

Format your pivot table by selecting Conditional Formatting, Data Bars to make it easier to spot the pattern.

Practicing with Other Time Intelligence Functions

There are a lot of inbuilt time intelligence functions, and it's easy to tell what most of them do. PREVI-OUSMONTH(), PREVIOUSQUARTER(), and PREVIOUSDAY(), for example, all return tables of dates referring to the previous period and probably don't need further explanation. To see how they work, set up a pivot table with contiguous months, as shown below.

CalendarYear 2003	
Row Labels ▼	**Total Sales**
January	$438,865
February	$489,090
March	$485,575
April	$506,399
May	$562,773
June	$554,799
July	$886,669
August	$847,414
September	$1,010,258
October	$1,080,450
November	$1,196,981
December	$1,731,788
Grand Total	**$9,791,060**

Practice Exercises: Time Intelligence, Cont.

Write the following formulas. Find the solutions to these practice exercises in Appendix A.

> **Tip:** As always, I suggest that you set up a suitable pivot table with a suitable column on Rows and [Total Sales] on Values before writing these measures. Doing this will help you check whether the measures are working and also should help you comprehend how the measures work. If you don't understand, go back and reread the section about SAMEPERIODLASTYEAR(). The functions in these practice exercises work in exactly the same way.

65. [Total Sales Previous Month]

Given that the PREVIOUSMONTH() function returns a table of dates, you need to embed the time intelligence formula inside a CALCULATE() function.

66. [Total Sales Previous Day]

You need to set up a suitable pivot table that gives you immediate feedback about whether your formula is working. Put 'Calendar'[DayNumberOfMonth] on Rows and make sure you filter for a single month.

67. [Total Sales Previous Quarter]

As with Practice Exercise 66, you need to set up a suitable pivot table for context. You can work out how to do this one yourself.

Writing Your Own Time Intelligence Functions

As mentioned earlier in this chapter, writing your own time intelligence functions is a bit harder than using the inbuilt time intelligence functions, particularly when you are learning. However, once you get the hang of it, you will find it quite easy, and this will also be a good sign of how much progress you are making in your understanding of DAX.

There are a couple strange things in the syntax that you need to get your head around before you can fully understand what you're doing. The good news is that I explain these things in this section. You will be writing your own custom time intelligence functions in no time at all. These are the two concepts you need to get your head around:

- Concept 1: Thinking "whole of table" when thinking about filter context
- Concept 2: Knowing how to use MIN() and MAX()

Let me cover these concepts before we get into any examples. That way, by the time you reach the examples, you will be primed and ready to go.

Concept 1: Thinking "Whole of Table" When Thinking About Filter Context

Consider the single row highlighted in the pivot table below. (This is the same pivot table you were just looking at above.)

CalendarYear	2003

Row Labels	Total Sales
January	$438,865
February	$489,090
March	$485,575
April	$506,399
May	$562,773
June	$554,799
July	$886,669
August	$847,414
September	$1,010,258
October	$1,080,450
November	$1,196,981
December	$1,731,788
Grand Total	**$9,791,060**

This pivot table is filtered for 'Calendar'[CalendarYear]=2003 in the filter. Also, the highlighted row (January) is also filtered—by 'Calendar'[MonthName]="January", which appears in the Rows area of the pivot table. When these two filters are combined, the single cell/value for [Total Sales] is filtered for the period January 2003. So, there are only 31 days that are used in the Calendar table in the data model for this cell. With this in mind, it is possible to *imagine* this filter applied on the back end. In fact, you can simulate what is happening by going into the Power Pivot window and manually applying these filters, as shown below.

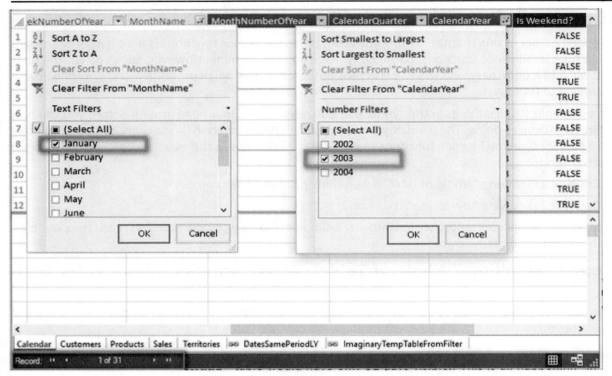

Applying a manual filter like this on a table in the Power Pivot window has no impact on any formula, but it does allow you to "see" what is happening behind the scenes (albeit in a simulation). Once you have done this a few times, you will begin to mentally visualise what is happening behind the scenes, which in turn will increase your understanding of how Power Pivot works.

> **Tip:** Always try to think about what these "filtered" tables would look like. (For example, in the example above, the Calendar table would have only 31 days visible.) This is all happening "in memory," on-the-fly. You can't open up Power Pivot and see this filtering happening (even though you can simulate it, as described above), but it is important that you be able to imagine it happening in your mind. Thinking about what is happening behind the scenes like this will make it easier to write custom time intelligence formulas.

When thinking about the filtering that is being applied, you should think about *the whole table*, not just the two columns with filters applied. It is clear that the table has only one month visible (January) and only one year visible (2003), but it is also true that there are 31 DayNumberOfMonth values visible (those from 1 through 31), and there are 4 different WeekNumberOfYear values (1 through 4). It is possible to reference any and all of these other columns and values in your DAX formulas after the initial filter context is applied, and this makes it very powerful indeed.

This is one of the main reasons you should also include an ID column in your Calendar table if you are going to write custom time intelligence functions. As you can see in the next image, after you filter the Calendar table based on January and 2003, there are actually 31 rows in the table, and the ID numbers of those rows run from 550 to 580. You can reference these ID values that remain in the filtered table in your DAX formulas to write very powerful DAX. But you need to be able to think "whole of table" to be able to understand how to do this.

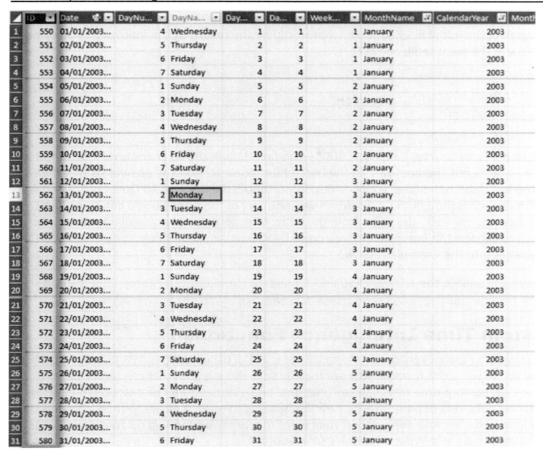

Concept 2: Knowing How to Use MIN() and MAX()

It is very common to use the MIN() and MAX() functions inside FILTER() when you write custom time intelligence functions. (You can also use FIRSTDATE() and LASTDATE() if you prefer.) You'll learn more detail in the examples that follow, but for now there is one key concept about MIN() and MAX() that you should understand: Whenever you use an aggregation function around a column in a DAX formula, *it always respects the initial filter context coming from the pivot table.*

So, let's go back to the pivot table from before, shown again below for convenience.

CalendarYear 2003	

Row Labels ▾	Total Sales
January	$438,865
February	$489,090
March	$485,575
April	$506,399
May	$562,773
June	$554,799
July	$886,669
August	$847,414
September	$1,010,258
October	$1,080,450
November	$1,196,981
December	$1,731,788
Grand Total	**$9,791,060**

You know that the pivot table has filtered the `Calendar` table so that only 31 days remain. Given that `MIN()` and `MAX()` always respect the initial filter context, what would be the results of the following DAX formulas for the highlighted row in the pivot table above?

1. `= MIN('Calendar'[Date])`

2. `= MAX('Calendar'[Date])`

3. `= MIN('Calendar'[ID])`

4. `= MAX('Calendar'[ID])`

The answer to Question 1 is, of course, January 1, 2003—the first date in the filter context. It's not the first date in the `Calendar` table but the first date in the initial filter context. And the answer to Question 2 is January 31, 2003, the last date in the filter context. But, importantly, the answers to Questions 3 and 4 are 550 and 580, respectively, even though this `ID` column was not part of the filter. So you can think of `MIN()` and `MAX()` as tools that can "harvest" the value from the initial filter context, in any available column across the whole table, and you can use this harvested value in your DAX formulas. Remember this fact about `MIN()` and `MAX()` when you get into the examples below.

> **Note:** If you want to validate the answers 550 and 580, go to the `Calendar` table, find the rows January 1, 2003, and January 31, 2003, and check `'Calendar'[ID]` for each row.

Writing Custom Time Intelligence Functions

Now you are going to write a custom version of `[Total Sales YTD]`, using `CALCULATE()` and `FILTER()`. I strongly encourage you to write this formula yourself for practice. There is a lot that can (and will) go wrong when you type your own custom time intelligence functions, and you need *lots* of practice to get it right. There are square bracket sets, sets of parentheses, new line spacing to make it easier to read, commas to be added in the right places, etc. *So make sure you actually write the following formula on your own computer.* Go ahead and do that now before moving on to the explanation:

```
Total Sales YTD Manual = CALCULATE([Total Sales],
    FILTER(ALL('Calendar'),
        'Calendar'[CalendarYear]=MAX('Calendar'[CalendarYear]) &&
        'Calendar'[Date] <=MAX('Calendar'[Date])
    )
)
```

Also make sure you set up a pivot table so that you can get immediate feedback about whether your formula is correct.

This formula needs a bit of explanation. I have used http://daxformatter.com in the following pages to make it easier to refer to the lines in the formula. I mentioned DAX Formatter in Chapter 9, and you can see here that it is a great tool for helping you read DAX formulas.

```
1  =
2  CALCULATE (
3      [Total Sales],
4      FILTER (
5          ALL ( 'Calendar' ),
6          'Calendar'[CalendarYear] = MAX ( 'Calendar'[CalendarYear] )
7              && 'Calendar'[Date] <= MAX ( 'Calendar'[Date] )
8      )
9  )
```

You can see that lines 4 through 8 above are all part of a `FILTER()` function because you can see that the `)` on line 8 is left aligned with the `F` in `FILTER()` on line 4.

This `FILTER()` function returns a table to the function `CALCULATE()`. `CALCULATE()` then applies a filter for this table of dates and propagates this filter to the `Sales` table prior to evaluating `[Total Sales]`. Let's look more closely at lines 6 and 7 in the `FILTER()` function. Line 6 reads:

```
'Calendar'[CalendarYear] = MAX('Calendar'[CalendarYear])
```

Okay, I hear you saying "How can the calendar year be equal to the MAX() of the calendar year?" What is really happening is that there is *a column name* on the left side of the equals sign, and there is *a* MAX() *function* on the right side. Remember from earlier in this chapter that whenever you see MIN() or MAX() in a formula like this, it always respects the initial filter context. So the way to read line 6 of this formula is as follows: "Add a filter to the table so that the column 'Calendar'[CalendarYear] is equal to the maximum value in my initial filter context coming from my pivot table."

For example, in the pivot table below, the maximum of the highlighted row is March 31, 2003, and hence MAX('Calendar'[CalendarYear]) = 2003.

CalendarYear	2003	🔽

Row Labels ▾	Total Sales	Total Sales YTD Manual
January	$438,865	$438,865
February	$489,090	$927,956
March	$485,575	$1,413,530
April	$506,399	$1,919,930
May	$562,773	$2,482,702
June	$554,799	$3,037,501
July	$886,669	$3,924,170
August	$847,414	$4,771,584
September	$1,010,258	$5,781,842
October	$1,080,450	$6,862,291
November	$1,196,981	$8,059,273
December	$1,731,788	$9,791,060
Grand Total	**$9,791,060**	**$9,791,060**

See how you need to think "whole of table" here? The initial filter context is applied over the month of March 2003, but the MAX() formula is working over the year column. Imagine this filter context acting on the table in your data model by mentally applying the filters: There were 31 rows left in the Calendar table, and for each of these rows, the value in 'Calendar'[CalendarYear] was 2003. As a result (in this case), the MIN() of 'Calendar'[CalendarYear] would also return 2003, as would SUM() and AVERAGE(), for that matter.

So line 6 is really saying "filter my table where 'Calendar'[CalendarYear]=*the initial filter context year*," which is 2003 in this case.

Let's move on. Line 7 starts with the double ampersand operator (which means *and* [i.e., do both line 6 *and* line 7]) and then says:

                    'Calendar'[Date] <=MAX('Calendar'[Date])

The same applies here as with line 6. MAX('Calendar'[Date]) reads the initial filter context from the pivot table and hence returns the value March 31, 2003, for the highlighted row in the pivot table. Therefore, this part of the formula adds an AND condition so that the underlying table is filtered for 'Calendar'[CalendarYear] = 2003 *and* also for the condition 'Calendar'[Date] *is on or before* March 31, 2003. As you can deduce, this is all the dates year to date.

As you go to the next row in the pivot table, the calendar year stays the same, but the month-end date moves to the end of the next month. So the number of days that are included increases as you work down the rows in the pivot table.

Now it is important to point out that you could not use MIN() in line 7 as you could do in line 6; this time it has to be MAX(). If you used MIN(), you would get March 1, 2003, as the last date, and the year-to-date result would be out by almost a full month of sales. It is important to think about what your formulas need and make sure you provide the right formulas to achieve the desired outcome (of course).

Now let's go back to ALL('Calendar'). Line 5 of the formula refers to ALL('Calendar') instead of just the Calendar table (which you have used previously). ALL(), as discussed in Chapter 13, is the "remove filter" function. (If necessary, go back and refresh your memory about ALL() before moving on.)

It is important to use the ALL() function here because you know that the pivot table reads the initial filter context before doing the calculation. Probably the easiest way to explain why you need the ALL() function is to consider what would happen if you didn't use ALL().

Consider again the highlighted row in the pivot table below.

CalendarYear	2003	▼	

Row Labels ▼	Total Sales	Total Sales YTD Manual
January	$438,865	$438,865
February	$489,090	$927,956
March	$485,575	$1,413,530
April	$506,399	$1,919,930
May	$562,773	$2,482,702
June	$554,799	$3,037,501
July	$886,669	$3,924,170
August	$847,414	$4,771,584
September	$1,010,258	$5,781,842
October	$1,080,450	$6,862,291
November	$1,196,981	$8,059,273
December	$1,731,788	$9,791,060
Grand Total	**$9,791,060**	**$9,791,060**

You know that the initial filter context for this row of the pivot table is for all 31 days in the month of March 2003. You can "imagine" that the Calendar table is filtered behind the scenes so that only these 31 days of March 2003 are visible.

Now let's look at why the [Total Sales YTD] formula does not work without the ALL() function. You should write the following formula and add it to your pivot table. (Don't miss the opportunity to practice now!)

```
=
CALCULATE (
    [Total Sales],
    FILTER (
        'Calendar',
        'Calendar'[CalendarYear] = MAX ( 'Calendar'[CalendarYear] )
            && 'Calendar'[Date] <= MAX ( 'Calendar'[Date] )
    )
)
```

CalendarYear	2003	⫪

Row Labels ▾	Total Sales	Total Sales YTD Does Not Work
January	$438,865	$438,865
February	$489,090	$489,090
March	$485,575	$485,575
April	$506,399	$506,399
May	$562,773	$562,773
June	$554,799	$554,799
July	$886,669	$886,669
August	$847,414	$847,414
September	$1,010,258	$1,010,258
October	$1,080,450	$1,080,450
November	$1,196,981	$1,196,981
December	$1,731,788	$1,731,788
Grand Total	$9,791,060	$9,791,060

You can see in the pivot table above (and in the one you have created yourself) that this formula is giving the sales *for the current month rather than YTD* in each row of the pivot table. The reason it doesn't work is related to the initial filter context discussed earlier. For the row of March 2003, the initial filter context applied a filter so that only the 31 days of March 2003 were "visible" in the `Calendar` table (behind the scenes). So how can the formula possibly return sales for all days "year to date," including the sales from January and February? The dates in January and February were already filtered out by the pivot table from the initial filter context, so you can't get the sales for these months to somehow reappear for the new formula if you write it this way.

If you want to include sales from January and February in the row next to the actual sales for March, you must first "remove the filter" created by the pivot table. This is what `ALL()` does when it is wrapped around the `Calendar` table in line 5: It removes the filter context that comes from the pivot table that is automatically applied to the `Calendar` table. You then reapply the filters you want to use in lines 6 and 7 so that you end up with all the dates YTD.

> **Note:** Custom time intelligence always uses some form of `ALL('Calendar')` to remove the initial filter context. The `FILTER()` function therefore iterates through an unfiltered copy of the `Calendar` table. But the `MIN()` and `MAX()` functions operate in the initial filter context *before* the `ALL()` function removes it.

> **Tip:** Go back and read this section again if necessary until you understand it well.

Now let me come back to that `ID` column I talked about earlier. A good `ID` column in a `Calendar` table starts at 1 and increments by 1 for each row in the table. So in the case of this `Calendar` table, each day of the year has an `ID` value that increments by 1. But the same applies to 445 calendars and weekly calendars. You should always have an `ID` column that increments by 1 for each row in the table (in chronological order, of course). This gives you a nice clean numeric column for moving backward and forward inside your formulas. To illustrate this point, the following formula will work for YTD:

```
Total Sales YTD Manual ID = CALCULATE([Total Sales],
    FILTER(ALL('Calendar'),
        'Calendar'[CalendarYear]=MAX('Calendar'[CalendarYear]) &&
        'Calendar'[ID] <=MAX('Calendar'[ID])
    )
)
```

Notice that here you replace the `Date` column with the `ID` column. Using the `ID` column like this is very powerful and allows you to jump back and forward in time, using your knowledge of the `Calendar` table structure by just doing numeric addition and subtraction on the `ID` column.

For one more example using the `ID` column, write a measure that returns the total sales for the same period last year. You did this earlier, using the function `SAMEPERIODLASTYEAR()`, but recall that this inbuilt time intelligence function works only for a standard calendar. You can also write a custom time intelligence function that works with a custom calendar using `FILTER()`. Note in the pivot table below that `[Total Sales LY ID]` works on both the month level and the year level.

CalendarYear	MonthName	Total Sales	Total Sales LY ID
⊟ 2001	July	$473,388	
	August	$506,192	
	September	$473,943	
	October	$513,329	
	November	$543,993	
	December	$755,528	
2001 Total		**$3,266,374**	
⊟ 2002	January	$596,747	
	February	$550,817	
	March	$644,135	
	April	$663,692	
	May	$673,556	
	June	$676,764	
	July	$500,365	$473,388
	August	$546,001	$506,192
	September	$350,467	$473,943
	October	$415,390	$513,329
	November	$335,095	$543,993
	December	$577,314	$755,528
2002 Total		**$6,530,344**	**$3,266,374**

Here is the formula you need to write for this:

```
Total Sales LY ID = CALCULATE([Total Sales],
    FILTER(ALL('Calendar'),
        'Calendar'[ID] >=MIN('Calendar'[ID]) -365 &&
        'Calendar'[ID] <=MAX('Calendar'[ID]) - 365
    )
)
```

Note that you can use the `ID` column to your advantage here to move back in time by 365 days. Also note how the first reference inside `FILTER()` is to `MIN('Calendar'[ID])`, and the second one is to `MAX('Calendar'[ID])`. It's time to think "whole of table" again. Let's take a look at two different areas of the following pivot table.

CalendarYear ▾	MonthName ▾	Total Sales	Total Sales LY ID
⊞ 2001		$3,266,374	
⊞ 2002		$6,530,344	$3,266,374
⊟ 2003	January	$438,865	$596,747
	February	$489,090	$550,817
	March	$485,575	$644,135
	April	$506,399	$663,692
	May	$562,773	$673,556
	June	$554,799	$676,764
	July	$886,669	$500,365
	August	$847,414	$546,001
	September	$1,010,25①	$350,467
	October	$1,080,450	$415,390
	November	$1,196,981	$335,095
	December	$1,731,78②	$577,314
2003 Total		$9,791,060	$6,530,344
⊟ 2004	January	$1,340,245	$438,865

In the pivot table cell marked #1 above (October 2003), you need to be able to visualise the `Calendar` table as it is currently filtered. In the case of October 2003, there are 31 rows that remain unfiltered. The first (earliest) of these rows is October 1, 2003, and it has an ID of 823. The last unfiltered row is October 31, 2003, and it has an ID of 853. So "October this year" can be thought of as:

        `'Calendar'[ID] >=823 && 'Calendar'[ID] <=853`

And October last year can be thought of as:

        `'Calendar'[ID] >=823 - 365 && 'Calendar'[ID] <=853 - 365`

When you write it this way, it is obvious why you use $>=$ MIN for the first filter line and $<=$ MAX for the second one. And the really great thing is that this works regardless of the time period you are looking at. In this first example, you are looking at a month, but if you look at #2 in the pivot table above, you see that this time the filter context is on an entire year. The formula therefore is filtering for all periods after the first date of the entire year (1/1/2003: `'Calendar'[ID]` = 550) and also for less than the last date of the calendar year (31/12/2003: `'Calendar'[ID]` = 914). Once you learn to trust this "whole of table" behaviour, you will be able to very quickly write custom time intelligence formulas by referencing the ID column alone.

What About Leap Years?

Astute readers will be crying foul about leap years by now. In fact, if you compare the measure [Total Sales LY ID] with the measure [Total Sales LY], you will notice that there is a different answer for leap years. Well, as I said earlier, every business is different, and different businesses handle these things in different ways. It is beyond the scope of this book to provide solutions to this problem, but you can read about some possible approaches at http://www.daxpatterns.com/time-patterns/.

A Final Word on ID Columns

In the examples above, we have used an ID column on the day level of granularity—the same level of granularity as the `Calendar` table. I also like to load integer ID columns for the other important columns of data in a `Calendar` table. For example, I like to add a `MonthID` column to my `Calendar` tables. It starts with 1 for the first January in the calendar, 2 for the first February, . . . 12 for the first December. But then it would become 13 for the second January, 14 for the second February, etc. Having a `MonthID` column like this makes it easy to reach back in time and grab the same monthly period from any time in the past.

Practice Exercises: Time Intelligence, Cont.

It's time for some more practice. Write the following formulas. First set up an appropriate pivot table so that you will get immediate feedback about whether your formula is correct. Find the solutions to these practice exercises in Appendix A.

68. [Total Sales Moving Annual Total]

With this DAX formula, you need to create a rolling 12-month total of sales. It will always show you 12 months' worth of sales, up to the end of the current month. Think about the problem using English words first and then convert that to DAX, using the techniques you have learnt here. I show my tips for writing this measure later in this chapter, but you should give it a go yourself before you peek.

69. [Total Sales Rolling 90 Days]

This is the same as the formula for Practice Exercise 68, but instead of delivering a rolling 12-month total, you will instead deliver a rolling 90-day total. Try to do this one from scratch, without referencing Practice Exercise 68. This is good practice to help you think like the DAX engine.

Tips for Writing a Moving Annual Total

This section walks through how to create the formula in Practice Exercise 69. Start by setting up a new pivot table with CalendarYear and MonthName on Rows and [Total Sales] on Values, as shown below.

Row Labels	Total Sales
⊟ 2001	$3,266,374
July	$473,388
August	$506,192
September	$473,943
October	$513,329
November	$543,993
December	$755,528
⊟ 2002	$6,530,344
January	$596,747
February	$550,817
March	$644,135
April	$663,692
May	$673,556
June	$676,764
July	$500,365
August	$546,001
September	$350,467
October	$415,390
November	$335,095
December	$577,314
⊟ 2003	$9,791,060
January	$438,865
February	$489,090
March	$485,575

Then write your formula, which might look like this:

```
Total Sales Moving Annual Total
= CALCULATE([Total Sales],
    FILTER(ALL('Calendar'),
       'Calendar'[ID] > MAX('Calendar'[ID]) - 365 &&
       'Calendar'[ID] <= MAX('Calendar'[ID])
    )
  )
```

Note: This is not the only way to write this formula. Just as in Excel, there are often multiple ways to write a formula in Power Pivot. If you have something different and it works, that's great. Also note that this formula may not work with leap years, depending on how your business handles the extra day. (Some businesses ignore the extra day and actually have 6 × 364-day years followed by 1 × 371-day extraordinary year, so it depends.)

Now check your formulas against the pivot table, as shown below. Select the sales for a period (e.g., #1 below) and then compare the total against the moving annual total at the end of December 2002 (see #2 below).

Row Labels	Total Sales	Total Sales MAT
⊟ 2001	$3,266,374	$3,266,374
July	$473,388	$473,388
August	$506,192	$979,580
September	$473,943	$1,453,523
October	$513,329	$1,966,852
November	$543,993	$2,510,846
December	$755,528	$3,266,374
⊟ 2002	$6,530,344	$6,530,344
January	$596,747	$3,863,120
February	$550,817	$4,413,937
March	$644,135	$5,058,072
April	$663,692	$5,721,764
May	$673,556	$6,395,321
June	$676,764	$7,072,084
July	$500,365	$7,099,061
August	$546,001	$7,138,871
September	$350,467	$7,015,395
October	$415,390	$6,917,456
November	$335,095	$6,708,557 ②
December	$577,314	$6,530,344
⊟ 2003	$9,791,0 ①	$9,791,060
January	$438,865	$6,372,462

ual | Sales LY | Sheet22 | **Total Sales MAT** | Sheet ... ⊕ ⋮

Average: $544,195   Count: 12   Sum: $6,530,344

One thing to note is that the first `FILTER()` line in the formula says *greater than*, and the last `FILTER()` line says *less than or equal to*. It is easy to get these things wrong when writing formulas, but you should not worry about this because it is easy to check and verify. As long as you set up a pivot table so that you can test the formulas you are writing, you can just take a guess and then change it if you need to (i.e., if you got it wrong). In this example, if you used *greater than or equal to*, you would end up with 366 days, which is incorrect.

But What About the First Year?

Now, if you want to get technical, the `[Total Sales Moving Annual Total]` result really doesn't make sense in the first 11 months of the sales data because you didn't have a full year of sales until the end of June 2002. There are many ways to solve this problem by using the `IF()` function. Here is one solution:

```
Total Sales MAT Improved =
    IF(MAX('Calendar'[ID])>=365,
        CALCULATE([Total Sales],
            FILTER(ALL('Calendar'),
                'Calendar'[ID] > MAX('Calendar'[ID]) - 365 &&
                'Calendar'[ID] <= MAX('Calendar'[ID])
```

```
            )
        )
    )
```

> **Tip:** By now you may have realised that it is easiest to copy one formula and then edit the copied version for the new formula. Indeed, this is a good idea, but try to keep the copying and changing to a minimum while you are learning. It's a good idea to get as much DAX writing practice as you can. Once you know how to do it, using copy and paste is a great way to go faster.

Researching DAX Functions

There are a lot of other time intelligence functions that you can use to write time-based DAX formulas. A key piece of advice as you learn how to use these other time intelligence functions (indeed, all other DAX functions) is to do a quick online search and read the relevant information in the documentation.

To do this, do a web search for the function name followed by the word DAX. In the example below, I have searched for "DATEADD DAX."

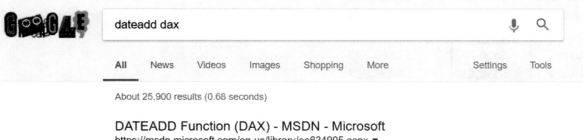

The first result returned is normally the official Microsoft documentation (MSDN) site. When you click on this MSDN link, you see something like the following.

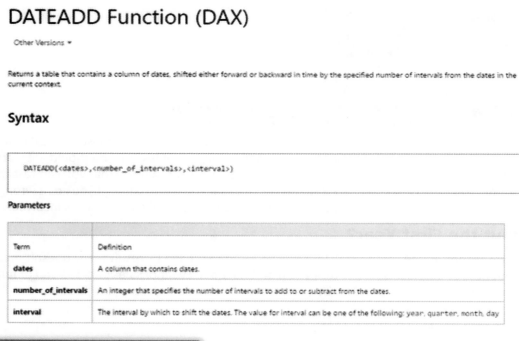

DATEADD Function (DAX)

Other Versions ▾

Returns a table that contains a column of dates, shifted either forward or backward in time by the specified number of intervals from the dates in the current context.

Syntax

```
DATEADD(<dates>,<number_of_intervals>,<interval>)
```

Parameters

Term	Definition
dates	A column that contains dates.
number_of_intervals	An integer that specifies the number of intervals to add to or subtract from the dates.
interval	The interval by which to shift the dates. The value for interval can be one of the following: year, quarter, month, day

Return Value

A table containing a single column of date values.

In many cases, the official documentation is not as useful as other websites. But there is some very important information that you can get from MSDN: the syntax, parameters, and return value. You can find the syntax and parameters by typing a function directly into the Measure dialog box in Excel, but sometimes the IntelliSense help doesn't clearly tell you the return value—and this is where doing a web search can help. The return value is a key piece of information that helps you understand how to use a function. In the case of DATEADD() above, the return value is a table, and hence you would use DATEADD() inside CALCULATE() to do a time shift. So you might write something like this:

```
Total Sales LY DATEADD =
    CALCULATE([Total Sales],
        DATEADD('Calendar'[Date],-1,Year)
    )
```

This formula works on various different time horizons, including quarters as well as years, as shown below.

CalendarYear		Row Labels	Total Sales	Total Sales LY DATEADD
2001		2002	$6,530,344	$3,266,374
2002		2003	$9,791,060	$6,530,344
2003		Grand Total	$16,321,404	$9,796,717
2004				

You may realise that this is basically the same as the SAMEPERIODLASTYEAR() example shown earlier in this chapter.

As another example, when you do a quick search for FIRSTDATE, you find the MSDN site the first time again.

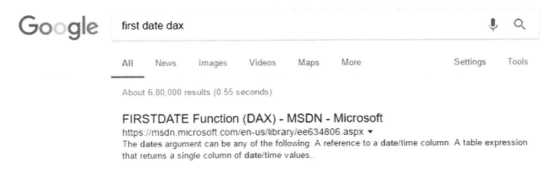

If you click through to the MSDN site, you can see that the returned value is a special table that has a single column and a single row, as shown below.

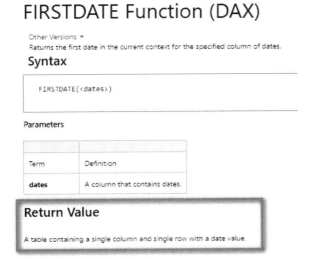

FIRSTDATE Function (DAX)

Other Versions ▾
Returns the first date in the current context for the specified column of dates.

Syntax

```
FIRSTDATE(<dates>)
```

Parameters

Term	Definition
dates	A column that contains dates.

Return Value

A table containing a single column and single row with a date value.

FIRSTDATE () returns a single value in a table. This is a special type of table that can be placed directly into a cell in a pivot table. (Normally you cannot do this.) So, you could write a formula like this:

```
First Date = FIRSTDATE('Calendar'[Date])
```

Row Labels ▼	Total Sales	Total Sales LY DATEADD	First Date
⊟ 2001	$3,266,374		01/07/2001
3	$1,453,523		01/07/2001
4	$1,812,851		01/10/2001
⊟ 2002	$6,530,344	$3,266,374	01/01/2002
1	$1,791,698		01/01/2002
2	$2,014,012		01/04/2002
3	$1,396,834	$1,453,523	01/07/2002
4	$1,327,799	$1,812,851	01/10/2002
⊟ 2003	$9,791,060	$6,530,344	01/01/2003
1	$1,413,530	$1,791,698	01/01/2003
2	$1,623,971	$2,014,012	01/04/2003
3	$2,744,340	$1,396,834	01/07/2003
4	$4,009,218	$1,327,799	01/10/2003
⊟ 2004	$9,770,900	$9,791,060	01/01/2004
1	$4,283,630	$1,413,530	01/01/2004
2	$5,436,429	$1,623,971	01/04/2004
3	$50,841	$2,744,340	01/07/2004
4		$4,009,218	01/10/2004
Grand Total	$29,358,677	$19,587,777	01/07/2001

Other Time Intelligence Functions

Here is a list of other time intelligence functions that you might want to explore:

```
DATESINPERIOD(date_column, start_date, number_of_intervals, intervals)
DATESBETWEEN(column, start_date, end_date)
DATEADD(date_column, number_of_intervals, interval)
FIRSTDATE (datecolumn)
LASTDATE (datecolumn)
LASTNONBLANKDATE (datecolumn, [expression])
STARTOFMONTH (date_column)
STARTOFQUARTER (date_column)
STARTOFYEAR(date_column [,YE_date])
ENDOFMONTH(date_column)
ENDOFQUARTER(date_column)
ENDOFYEAR(date_column)
PARALLELPERIOD(date_column)
PREVIOUSDAY(date_column)
PREVIOUSMONTH(date_column)
PREVIOUSQUARTER(date_column)
PREVIOUSYEAR(date_column)
NEXTDAY(date_column)
NEXTMONTH(date_column)
NEXTQUARTER (date_column)
NEXTYEAR(date_column [,YE_date])
DATESMTD(date_column)
DATESQTD (date_column)
DATESYTD (date_column [,YE_date])
TOTALMTD(expression, dates, filter)
TOTALQTD(expression, dates, filter)
```

A Free Quick Reference Guide

I have produced (and I maintain for new functions) a quick reference guide of all DAX functions in PDF format that you may like to download and use. The *DAX Reference Guide* PDF is not meant to replace the online documentation but to supplement it. As shown below, the PDF is fully indexed, and you can jump to the relevant sections by clicking on the hyperlinks in the table of contents.

You can download the *DAX Reference Guide* for free by visiting my online shop at http://xbi.com.au/shop and then navigating to the Books section.

DAX Functions List

This DAX functions quick reference guide has been prepared by Matt Allington from http://exceleratorbi.com.au and contains a list of all current DAX functions in a summarised and easy to use format. You can print the document and/or use the search features for PDF documents to search for the function you are looking for.

This document is a supplement and is not intended to replace the more detailed documentation that is available online.

When looking for online documentation it is best to do a web search from your favourite search engine by specifying the function name followed by the word DAX i.e. "**FunctionName DAX**".

Tip: If you are going to search this document for a function name using search, then type the function name followed by a space then an open bracket. E.g. instead of searching for VALUES you should search **VALUES (**, including the space.

Contents

DAX Functions List

DAX Aggregation Functions (Aggregators)

DAX Date and Time Functions

DAX Filter Functions

DAX Information Functions

DAX Logical Functions

16: DAX Topic: RELATED() and RELATEDTABLE()

The functions RELATED() and RELATEDTABLE() are typically used in calculated columns to reference relevant records in other tables, although they can be used in measures, too. They are a bit like VLOOKUP() for tables that have a relationship. As mentioned briefly in Chapter 10, a row context does not follow a relationship. So even though there may be a relationship between two tables, a row context cannot use this relationship—unless you use one of these two functions that can. Basically, RELATED() and RELATEDTABLE() allow a row context to leverage an existing relationship so it can access columns in related tables.

When to Use RELATED() vs. RELATEDTABLE()

To understand when to use the RELATED() and RELATEDTABLE() functions, you need to understand what each one returns. As you know, you can use IntelliSense in the formula bar in the Power Pivot window to find out what each of these functions returns.

You can see below that RELATED() returns a single value from another table.

As shown below, RELATEDTABLE() returns a table.

Remember from Chapter 2 that relationships between tables in Power Pivot are normally of the type "one to many." Also remember from Chapter 2 that best practice for Excel users is to lay out tables in Diagram view with the lookup tables at the top (the "one" side of the relationship) and the data tables at the bottom (the "many" side of the relationship), as shown below.

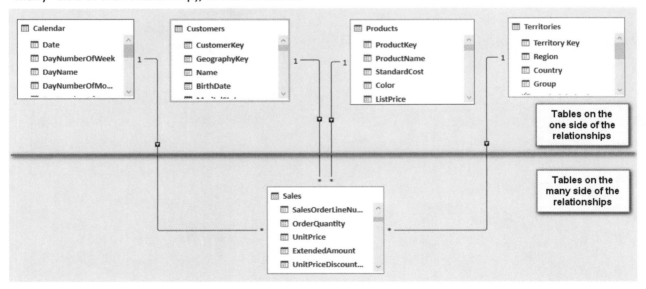

The two RELATED() functions allow you to refer to columns in another connected table. So when you think about it, if you want to add a custom column in a table on the "one" side of the relationship—i.e., add a new column in a lookup table (a table above the line in the image above)—then it is highly likely that there will be multiple rows on the "many" side of the relationship. So when writing a formula in a calculated column on a lookup table, you must use the RELATEDTABLE() function *because it will fetch a table of values*, including all the matching values in the data table. Conversely, if you are writing a calculated column in a table on the "many" side of the relationship (i.e., a data table), then there will be only one matching row in the lookup table, and hence you use RELATED() to return that single value.

The RELATED() Function

This section provides an example of bringing a value from a column in a lookup table into a table on the "many" side of the relationship. For the sake of this example, assume that your business has a new management layer, and you want to add a new level of reporting to cover this new management layer. In effect, you need to enhance the Territories table to add a new geographic region. To achieve this, you could do the following:

- Create a new table that contains the logic of the new management layer.
- Import the new table into the data model.
- Join the new table to the existing Territories table (in this example).
- Create a new calculated column in the Territories table (on the "many" side of the relationship) and bring in the new management layer from the new table into the Territories table as a new column.

This will all make more sense as you work through the following example, which also shows how you can manually add new tables of data in Power Pivot.

Here's How: Manually Adding Data to Power Pivot from a New Linked Table

Sometimes you don't have the data in your data model that you need to complete a task. Say you wanted to create a new management level in the Territories table. You could do that with a calculated column, but you could also do it by loading another table of data local to your Excel workbook. In this example, you are going to create a new management level for the Northern and Southern Hemispheres of the world and learn how to create a linked table at the same time:

1. Insert a new worksheet in your workbook and add the following data to the sheet.

Group	Hemisphere
Europe	Northern
NA	NA
North America	Northern
Pacific	Southern

2. Select one of the cells in the data and press Ctrl+L (or press Ctrl+T or select Insert, Table). To help Excel auto-detect the table, ensure that there is no other data in the surrounding cells.

3. While you still have the new table selected, go to the Table Name box on the File tab and rename the table Hemisphere.

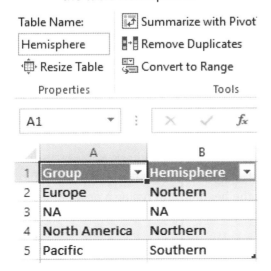

Note: You must rename your linked tables inside Excel. Unlike with other imported tables, you can't change linked table names inside Power Pivot.

4.   From the Power Pivot tab select Add to Data Model. (In Excel 2010, from the Power Pivot tab select Create Linked Table.)

5.   Switch to the Power Pivot window and then switch to the Diagram view and rearrange the tables so that the new table (which is a lookup table to another lookup table and will be on the "one" side of the relationship) is sitting above the current `Territories` table, as shown below.

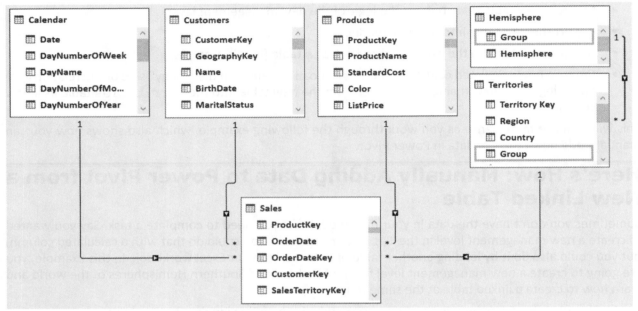

6.   Join the tables by dragging the `Group` column from the `Territories` table up and dropping it on top of the `Group` column in the new `Hemisphere` table.

Note: The `Territories` table now has two roles. It is now acting as a lookup table to the `Sales` table and as a data table to the new `Hemisphere` table.

7.   Bring the data that resides in the `Hemisphere[Hemisphere]` column into a new calculated column inside the `Territories` table. Switch to the Data view, navigate to the `Territories` table, and then add a calculated column by typing the formula shown below.

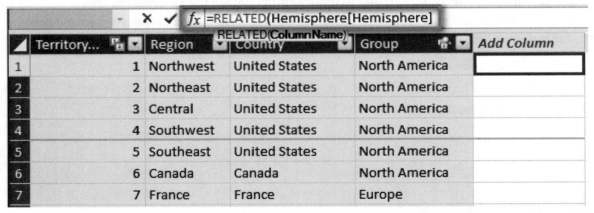

8.   Press Enter, and you see all the values appear in the new calculated column. It is a lot like a VLOOK-UP()! You can rename the new column by double-clicking the heading and typing a new name.

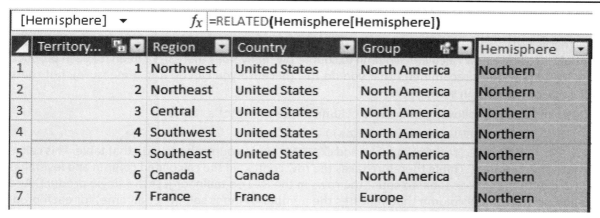

[Hemisphere] ▼		f_x =RELATED(Hemisphere[Hemisphere])			
◢ Territory... 🔲 ▼	Region ▼	Country ▼	Group 🔲 ▼	Hemisphere ▼
1	1 Northwest	United States	North America	Northern
2	2 Northeast	United States	North America	Northern
3	3 Central	United States	North America	Northern
4	4 Southwest	United States	North America	Northern
5	5 Southeast	United States	North America	Northern
6	6 Canada	Canada	North America	Northern
7	7 France	France	Europe	Northern

9. Finally, to hide the `Hemisphere` table from the client tools, in the Diagram view, right-click the `Hemisphere` table and select Hide from Client Tools, as shown below.

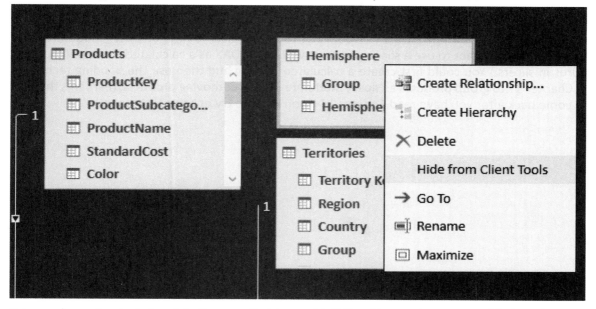

It is good practice to bring data from an "add-on table" like this `Hemisphere` table into the main `Territories` table as an additional column rather than use the data in an additional lookup table. It is possible to leave the `Territories` table untouched and use the columns from the `Hemisphere` table in your pivot tables. But the problem is that this can be confusing to users. It doesn't make business sense to have all the geographic information *except* for the hemisphere information in the `Territories` table but instead store it in the `Hemisphere` table. So for consistency and simplicity for the end user, it is better to bring all the "like data" into the same table (or simply create the new data as a calculated column without the linked table at all).

> **Note:** Better practice is to bring all the "like data" into the same table when you load the data using Power Query, but you can also do it as shown here. And best practice is to change the `Territories` table back at the source to include the new `Hemisphere` column in the `Territories` table, but that is not always possible in a timely manner.

The RELATEDTABLE() Function

As discussed earlier, RELATEDTABLE() is used to reference a table on the "many" side of the relationship. A simple example is to add a new calculated column to count how many sales there have been for each product. Once again, I generally don't recommend that you do this (because you can do it in a measure), but there may be valid reasons to do it in some cases.

Go ahead now and add the following calculated column in the Products table:

```
= COUNTROWS (RELATEDTABLE (Sales))
```

As you know, RELATEDTABLE() returns a table, and COUNTROWS() counts the rows in that table. This calculated column in the Products table therefore takes the row context in the calculated column and leverages the relationship with the Sales table to count the rows in the Sales table for just the single product. As a result, you end up with a new column that indicates the number of items sold (over all time) for each product in the Products table. (The quantity for each line in the Sales table is always 1 in this sample data.)

> **Note:** You do not need to use CALCULATE() with RELATEDTABLE() to force context transition and convert the row context to a filter context. RELATEDTABLE() will work on its own.

One valid use case for using RELATEDTABLE() would be to create a slicer to filter on slow-, moderate-, and fast-selling products. If you want to use a slicer, you must write your DAX as a calculated column. (You can't place measures in slicers.) You could first create a calculated column and then use the banding technique discussed in Chapter 17 to group products as slow-, moderate-, and fast-moving products. (Park this thought for now and come back after you have read Chapter 17 if you want to try out this technique.)

17: Concept: Disconnected Tables

So far as you have worked through this book, you have always loaded tables into the data model and then connected them to other tables. This is a fundamental technique with Power Pivot that allows you to work across multiple tables without using VLOOKUP(). However, you are not required to join tables together in the data model, and indeed there are some instances when it doesn't make sense to do so. This chapter discusses two techniques that do not involve connecting tables:

- Using harvester measures
- Using banding

Using Harvester Measures

Rob Collie taught me the technique of manually creating a table of values and then writing a special measure to "harvest" the value selected by the user from that table so it can be used inside a formula, and I have borrowed his name for it: *harvester*. As the name suggests, a *harvester measure* is used to "harvest" something, such as input from a user. Let's look at an example to demonstrate.

Imagine that in your data, the sales result is directly proportional to the profit result. You have sales data and want to see what impact an increase in sales will have on your total profit. You could write a new measure hard-coded at a 10% increase, as shown below.

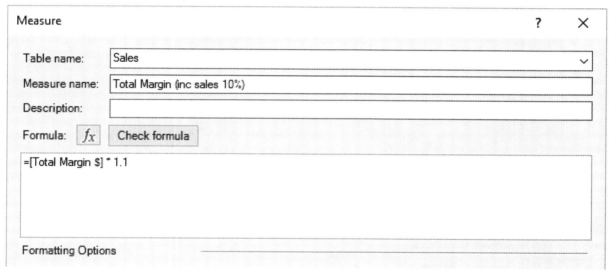

And it would look as shown below in a pivot table.

CalendarYear	2003	

Row Labels	Total Sales	Total Margin $	Total Margin (inc sales 10%)
Accessories	$293,710	$183,862	$202,248
Bikes	$9,359,103	$3,833,345	$4,216,680
Clothing	$138,248	$55,526	$61,078
Grand Total	**$9,791,060**	**$4,072,733**	**$4,480,006**

But what if you wanted to see what it looks like for a 5% increase in sales, or 15%, or some other percentage? It would not be efficient to create lots of new measures, one for each value. A better approach is to create a table of possible values and then create a harvester measure to receive input from the user on which value to use.

Here's How: Creating a Harvester Measure

Follow these steps to create a harvester measure:

1. Start with a blank worksheet in your workbook and create a list of possible values, such as a range of integers from 1 to 15, with the header Value, as shown below left.

2. Click anywhere in the list and press Ctrl+L to create an Excel table. You get something like the table shown below right.

Value
1
2
3
4
5
6
7
8
9
10
11
12
13
14
15

Value ▼
1
2
3
4
5
6
7
8
9
10
11
12
13
14
15

3. Click inside the table, make sure the Design tab is selected (it should be automatically) and then in the Table Name box, change the name of the table to `Increase`.

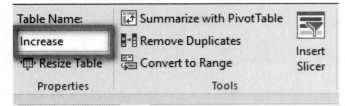

4. Add this table to the data model. To do this, select any cell in the table and then go to the Power Pivot tab and select Add to Data Model (or, in Excel 2010, select Create Linked Table). After you do this, the Data view opens, and you see the new linked table inside Power Pivot.

5. Switch to the Diagram view so you can see your new table. (You may need to select Fit to Screen to be able to see it.) This time the table is not joined to any other table; it is a disconnected table. Just position it somewhere so it is easy to see on the screen, as shown below.

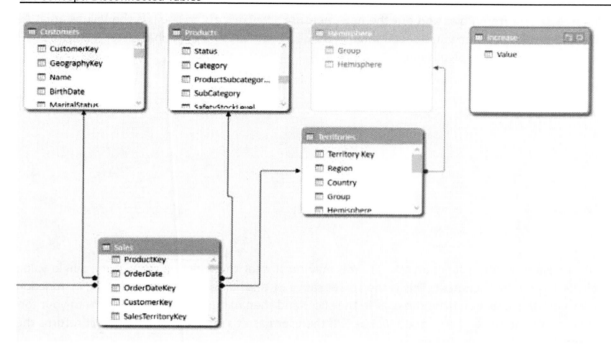

6. Now create a new pivot table and put `Increase[Value]` on Rows (just for this demo). Then add `Increase[Value]` as a slicer as well. You should have a pivot table like the one below.

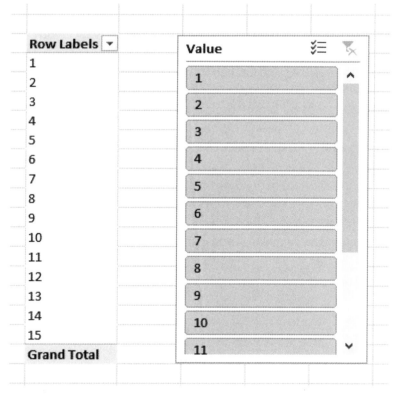

7. Note what happens when you click on one of the values in the slicer. It filters the pivot table so that only that single value is visible in Rows. The slicer thus allows the user to select a single value to represent the increase in sales required for analysis. What you now want to do is "harvest" this selection into a measure.

8. Click inside the pivot table and write the following measure:

```
Selected Value = MAX(Increase[Value])
```

9. Remove `Value` from Rows and put the new measure `[Selected Value]` in the Values area. As you can see below, when you select a value in the slicer, it is shown in your harvester measure (Selected Value) in the pivot table.

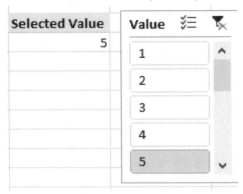

10. This measure uses the function `MAX()`. You may recall that this function returns the single value selected in the filter context. This is the secret sauce of this harvest measure. The `MAX()` function "harvests" the selection from the user in the slicer and then passes that selected value to your formula for the measure `[Selected Value]`. If the user hasn't selected a single value, it returns the maximum of all the selected values.

Note: This is what is happening here:

*   The slicer is connected to the table called `Increase` in the data model.
*   When you select a single item in the slicer, the slicer filters the `Increase` table in the data model so that only that single row is left unfiltered. (You can imagine this table filtered this way or you can simulate what is happening by applying a filter to the table inside Power Pivot.)
*   The measure `[Selected Value]` respects the pivot table filter context. (Remember that the slicer is part of the filter context.) Then the measure finds the maximum of `Value` in the initial filter context.
*   You can make sure only a single selection is made by setting the multi-select icon on the top-right corner of corner of the slicer to Off.
*   Given that there is only one value that is unfiltered, the measure returns that value.

So it should be obvious that you can use almost any aggregation formula in place of `MAX()`. `MIN()`, `AVERAGE()`, and `SUM()` all work just as well because the slicer selection has only a single item selected. These other aggregation approaches give you different results if you select more than one item from the slicer, but in this scenario, you are only expecting the user to select a single value.

Once you have the value selected in the slicer available as a measure, you can write a new DAX formula that uses it:

```
Total Margin with Selected Increase =
    [Total Margin $] * (100 + [Selected Value])/100
```

11. To tidy this up a bit, change the description in the slicer by right-clicking the slicer and selecting Slicer Settings. Then change the title to read `% Sales Increase`.

Row Labels ⌄	Total Sales	Total Margin $	Total Margin with Selected Increase
Accessories	$293,710	$183,862	$191,216
Bikes	$9,359,103	$3,833,345	$3,986,679
Clothing	$138,248	$55,526	$57,747
Grand Total	**$9,791,060**	**$4,072,733**	**$4,235,642**

Practice Exercise: Harvester Measures

In Chapter 9, you created the following DAX formula:

```
Total Customers Born Before 1950 =
    CALCULATE([Total Number of Customers],
        Customers[BirthDate] <DATE(1950,1,1)
    )
```

In the next practice exercise, you will write a measure that allows you to change the "before year" by using the harvester measure technique described above.

Find the solution to this practice exercise in Appendix A.

70. [Total Customers Born Before Selected Year]

Create a new pivot table that allows the user to select from a list of years in a slicer. Change the `[Total Customers Born Before 1950]` measure from being hard-coded to 1950 and instead make the year selectable from the slicer.

This is quite a difficult problem, and you will have to think back on what you have learnt in previous chapters to make it work. You should try to do it yourself, and if you get stuck, read the start of the worked-through solution below and then try to solve the problem again.

Here's How: Solving Practice Exercise 70

There is a trick to Practice Exercise 70. The original measure you created used a "simple filter" in CALCU-LATE(). If you replace the "year value" from the first formula with the harvester measure [Selected Year], you get the error message shown below.

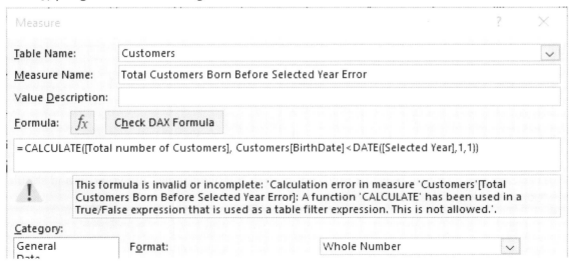

The problem is that you cannot use measures in a "simple" CALCULATE() formula. If you want to use measures (as you do in this case), you must use the FILTER() function inside CALCULATE(). So instead of writing this:

```
Customers[BirthDate] < DATE ([Selected Year], 1, 1)
```

you need to write a FILTER() function that filters the Customers table to replace the line above.

Go back and give it a go: See if you can write the correct formula by using the FILTER() function. If you still need more help, read on to see the correct formula.

Here is the worked-through solution for Practice Exercise 70:

1. Create a list of values in Excel for years (say 1900 through 2000). Give the column a header such as Year.

2. Convert the list to an Excel table, give it a name like YearTable, and add it to the data model. Do not connect the table to any other tables.

3. Create a new pivot table and put Customers[Occupation] on Rows.

4. Insert a slicer for the new table. Find the new table YearTable in the PivotTable Fields list, right-click the column Year, and select Add as Slicer.

5. Click inside the new pivot table and then write a new measure to harvest the selected value from the slicer:

    ```
    Selected Year = MAX(YearTable[Year])
    ```

6. Write the following measure to put into your pivot table:

    ```
    Total Customers Born Before Selected Year
        = CALCULATE ([Total Number of Customers],
            FILTER (Customers,
                Customers[BirthDate] < DATE ([Selected Year], 1, 1)
            )
        )
    ```

7. You should end up with something that looks as shown below. When you click on a year in the slicer, the [Selected Year] measure updates in the pivot table, and the results for [Total Customers Born before Selected Year] update to show the values for the year you have selected in the slicer.

Row Labels ▼	Selected Year	Total Customers Born Before Selected Year	Year
Clerical	1965	1,567	1963
Management	1965	2,229	1964
Manual	1965	860	1965
Professional	1965	3,382	1966
Skilled Manual	1965	2,071	1967
Grand Total	1965	10,109	1968
			1969
			1970

8. The [Selected Year] measure is not required to be in the pivot table, and you can and should remove it once you know the pivot is working.

The SWITCH() Function Revisited

In Chapter 11, I introduced you to the SWITCH() function. One really cool feature of SWITCH() is that you can create a switch measure that allows you to toggle between multiple other measures. Take a look at the pivot tables shown below.

The first pivot table (see #2 above) has Total Sales selected in the slicer (#1). When Total Sales is selected, the pivot table updates to show [Total Sales] (#2). When the user selects Total Cost (#3), the pivot table changes to show [Total Cost] (#4), and when Total Margin (#5) is selected, the pivot table shows the [Total Margin $] results (#6). This toggle effect, which is really engaging for the user, can be used to create very complex and useful interactive reports.

Here's How: Creating a Morphing Switch Measure

You need to create a disconnected table and a harvester measure to be able to complete this technique:

1. Create a table of values in Excel as shown below.

2. Name the table DisplayMeasure.
3. Add the table to the data model. Do not connect the table to any other tables.
4. Switch to Data view in the Power Pivot window, click in the DisplayMeasure[Measure] column, and click the Sort by Column button (see #1 below) and then Sort by Column (#2).

5. Ensure that the Sort column (see #1 below) has Measure selected and select Measure ID from the Column drop-down (#2). Click OK (#3).

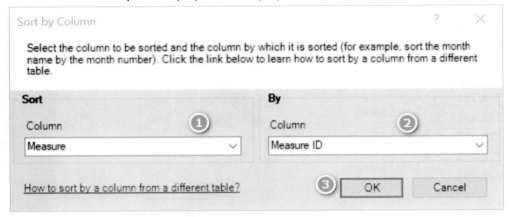

6. Go back to the Excel window. Create a new pivot table and put `'Calendar'[CalendarYear]` on Rows.

7. Insert a slicer for the `DisplayMeasure` table. Find the `DisplayMeasure` table in the PivotTable Fields list, right-click the column `Measure`, and select Add as Slicer.

8. Click inside the new pivot table and then write a new measure to harvest the selected value from the slicer:

    ```
    Selected Measure = MAX(DisplayMeasure[MeasureID])
    ```

9. This is the harvester measure that you use to select the column that is to be displayed in the pivot table.

10. Create a new measure in the `Sales` table as follows:

    ```
    Total Measure = SWITCH([Selected Measure],
            1,[Total Sales],
            2,[Total Cost],
            3,[Total Margin $]
        )
    ```

11. Change the slicer title to `Total Measure`. You now have an interactive pivot table as shown below, with the `Total Measure` column displaying values based on the measure selected in the slicer.

Row Labels ▼	Total Measure
2001	$3,266,374
2002	$6,530,344
2003	$9,791,060
2004	$9,770,900
Grand Total	$29,358,677

Total Measure ⌕≡ ▼

- Total Sales
- Total Cost
- Total Margin

Using Banding

Another disconnected table technique is banding; I learnt this technique from Marco Russo and Alberto Ferrari at http://sqlbi.com.

To understand banding, think about the earlier example in this chapter in which you created a slicer based on the year the customer was born. A more common and practical need is to be able to analyse customers based on their age group rather than their actual age, like this:

- Under 20
- 20 to less than 30
- 30 to less than 40
- 40 to less than 50
- 50 to less than 60
- 60 and over

It is possible to write a calculated column in the `Customers` table that creates these age group bands. But it would be a very complex formula, and it would be hard to edit.

> **Note:** For the sake of the exercise, I use January 1, 2003, as the "current date" from which to work out the age of each customer. Of course, in reality, each customer's age band will change over time, but I have ignored that fact for this example so that the results you see onscreen will be the same as my results shown below. If I used `TODAY()` in this exercise, my results would be different to yours.

A hard-coded calculated column formula for age group might look like this:

```
= IF(((date(2003,1,1) - Customers[BirthDate])/365)<20,"Less than 20",
IF(((date(2003,1,1) - Customers[BirthDate])/365)<30,"20 to less than
30", IF(((date(2003,1,1) - Customers[BirthDate])/365)<40,"30 to less
than 40", IF(((date(2003,1,1) - Customers[BirthDate])/365)<50,"40 to
less than 50", IF(((date(2003,1,1) - Customers[BirthDate])/365)<60,"50
to less than 60","Greater than 60")))))
```

This DAX works, but it is not very user friendly, it is hard to write, and it is even harder to read and maintain. A better approach is to use banding.

Here's How: Applying Banding

The first step in banding is to create a linked table in Excel that contains the upper and lower values for each band, as well as a text description. Follow these steps:

1. Create a list of values in Excel and convert it to a table (by pressing Ctrl+L). You should have something that looks like the table below.

2. Inside Excel, go to the Table Design tab and rename the table `AgeBands`. (You can't change a linked table name inside Power Pivot, so you need to change it in Excel.)

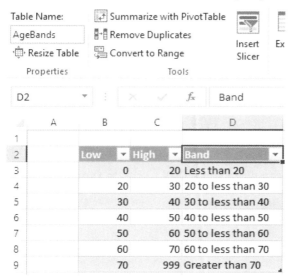

3. To add your table to the data model, go to the Power Pivot tab and select Add to Data Model. (In Excel 2010, select Create Linked Table.)

Note: It is important to set up the banding table so there is no crossover of ages between the low and high ranges. The table above covers all possible ages between 0 and 999, without any duplication. Of course, the 999 value is any arbitrarily large value to catch everyone.

Note: There is no need to join this table to any other table in the data model. In fact, there is no workable way you can do that anyway. Even if there were an age column in the Customers table, you still couldn't join this table to the age column. This banding table doesn't contain all the possible ages for customers; it just has the age bands. So if you first create a customer age column and then join the Low column to this new column, the data will only match for customers who are 20, 30, 40, etc. There will be no match for customers with ages that don't end in a zero (e.g., 21, 22, 23, etc.). So that is not going to work. This table is not joined; hence, it is called a *disconnected table*.

4. Go to the Customers table in Data view and scroll all the way to the right of the table until you see Add Column as the next column name.
5. Click in the first cell in this blank column and type the following formula in the formula bar:
        =(DATE(2003,1,1) - Customers[BirthDate])/365
6. Press Enter, and Power Pivot automatically renames the column Calculated Column 1. Just double-click that column name and rename it Age.

Note: Although it is not required to make this banding technique work, you could enhance this formula with some rounding, as follows:

    = ROUNDDOWN((DATE(2003,1,1) - Customers[BirthDate])/365,0)

	Custome...	GeographyKey	Name	BirthDate	Age
1	13152	348	Gabrielle Butler	16/02/1978 ...	24
2	14095	343	Paige Griffin	10/09/1976 ...	26
3	14349	546	Nicole Griffin	11/05/1976 ...	26
4	15252	547	Jada Murphy	14/02/1980 ...	22
5	15258	607	Chloe Reed	07/05/1978 ...	24
6	15816	50	Victoria Miller	20/05/1976 ...	26
7	17338	62	Jordyn Long	17/02/1976 ...	26
8	17359	637	María Flores	08/03/1975 ...	27
9	18345	53	Samantha Bryant	19/09/1975 ...	27
10	18762	345	Arthur Wilson	22/05/1978 ...	24
11	18775	546	Andrea Bell	18/05/1975 ...	27
12	18790	635	Julia Martin	26/09/1979 ...	23
13	18915	316	Sydney Gonzalez	05/01/1975 ...	28
14	19636	536	Jessica Lee	17/11/1976 ...	26

7. Now that you have this new calculated column, you can write some DAX to create the banding column.
8. Move to the right of the Customers table until you see Add Column, click in the first cell of this empty column and enter the following formula:
        = CALCULATE(VALUES(AgeBands[Band]),
            FILTER(AgeBands,

```
            Customers[Age] >= AgeBands[Low] &&
            Customers[Age] < AgeBands[High]
        )
    )
```

9. Double-click the column heading and name this column Age Group.

The key to this formula is the FILTER() function. This FILTER() function iterates over the AgeBands table and checks each customer's age against the low and high values for each band. There is only ever one single row in the AgeBands table that matches the age of the customer. The FILTER() function inside CALCU-LATE() first filters the AgeBands table so that only the one row that matches the age band is left visible. Then CALCULATE() evaluates the expression VALUES(AgeBands[Band]), and because there is only one row visible, VALUES() returns the name of the band as a text value into the column.

> **Note:** There are two main benefits of taking this approach to banding:
>
> - The DAX formula is easier to read and understand. Once you get used to the concept, it is easier to write, too.
>
> - It is easy to make changes in the future. For example, if you want to add another age band to your analysis (e.g., a new "Greater than 80" age band), all you need to do is add another row to your AgeBands table and then click Refresh.

Here's How: Editing a Manually Created Table

After you have created a linked table, you may need to go back and change the data in the table. Follow these steps to edit a manually created table (linked table):

1. Add new rows to the table, as shown below. Note that one new row is added to the bottom of the table, and the last row is changed from the original table:

Low	High	Band
0	20	Less than 20
20	30	20 to less than 30
30	40	30 to less than 40
40	50	40 to less than 50
50	60	50 to less than 60
60	70	60 to less than 70
70	80	70 to less than 80
80	999	Greater than 80

2. In the Power Pivot window, select Refresh, Refresh All.

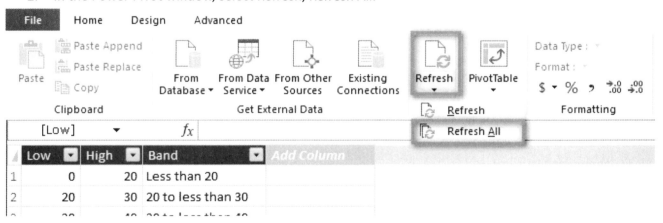

> **Note:** In Excel 2013, all you need to do is open the Power Pivot window, and it should update automatically.

3. Maintaining a banding table like this is much easier than editing a complex nested IF statement.

4. It's time to use this new calculated column in a pivot table, so create a new pivot table on a new worksheet. Put `Customers[Age Group]` on Rows and then add these measures that you wrote in Practice Exercises 1 and 15):

    ```
    [Total Sales]
    [Customers That Have Purchased]
    ```

5. Add some conditional formatting so that the pivot table is easier to read. You should end up with a pivot table something like the one shown below.

Row Labels	Customers That Have Purchased	Total Sales
20 to less than 30	3,319	$4,356,580
30 to less than 40	6,301	$11,537,347
40 to less than 50	4,937	$8,585,476
50 to less than 60	2,727	$3,685,270
60 to less than 70	1,076	$1,117,530
70 to less than 80	96	$71,747
Greater than 80	28	$4,728
Grand Total	**18,484**	**$29,358,677**

It is easy to see the power of banding. It is unlikely that you will ever want to analyse a business based on sales to customers who are 20, 21, 22, etc. Grouping customers into age brackets is more practical, and this disconnected table banding technique makes it a snap.

Interim Calculated Columns

In the banding example, you first created an Age calculated column and then created an Age Group calculated column. Breaking the problem into parts like this makes the DAX easier to read, write, and debug. However, you should be aware that it is generally not considered good practice to leave interim calculated columns in your data model as they inefficiently take up extra space (unless you want to use the interim column in your data model as well, of course).

What you really should do after you get the final calculated column working as expected is combine all the unwanted interim columns into a single final calculated column and then delete the unwanted interim columns. This will save space in your workbook, which will improve efficiency. Making this change could also make the formula harder to read. To solve this problem, I am going to introduce you to the concept of variables in DAX. Let me first explain the variables syntax, and then I will show you how to remove the interim column.

Variables Syntax

Two keywords in DAX allow you to create and refer to variables in your DAX formulas. The first keyword is VAR (which stands for *variable*).

> **Note:** In reality, VAR is more like a constant than a variable as its value cannot change during evaluation.

VAR is always accompanied by a second keyword, RETURN.

Here is the syntax for VAR:

My Column (or Measure) =

VAR *FirstVariableName* = *<valid DAX expression>*

VAR *SecondVariableName* = *<another DAX expression>*

Return

<another DAX expression that can reference the variables>

The above generic syntax can be a bit confusing, so the image below shows a real example using the formula from above.

```
Age Group =
VAR Age =
    ROUNDDOWN ( ( DATE ( 2003, 1, 1 ) - Customers[BirthDate] ) / 365, 0 )
RETURN
    CALCULATE (
        VALUES ( AgeBands[Band] ),
        FILTER ( AgeBands, Age >= AgeBands[Low] && Age < AgeBands[High] )
    )
```

Note how lines 2 and 3 in the formula above set the value of the variable Age to be the value that was previously stored in the original Age calculated column from earlier in this chapter. Once the variable has been set, it is referred to again (twice) in line 7.

A variable can refer to another variable, as shown in line 4 below.

```
Age Group =
VAR AgeInDays =
    ROUNDDOWN ( ( DATE ( 2003, 1, 1 ) - Customers[BirthDate] ), 0 )
VAR Age = AgeInDays / 365
RETURN
    CALCULATE (
        VALUES ( AgeBands[Band] ),
        FILTER ( AgeBands, Age >= AgeBands[Low] && Age < AgeBands[High] )
    )
```

A variable can contain a table as well as a value, as shown in row 5 below.

```
Age Group =
VAR AgeInDays =
    ROUNDDOWN ( ( DATE ( 2003, 1, 1 ) - Customers[BirthDate] ), 0 )
VAR Age = AgeInDays / 365
VAR BandsTable =
    FILTER ( AgeBands, Age >= AgeBands[Low] && Age < AgeBands[High] )
RETURN
    CALCULATE ( VALUES ( AgeBands[Band] ), BandsTable )
```

Variables are set in the initial filter and row context. It doesn't matter if the filter and/or row context changes after the RETURN keyword; the variables have already been assigned, and hence they will not change as a result of any changing filter or row context.

Now that you know how the VAR syntax works, you are ready to remove the interim calculated column and move everything into the final banding column.

Here's How: Deleting Interim Calculated Columns

Follow these steps to combine the interim columns into the final banding calculated column and then delete the interim column:

1. Navigate to the interim calculated column in the table (Age in this example).

2. Highlight the formula and press Ctrl+C to copy the entire formula from the interim column, as shown below.

3. Navigate to the final banding calculated column (Age Group in this example). You can enlarge the formula bar by clicking the drop-down arrow in the top right if needed.

```
=CALCULATE(VALUES(AgeBands[Band]),
     FILTER(AgeBands,
          Customers[Age] >= AgeBands[Low] &&
          Customers[Age] < AgeBands[High]
     )
)
```

> **Hover mouse and then click and drag down to create a larger editing window.**

hyKey	Name	BirthDate	Age	Age Group
348	Gabrielle Butler	16/02/1978 ...	25	20 to less than 30
343	Paige Griffin	10/09/1976 ...	26	20 to less than 30

4. Create two new blank lines after the = in the formula (by pressing Shift+Enter). At this point in the process, you should have a few blank spaces in your formula, as shown below.

```
fx =

CALCULATE(VALUES(AgeBands[Band]),
     FILTER(AgeBands,
          Customers[Age] >= AgeBands[Low] &&
          Customers[Age] < AgeBands[High]
     )
)
```

5. Type the keyword VAR and Age (see #1 below), paste the Age column code (#2), and then type the RETURN keyword (#3) as shown below.

```
fx = VAR Age = ROUNDDOWN((DATE(2003,1,1) - Customers[BirthDate])/365,0)
①       RETURN                                                    ②
③
CALCULATE(VALUES(AgeBands[Band]),
     FILTER(AgeBands,
          Customers[Age] >= AgeBands[Low] &&
          Customers[Age] < AgeBands[High]
     )
)
```

6. Replace the two instances of the original column name Customers[Age] with the reference to the variable Age, as shown below.

```
fx  = VAR Age = ROUNDDOWN((DATE(2003,1,1) - Customers[BirthDate])/365,0)
        RETURN
    CALCULATE(VALUES(AgeBands[Band]),
            FILTER(AgeBands,
                Customers[Age] >= AgeBands[Low] &&
                Customers[Age] < AgeBands[High]
            )
    )
```

Replace these with the variable Age

```
fx  = VAR Age = ROUNDDOWN((DATE(2003,1,1) - Customers[BirthDate])/365,0)
        RETURN
    CALCULATE(VALUES(AgeBands[Band]),
            FILTER(AgeBands,
                Age >= AgeBands[Low] &&
                Age < AgeBands[High]
            )
    )
```

7.   Delete the interim column `Customers[Age]`.

Note: Of course, if you need the interim column in your table, you should keep it. But if you don't need it, you should remove it by using the process shown above.

Note: For deeper coverage of the use of variables, see my blog: https://exceleratorbi.com.au/using-variables-dax/.

18: Concept: KPIs

Power Pivot has a feature called *KPIs* (*key performance indicators*). A KPI is basically a visualisation tool that uses graphical icons to indicate how well a value compares to some target value. You can use KPIs to add interesting visualisations to your pivot tables so the reader can instantly see if things are on track. To see how it works, let's look at an example.

In the following pivot table, I have created a KPI against the [Margin %] measure. Note that the icons visually indicate the status.

Row Labels ▼	Total Sales	Margin %	Margin % Status
Bike Racks	$39,360	62.6%	✓
Bike Stands	$39,591	62.6%	✓
Bottles and Cages	$56,798	62.6%	✓
Caps	$19,688	23.0%	✗
Cleaners	$7,219	62.6%	✓
Fenders	$46,620	62.6%	✓
Gloves	$35,021	62.6%	✓
Helmets	$225,336	62.6%	✓
Hydration Packs	$40,308	62.6%	✓
Jerseys	$172,951	23.0%	✗
Mountain Bikes	$9,952,760	45.4%	✓
Road Bikes	$14,520,584	38.1%	✗
Shorts	$71,320	62.6%	✓
Socks	$5,106	62.6%	✓
Tires and Tubes	$245,529	62.6%	✓
Touring Bikes	$3,844,801	37.8%	✗
Vests	$35,687	62.6%	✓

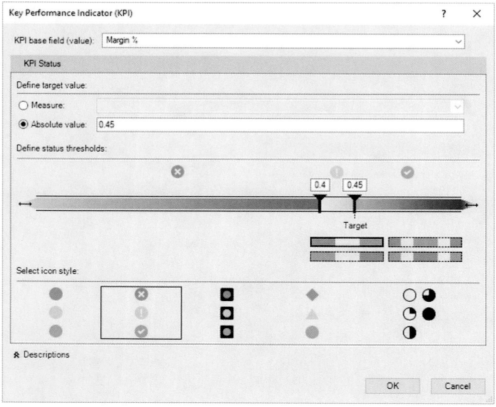

Here's How: Creating a KPI

Follow these steps to create a KPI:

1. Set up a new pivot table with `Products[SubCategory]` on Rows and then add `[Total Sales]` and `[Margin %]` on Values.

2. Click inside the pivot table, navigate to the Power Pivot tab, and select KPIs (see #1 below), New KPI (#2).

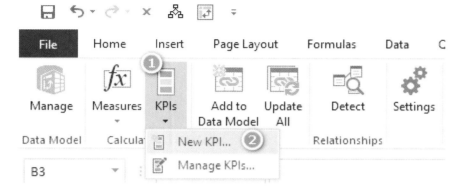

Select Margin % from the KPI Base Field (Value) drop-down (see #1 below).

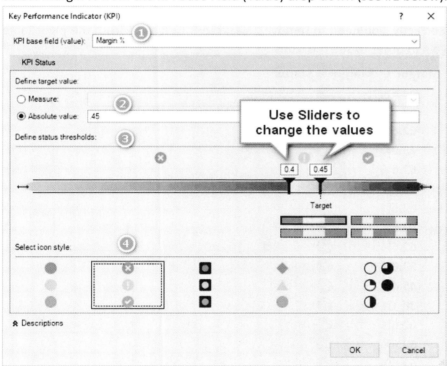

3. In the section Define Target Value, where you have two choices, select Absolute Value and set it to `.45` (see #2 above). (Note that 45% is actually 0.45; if you type 45 instead of .45, it won't work.)

4. Under Define Status Thresholds (#3), set the lower slider to 0.4 and the upper slider to 0.45.

5. Select an icon set (#4) that works in black and white. At this point, you come across a bug (as of this writing in both Excel 2013 and Excel 2016). When you finish writing this KPI, the pivot table looks as shown below.

Note: Best practice with visualisations like this is to use an icon set that makes sense in colour as well as black and white (so it can be understood by people who are colour-blind or for black-and-white printed copies of the report).

Row Labels	Total Sales	Margin %	Margin % Status
Bike Racks	$39,360	62.6%	1
Bike Stands	$39,591	62.6%	1
Bottles and Cages	$56,798	62.6%	1
Caps	$19,688	23.0%	-1
Cleaners	$7,219	62.6%	1
Fenders	$46,620	62.6%	1
Gloves	$35,021	62.6%	1
Helmets	$225,336	62.6%	1
Hydration Packs	$40,308	62.6%	1
Jerseys	$172,951	23.0%	-1
Mountain Bikes	$9,952,760	45.4%	1
Road Bikes	$14,520,584	38.1%	-1
Shorts	$71,320	62.6%	1
Socks	$5,106	62.6%	1
Tires and Tubes	$245,529	62.6%	1
Touring Bikes	$3,844,801	37.8%	-1
Vests	$35,687	62.6%	1

6. To make the KPI display correctly, you need to remove [Margin % Status] from the pivot table and then put it back in again in order to see the icons.

Row Labels	Total Sales	Margin %	Margin % Status
Bike Racks	$39,360	62.6%	✓
Bike Stands	$39,591	62.6%	✓
Bottles and Cages	$56,798	62.6%	✓
Caps	$19,688	23.0%	✗
Cleaners	$7,219	62.6%	✓
Fenders	$46,620	62.6%	✓
Gloves	$35,021	62.6%	✓
Helmets	$225,336	62.6%	✓
Hydration Packs	$40,308	62.6%	✓
Jerseys	$172,951	23.0%	✗
Mountain Bikes	$9,952,760	45.4%	✓
Road Bikes	$14,520,584	38.1%	✗
Shorts	$71,320	62.6%	✓
Socks	$5,106	62.6%	✓
Tires and Tubes	$245,529	62.6%	✓
Touring Bikes	$3,844,801	37.8%	✗
Vests	$35,687	62.6%	✓

This problem does not exist in Excel 2010, where you see the icon set you selected.

19: Concept: Multiple Data Tables

So far in this book, we have used only a single data table, the `Sales` table. It is quite likely that you will want or need to use multiple data tables in your data models. When you bring a second data table into Power Pivot, it is common for people to think that they should join the new data table to the original data table, but that is not the case. The correct way to join a second data table to a data model is to treat the new data table exactly the same as the first data table.

To help you understand how to do this, the following "Here's How" looks at a common business scenario in which a business wants to load a budget table as well as a sales table. One of the challenges of this scenario is that the budget is often at a different level of granularity than actual sales. For example, sales may be captured and reported every day for every individual product, but budgets may be set only for each month and for each product category.

Here's How: Adding a Budget Table

The following steps walk you through the process of importing a `Budget` table, creating a new `BudgetPe-riod` table, and then creating a measure for the budget:

1. To bring in the budget data and a new `BudgetPeriod` table, in the Power Pivot window, select Home, Existing Connections.

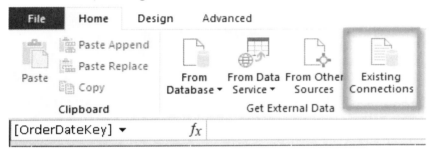

2. Select the Access database you have been using (see #1 below) and then click Open (#2).

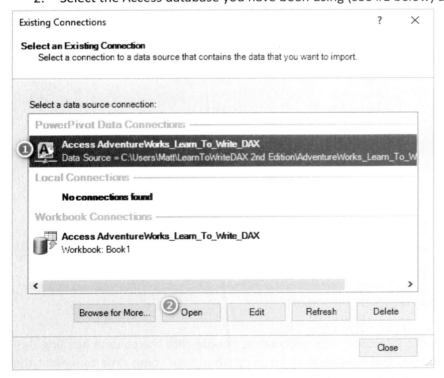

3. Select the first option, Select from a List of Tables, and click Next.

4. Select the `Budget` table, the `BudgetPeriod` table, and the `dimProductCategory` table. Rename the `dimProductCategory` table `ProductCategory`, as shown below, and click the Preview & Filter button.

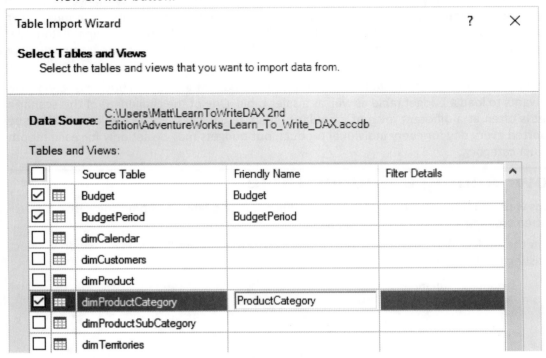

5. Deselect all the columns (see #1 below) and then just select the `EnglishProductCategoryName` column (#2) and click OK.

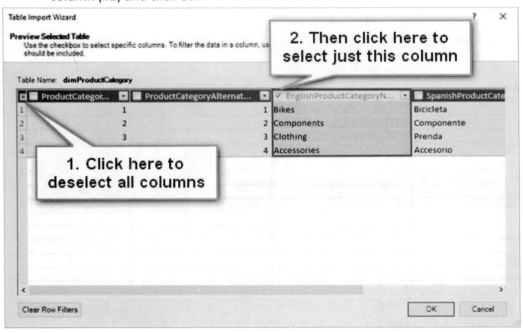

6. Click OK and then click Finish to complete the import.
7. Click Close.
8. To tidy things up a bit, go to the `ProductCategory` table, double-click the column heading `EnglishProductCategoryName`, and rename it `Category`. Then take some time to look at the data in these three tables:

• **Budget table**—The `Budget` table has a monthly sales budget for each category. The `Period` column is in the format YYYYMM for year and month, as shown below.

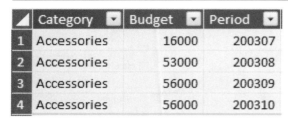

Category	Budget	Period
1 Accessories	16000	200307
2 Accessories	53000	200308
3 Accessories	56000	200309
4 Accessories	56000	200310

- **BudgetPeriod table**—The BudgetPeriod table is a type of calendar table and is different to what you have used so far. Like the Budget table, it contains a Period column in the format YYYYMM, as shown below.

CalendarYear	MonthName	Month Number	Period
1	2003	July	7	200307
2	2003	August	8	200308
3	2003	September	9	200309
4	2003	October	10	200310
5	2003	November	11	200311
6	2003	December	12	200312
7	2004	January	1	200401

- **ProductCategory table**—The ProductCategory table has a list of the four possible product categories, as shown below.

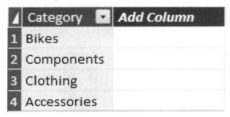

Category	Add Column
1 Bikes	
2 Components	
3 Clothing	
4 Accessories	

9. The reason you need all these new tables will make sense shortly.

10. Switch to Diagram view. If necessary, click the Fit to Screen button (as shown below) so that you can see all the tables on the screen.

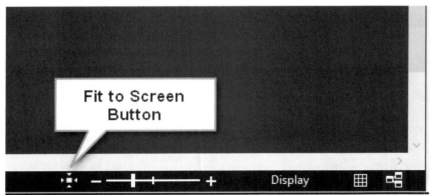

Fit to Screen Button

11. Rearrange your tables as shown below. Place the BudgetPeriod table (see #1 below) above the Calendar table and place the Budget table (#2) next to the Sales table. Put the ProductCategory table (#3) above the Products table, as shown below.

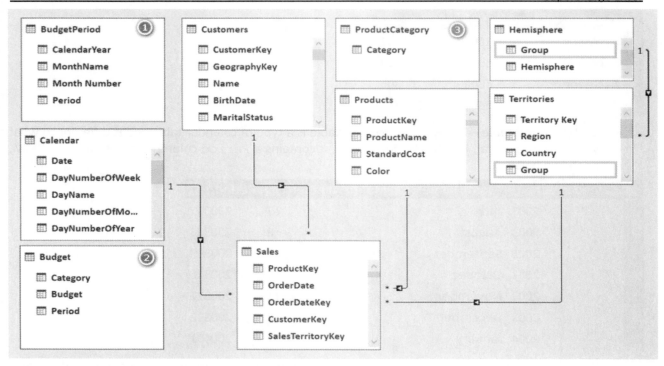

Note: To see why you need the `BudgetPeriod` table, try to join the `Budget` table to the `Calendar` table. Click on the `Period` column in the `Budget` table and drag and drop it on the `Period` column in the `Calendar` table.

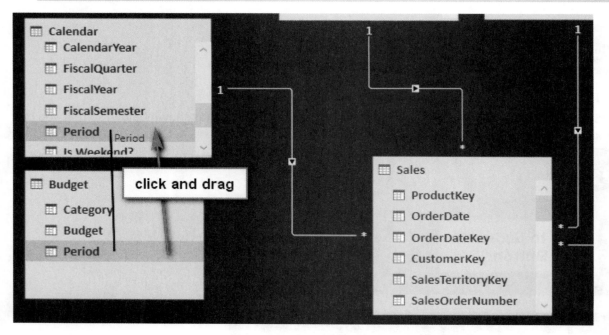

When you do this, you get the following error.

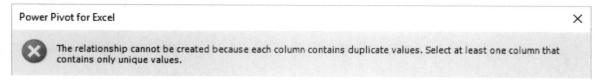

Do you see the issue? The `Calendar` table is a daily calendar, but the `Budget` table is a monthly budget (a very common business scenario). There are between 28 and 31 entries for each month in the `Period` column in the `Calendar` table. *But Power Pivot supports only one-to-many relationships.* The lookup table (`Calendar`) at the top simply must have a single value for `Period` if you are to make the join, so this is not going to work. This is why you need the `BudgetPeriod` table. There is only one value for each `Period` in the `BudgetPeriod` table, and hence you are able to join the `Budget` table to the `BudgetPeriod` table (see #1 below).

12. Join the `Calendar` table to the `BudgetPeriod` table by dragging the `Period` column from the `Calendar` table to the `Period` column in the `BudgetPeriod` table (see #2 below).

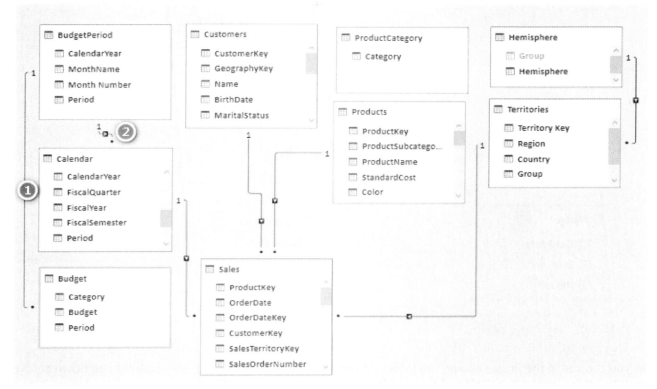

13. Now you need to do the same again and this time join the `ProductCategory` table to the `Budget` table. If you try to join the `Budget[Category]` column to the `Products` table, you get the same error as before.

14. To join the `Budget` table to the `ProductCategory` table, click and drag the column `Budget[-Category]` to `ProductCategory[Category]`.

15. To join the `Products` table to the `ProductCategory` table, click and drag the column `Products[Category]` to the `ProductCategory[Category]` column.

When you are finished, you will have a layout similar to the layout shown below. Notice that it becomes difficult to keep track of all the relationships when you have lots of tables in your data model. This is one reason I recommend arranging the tables using the Collie layout methodology, as shown below.

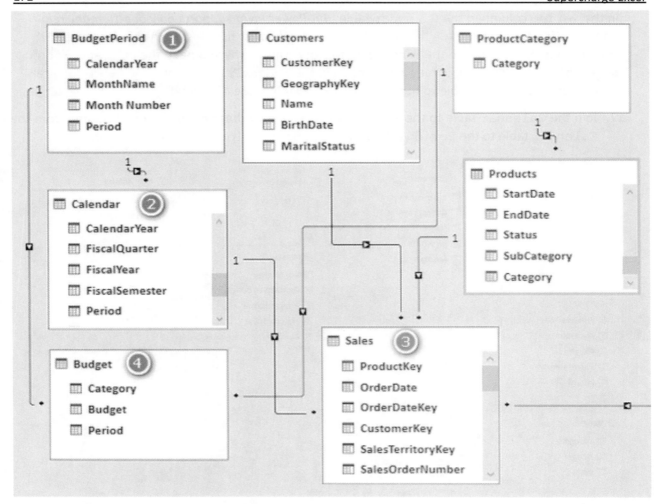

As you can see in the image above, the tables on the "many" side of the relationship should be down below, and the tables on the "one" side of the relationship should be up high. The filters always flow downhill, and this layout makes it much easier to understand how the filters flow. So, if you filter on the `BudgetPeriod` table (see #1 above), this table directly filters the `Budget` table (#4) via the direct relationship. In addition, the `BudgetPeriod` table (see #1) directly filters the `Calendar` table (#2), and the `Calendar` table (#2) filters the `Sales` table (#3). So, the net result is that any filter you apply to the `BudgetPeriod` table (#1) filters both the `Sales` table (#3) and the `Budget` table (#4). The same concept applies with the `Product-Category` table.

When working with data tables of differing granularities, as in this case, it is important to use the correct tables and columns in your pivot table filters. So, when working with both the `Sales` table and the `Budget` table, you must use the columns from the `BudgetPeriod` table in your pivot tables; *columns from the* `Calendar` *table will not work.*

Practice Exercises: Multiple Data Tables

It's time to get some practice writing new DAX formulas across the two data tables: Budget and Sales. First, create a new pivot table. Then put ProductCategory[Category] on Rows, BudgetPeriod[Period] on Rows, and [Total Sales] on Values. Make sure you select the correct columns from the two new tables (ProductCategory and BudgetPeriod). Your pivot table should look like the one below.

Row Labels ▾	Total Sales
⊟ Accessories	$700,760
200307	$14,468
200308	$52,057
200309	$52,150
200310	$54,595
200311	$54,832
200312	$65,608
200401	$56,457
200402	$56,996
200403	$60,098
200404	$62,674
200405	$71,880
200406	$65,201
200407	$33,745
⊟ Bikes	$28,318,145
200107	$473,388
200108	$506,192
200109	$473,943

Once your pivot table is set up, click in the pivot table and then write the following new measures. Find the solutions to these practice exercises in Appendix A.

71. [Total Budget]

72. [Change in Sales vs. Budget]

73. [% Change in Sales vs. Budget]

The image below shows what the pivot table looks like with these formulas and the addition of conditional formatting.

Row Labels ▾	Total Sales	Total Budget	Change in Sales vs. Budget	% Change in Sales vs. Budget
⊟ Accessories	$700,760	$739,000	-$38,240	-5.2%
200307	$14,468	$16,000	-$1,532	-9.6%
200308	$52,057	$53,000	-$943	-1.8%
200309	$52,150	$56,000	-$3,850	-6.9%
200310	$54,595	$56,000	-$1,405	-2.5%
200311	$54,832	$54,000	$832	1.5%
200312	$65,608	$72,000	-$6,392	-8.9%
200401	$56,457	$61,000	-$4,543	-7.4%
200402	$56,996	$63,000	-$6,004	-9.5%
200403	$60,098	$63,000	-$2,902	-4.6%
200404	$62,674	$68,000	-$5,326	-7.8%
200405	$71,880	$78,000	-$6,120	-7.8%
200406	$65,201	$63,000	$2,201	3.5%
200407	$33,745	$36,000	-$2,255	-6.3%

Here's How: Creating a Budget KPI

Here is how you can use your new Budget table to create a KPI:

1. Click in the pivot table you created for Practice Exercises 71–73 and select Power Pivot, KPI, New KPI.

2. Select Total Sales for the KPI base field.

3. Select Total Budget in the Define Target Value section as the measure.

4. Adjust the sliders so that they are set to 95% and 100%.

5. Click OK.

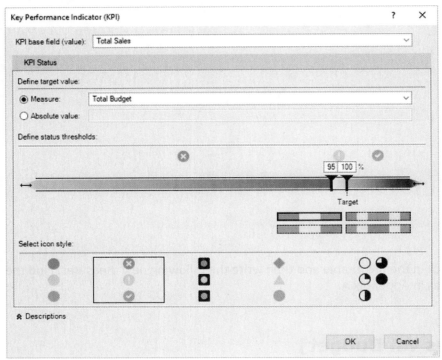

6. If you are using Excel 2013/Excel 2016, remove this new KPI from your pivot table and then add it back. Once you have done that, it should look as shown below. The new KPI shows red, yellow, and green to indicate how close the actual sales were to the budget.

Row Labels ▾	Total Sales	Total Budget	Change in Sales vs. Budget	% Change in Sales vs. Budget	Total Sales Status
⊟ Accessories	$700,760	$739,000	-$38,240	-5.2%	⊗
200307	$14,468	$16,000	-$1,532	-9.6%	⊗
200308	$52,057	$53,000	-$943	-1.8%	◐
200309	$52,150	$56,000	-$3,850	-6.9%	⊗
200310	$54,595	$56,000	-$1,405	-2.5%	◐
200311	$54,832	$54,000	$832	1.5%	✓
200312	$65,608	$72,000	-$6,392	-8.9%	⊗
200401	$56,457	$61,000	-$4,543	-7.4%	⊗
200402	$56,996	$63,000	-$6,004	-9.5%	⊗
200403	$60,098	$63,000	-$2,902	-4.6%	◐
200404	$62,674	$68,000	-$5,326	-7.8%	⊗
200405	$71,880	$78,000	-$6,120	-7.8%	⊗
200406	$65,201	$63,000	$2,201	3.5%	✓
200407	$33,745	$36,000	-$2,255	-6.3%	⊗

20: Concept: Cube Formulas

This chapter covers one of my favourite topics: cube formulas. Cube formulas have been around for many years. But before Power Pivot was launched, the only way you could use cube formulas was to connect to a SQL Server Analysis Services (SSAS) multidimensional cube. Some large companies have SSAS set up, and some of those companies may connect directly to SSAS from Excel, and some of those that do may have discovered cube formulas. But given how rare the above scenario is, most people have never come across cube formulas prior to discovering Power Pivot.

What Is a Cube Formula?

So far in this book, you have always consumed and visualised the information from the data model in a pivot table. Pivot tables are great, and I use them all the time, but they do have some limitations. The biggest limitation is that you are locked in to the format that the pivot table gives you. But what if you want to put a single value in a single cell in a workbook? In that case, you could create a pivot table and then point the cell in question to the pivot table, but that involves a lot of overhead. In addition, if the pivot table changes shape at any time (e.g., on refresh), then chances are the cell positions will change, and your formula may point to the wrong cell. The best-case scenario is that you realise there is a problem. The worst-case scenario is that your formula points to another similar cell in the pivot table, and you don't even notice!

"What about GETPIVOTDATA()?" I hear some of you say. Well, yes, you can use GETPIVOTDATA(), but with it, you still have the overhead of the pivot table, and the bottom line is that cube formulas are much better. The easiest way to get started with cube formulas is to convert an existing pivot table to cube formulas. The following pages walk you through how to do that.

Here's How: Converting a Pivot Table to Cube Formulas

Follow these steps to convert a pivot table to cube formulas:

1. Create a new blank sheet in your workbook and insert a pivot table like the one shown below, with 'Calendar'[CalendarYear] on Rows, Products[Category] on Columns, and [Total Sales] on Values. Also, add a slicer for Customers[Occupation]. Click on the slicer and make sure it works before proceeding.

Occupation		Total Sales	Column Labels			
		Row Labels	Accessories	Bikes	Clothing	Grand Total
Clerical		2001		$3,266,374		$3,266,374
Management		2002		$6,530,344		$6,530,344
Manual		2003	$293,710	$9,359,103	$138,248	$9,791,060
Professional		2004	$407,050	$9,162,325	$201,525	$9,770,900
Skilled Manual		Grand Total	$700,760	$28,318,145	$339,773	$29,358,677

2. To convert the pivot table to cube formulas, click inside the pivot table and then select Analyze (see #1 below), OLAP Tools (#2), Convert to Formulas (#3).

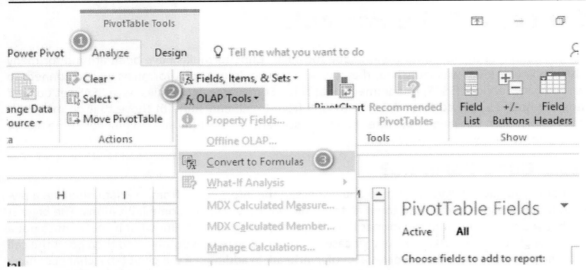

3. And then BAM! Your pivot table is converted to a stack of standalone formulas that you can move around as you want on the spreadsheet. What's more, the slicer still works! Go ahead and drag the formulas around to a new location in your spreadsheet and then click on the slicer to verify that it works.

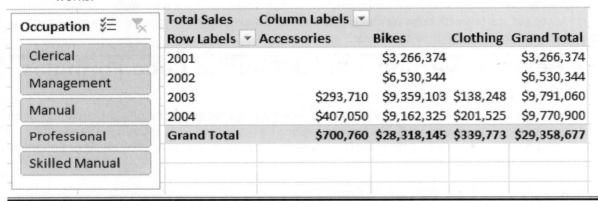

Occupation		
Clerical		
Management		
Manual		
Professional		
Skilled Manual		

Total Sales	Column Labels			
Row Labels	Accessories	Bikes	Clothing	Grand Total
2001		$3,266,374		$3,266,374
2002		$6,530,344		$6,530,344
2003	$293,710	$9,359,103	$138,248	$9,791,060
2004	$407,050	$9,162,325	$201,525	$9,770,900
Grand Total	$700,760	$28,318,145	$339,773	$29,358,677

Writing Your Own Cube Formulas

There are seven cube formulas in total, and they all start with the word CUBE. You can see the list by typing =CUBE into a cell in a workbook.

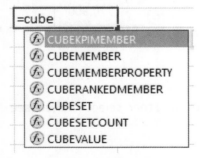

This book covers the two most-used formulas, CUBEVALUE() and CUBEMEMBER(). Once you have mastered these two formulas, you can do some research to learn about the other five.

CUBEVALUE() vs. CUBEMEMBER()

Go back to the pivot table that you just converted and double-click inside the grand total cell (see #1 below) so that Excel is in Edit mode. Notice in the formula bar (#2) that this grand total cell is a CUBEVALUE() formula, and it points to a number of other cells (#3). The formulas inside each of these other cells are CUBEMEMBER() formulas.

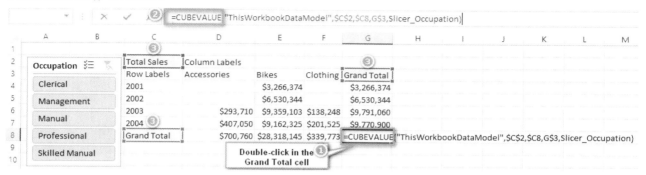

CUBEVALUE() is used to extract the value of a measure from the data model, and CUBEMEMBER() is used to extract a value from a column in a data/lookup table. When they are used together, CUBEMEMBER() filters the data model before calculating the CUBEVALUE() expression.

Now that you know about cube formulas, you can build a pivot table that contains the cube formulas you want in your spreadsheet and then simply select Analyze, OLAP Tools, Convert to Formulas. Once you have done this, you can copy and paste the resulting formulas wherever you want. But it actually isn't very hard to write cube formulas from scratch, so let's do that together now.

Here's How: Writing CUBEVALUE() from Scratch

The important keyboard keys when writing cube formulas are the double quote, the square brackets, and the full stop (period in the United States). This information will make sense as you work through these steps. Be sure to follow these steps exactly:

1. Click in an empty cell in a workbook and type **=CUBEVALUE(**. Notice the tooltip that pops up. It is asking for a connection and one or more member expressions. The member expressions can be either measures or table columns from your data model.

2. Type " (a double quote). You are presented with a list of connections available to the workbook. Normally there is only one for a Power Pivot workbook. In Excel 2013 and Excel 2016 it is called ThisWorkbookDataModel, and in Excel 2010 it is called PowerPivotData.

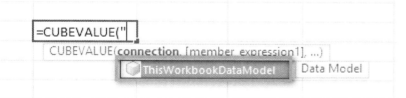

3. Press the Tab key to select the connection and then type " again.

4. Type **,** (a comma).

5. Type " (a double quote) again to start the next parameter. This time notice that the tooltip shows a list of all the tables in the data model (see below). There is also one additional item in the list, [Measures]. All your DAX formulas are stored in [Measures].

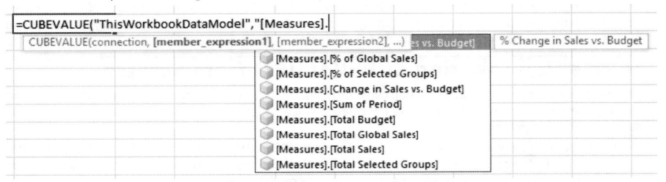

6. Type **[** and then **M** and press Tab to select [Measures].

7. Type **.** (a period), and you see a list of all the measures that exist in the data model. From here you can either keep typing **[** followed by the name of the measure or use the up and down arrow keys on the keyboard to navigate to the measure you want to select.

8. Type **[** and then type **Total S**. This brings the [Total Sales] measure to the top.

9. Press Tab, type **")**, and press Enter

10. If you have followed these instructions exactly, you end up with a value in a cell, as shown below. This is your first hand-written cube formula:

        = CUBEVALUE("ThisWorkbookDataModel","[Measures].[Total Sales]")

        $29,358,677

You probably noticed that the value you end up with after writing this cube formula is the grand total for all the data in the data model. It should therefore be clear that the data model is completely unfiltered. It is possible to filter this formula just as in a pivot table by adding some CUBEMEMBER() functions to the formula (sort of like adding a column from a data model to Rows in a pivot).

> **Note:** Before moving on, you should rewrite the formula above a couple of times for practice. Remember that the most important keys on your keyboard in this process are double quotes, square brackets, and the period, along with Tab to select the highlighted selection. Practice the rhythm of writing these formulas using these keys on the keyboard.

Here's How: Applying Filters to Cube Formulas

To filter an existing formula, follow these steps:

1. Select one of the formulas you have already written and start to edit it.

2. Delete the last **)** and then type **,** (a comma). The tooltip asks for `member_expression2`.

3. Type **"[**.

4. Use the down arrow key to select `[Calendar]`. Then press Tab.

5. Type **.** (full stop/period) and use the down arrow to select `[CalendarYear]`. Then press Tab.

6. Type **.** (full stop/period) and notice that the tooltip offers only a single choice, `[All]`. Select `[All]`.

7. Type **.** (full stop/period) and notice that the tooltip prompts you for the year. Select `[2003]`.

8. Finish the formula by typing **")** and pressing Enter. This is the final formula:

   ```
   = CUBEVALUE("ThisWorkbookDataModel","[Measures].[Total Sales]", "[Calen-
   dar].[CalendarYear]. [2003]")
   ```

9. Go back into this formula again and delete the **)**, add another **,** (a comma), and then follow the same process as above to add another cube member, this time for `Products[Category] = "Cloth-ing"`. This is the formula you need:

   ```
   = CUBEVALUE("ThisWorkbookDataModel", "[Measures].[Total Sales]", "[Calen-
   dar].[CalendarYear]. [2003]", "[Products].[Category]. [Clothing]"
   )
   ```

10. You can add any measure from your data model into your spreadsheet by writing a cube formula like this. You can further filter the measure in your cube formula by adding additional `CUBEMEMBER()` expressions inside the cube formula you are writing.

Here's How: Adding a Slicer Without a Pivot Table

Connecting your formulas to slicers is easy. You should have a slicer for `Customers[Occupation]` on the worksheet. If you don't have this slicer, then go ahead and add it now. Here are the steps to add a slicer when there is no pivot table:

1. Select Insert, Slicer.

   Note: In this case, you can't right-click on a column in the PivotTable Fields list because there is no pivot table.

2. In the Existing Connections dialog that appears, select the Data Model tab (see #1 below), select Tables in Workbook Data Model (#2), and click Open (#3).

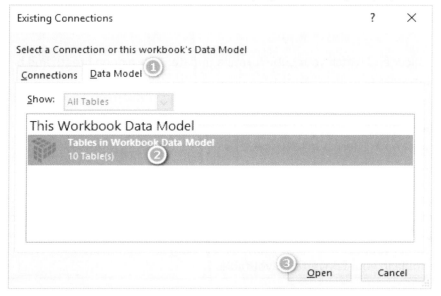

3. Find the `Customers[Occupation]` slicer in the list, select its check box, and click OK. You now have a slicer on your sheet, but it is not connected to your formula.

Here's How: Connecting a Slicer to a Cube Formula

Follow these steps to connect a slicer to a cube formula:

1. Check the unique name for the slicer you just created by right-clicking the slicer and selecting Slicer Settings.

2. In the Slicer Settings dialog that appears, note and memorise the value that appears in the second line, Name to Use in Formulas. You will need the name of the slicer in the next step. In my case it is called `Slicer_Occupation`. In your case it may be called something different. Click Cancel.

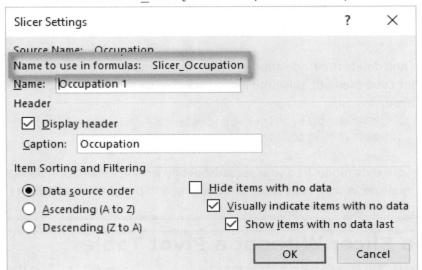

3. Go back into the cube formula you were working on earlier and delete the last **)** and add **,** (a comma) followed by the slicer name from step 2 and then type **)**.

4. Your formula should now look something like this (though your slicer may have a slightly different name):

```
= CUBEVALUE("ThisWorkbookDataModel", "[Measures].[Total Sales]", "[Calen-
dar].[CalendarYear].&[2003]",
"[Products].[Category].&[Clothing]", Slicer_Occupation1
)
```

> **Note:** You do not use double quotes around slicer names. This is an unfortunate inconsistency, but it is just how it works.

5. Now test it out: Click on your slicer and watch your cube formula update. Take a deep breath and be amazed. How cool are cube formulas?!

Writing CUBEMEMBER() Formulas

In addition to referencing a column name inside a CUBEVALUE() formula, it is possible to write a CUBEMEMBER() formula directly in a cell in a workbook. Here is an example of a CUBEMEMBER() formula:

```
= CUBEMEMBER("ThisWorkbookDataModel", "[Customers].[Occupation].[All].
[Manual]"
)
```

You can see a lot more of these formulas if you go back to the original pivot table that you converted and click in the column and row headings. If you write a CUBEMEMBER() formula as a standalone formula in a cell, you can reference that cell from within your CUBEVALUE() formula by using cell references. Once again, you can see this by examining the formula in your converted pivot table.

21: Moving from Excel to Power BI

PowerBI.com is a relatively new service from Microsoft. If first became generally available in July 2015, after the first edition of this book was already completed. As of this writing, the product is almost three years old, and it has become the leading product in its class (as judged by Gartner). There is no doubt that Excel users will increasingly want to use PowerBI.com as a tool to share workbooks and leverage the modern visualisations that are quickly becoming available.

This chapter provides the information you need to get started with Power BI. The good news is that all the skills you have learnt in this book are fully transferable to Power BI. Even better, writing DAX will help you get value from Power BI, and you already have skills in that area.

There are three tools that you need to know about to take advantage of Power BI: PowerBI.com, Power BI Desktop, and Power BI Mobile.

PowerBI.com

PowerBI.com is Microsoft's cloud-hosted solution. A free version allows you to upload 1 GB of workbooks and reports to the cloud and to share reports and dashboards with other people. There are some limitations to the free version, though, the main one being that you can only share individual reports with single visualisations via a dashboard. If you want to have anything more sophisticated, such as multiple visualisations on the same page that interact together, you need to purchase the subscription service.

At this writing, the PowerBI.com subscription costs US$9.99 per user per month. With this paid service, each user has access to 10 GB of online storage. At this price, the service is a bargain compared to the alternatives that exist.

Power BI Desktop

Power BI Desktop is a free tool that you can download from PowerBI.com and use to author your own data models and reports locally on your PC. It is an incredible piece of software that offers all the capabilities of Power Pivot and Power Query (Excel version) as well as all the visualisation capability of PowerBI.com, bundled up in a desktop tool that is completely free to download and use. You can import the data models from your Excel workbooks and create new reports, or you can create standalone data models and reports from scratch. When you are done, you can simply keep using the reports natively on your PC, or you can upload the reports to PowerBI.com and share them with others from there.

Power BI Mobile

Power BI Mobile, as its name suggests, is a mobile app. It is available for Microsoft tablets and phones, Apple iPads and iPhones, and Android tablets and phones. The app is native to each individual device, which means the end user gets the best possible experience when looking at reports published at PowerBI.com. Power BI Mobile is used only to consume reports; at this time, it cannot be used to author reports.

Differences Between Power BI and Excel 2010/2013/2016

There are a couple of important differences between Power Pivot for Excel (2010/2013/2016) and the Power BI version of Power Pivot:

- More than 20 new functions further enhance the DAX language. You can find out more about them by searching the web for "new DAX functions for Power BI."
- There is no longer a limitation requiring all relationships to be of the type "one to many." It is possible to edit relationships and change them to "one to one" or "many to many."

- It is possible to change the cross-filtering behaviour of relationships so that filters propagate from the "many" side of the relationship to the "one" side of the relationship. Put another way, with Power BI (and Excel 2016), it is possible to have filters propagate "uphill."

- Calculated fields have been renamed *measures* (as in Excel 2010 and 2016). Thankfully, only Excel 2013 used the term *calculated fields*.

The Power BI Desktop Relationships View

If you know how to use Power Pivot for Excel, using Power BI will be easy for you. As you can see in the image below, the Relationships view in Power BI is very similar to the Diagram view in Power Pivot.

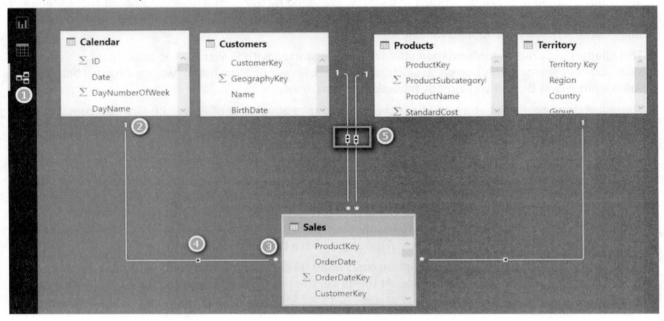

A few things are worth noting here:

- There is a menu on the left-hand side (see #1 above) that switches between the Report, Data, and Relationships views.

- The relationship visualisations have been improved. For example, the "one" side of a relationship is now indicated by a number 1 (#2), and the "many" side is indicated with an * (#3).

- The direction of filter propagation is now indicated with arrows (#4).

- When a filter is configured to work in both directions, there are arrows pointing in both directions (#5).

Here's How: Installing Power BI Desktop

To download Power BI Desktop, follow these steps:

1. Go to http://powerbi.com.

2. Select Products, Power BI Desktop.

3. Download and install Power BI Desktop on your PC.

Here's How: Importing Data to Power BI Desktop

Once you have Power BI Desktop installed on your PC, you're ready to import data into it. This process is very similar to importing data into Excel, as you can see in these steps:

1. Open Power BI Desktop.

2. If the startup page appears, dismiss it by clicking the X in the top-right corner.

3. Select Home, Get Data, More, Access Database.

4. Navigate to the AdventureWorks database you have been using throughout this book and import the first five items in the Navigator list (shown below).

Navigator

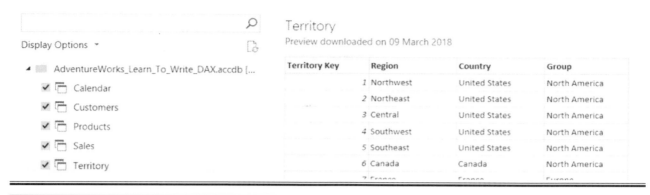

Here's How: Creating Relationships

The process of creating relationships in Power BI is the same as the process of creating relationships in Excel:

1. Switch to the Relationships view by clicking the Relationships icon on the left side of the screen.

2. Move the tables so they are laid out using the Collie layout methodology discussed in Chapter 2. Notice that two relationships have been automatically created, and they are both set to cross-filter in both directions. (You know this because of the double arrows pointing up and down.)

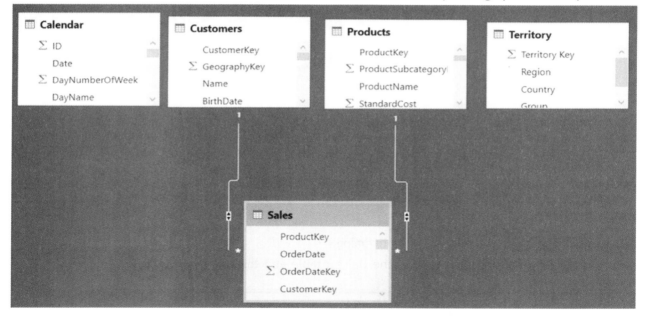

3. Double-click the relationship between the Customers table and the Sales table.

4. In the Edit Relationship dialog that appears, select Single from the Cross Filter Direction drop-down, as shown below.

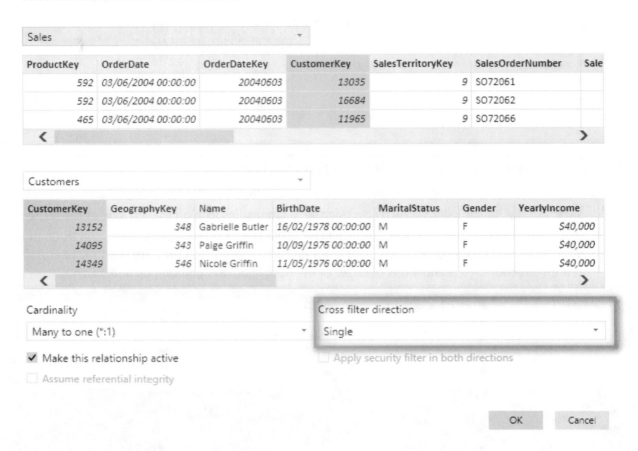

Edit relationship

Select tables and columns that are related.

Sales

ProductKey	OrderDate	OrderDateKey	CustomerKey	SalesTerritoryKey	SalesOrderNumber	Sale
592	03/06/2004 00:00:00	20040603	13035	9	SO72061	
592	03/06/2004 00:00:00	20040603	16684	9	SO72062	
465	03/06/2004 00:00:00	20040603	11965	9	SO72066	

Customers

CustomerKey	GeographyKey	Name	BirthDate	MaritalStatus	Gender	YearlyIncome
13152	348	Gabrielle Butler	16/02/1978 00:00:00	M	F	$40,000
14095	343	Paige Griffin	10/09/1976 00:00:00	M	F	$40,000
14349	546	Nicole Griffin	11/05/1976 00:00:00	M	F	$40,000

Cardinality

Many to one (*:1)

Cross filter direction

Single

☑ Make this relationship active   ☐ Apply security filter in both directions

☐ Assume referential integrity

OK   Cancel

Note: You can change the relationship type (cardinality) and also the cross-filter direction in the Edit Relationship dialog.

5. Click OK to close the Edit Relationship dialog.

6. Create the relationships between the `Sales` table and the other two tables as you would do in Excel.

Here's How: Creating New Measures

The process of creating a new measure in Power BI Desktop is almost identical to the process of creating measures in Power Pivot for Excel 2016. You can write measures from either the Report view or the Data view, just as in Excel. Follow these steps to create a new measure (and notice that it's the same approach you have used elsewhere in this book):

1. Navigate to the Report view.

2. On the right side of the screen, go to the Visualizations section (see #1 below) and click the Matrix icon (#2). Power BI adds a new matrix visualisation object on the report canvas on the left (#3). (A matrix is similar to a pivot table.)

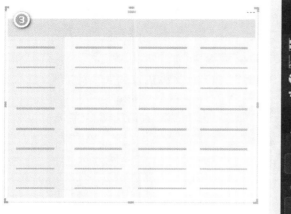
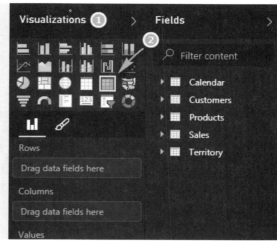

3. Select the matrix on the report canvas (#3 above).

4. On the right side of the screen, open the Products table (see #1 below) and place a check mark in Category from the list of columns (#2). Power BI adds the `Products[Category]` column to the matrix (#3), just as would happen in Excel.

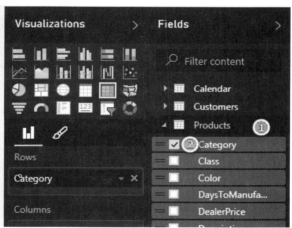

5. From the Fields list on the right side, right-click the `Sales` table (see #1 below) to ensure that the new measure you are about to write is placed in the `Sales` table and click New Measure (#2).

6. You can see Measure in the Fields list (see #1 below) and highlighted text `Measure =` in the formula bar (#2).

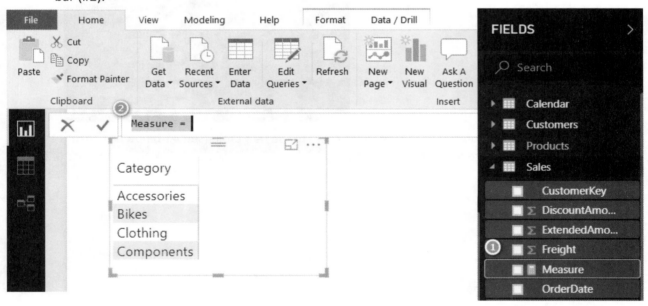

7. Overwrite the highlighted text with the measure name and formula and press Enter. (Note that with Power BI, you need to specify the name of the measure and the formula in the formula bar, as shown below.)

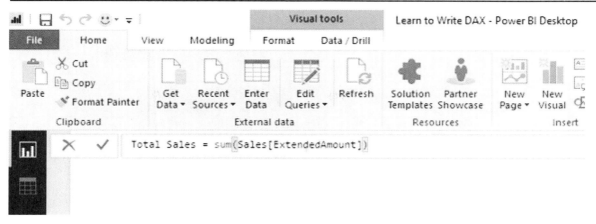

Total Sales = sum(Sales[ExtendedAmount])

Note: There are some significant improvements in the Power BI user interface over the Excel interface, including the following:

- You do not have to place a colon before the equal sign as you do if you write the formula in the Power Pivot window in Excel 2013 or Excel 2016.
- You can type the name of a column, and Power BI automatically prepends the table name to the front of the column name.
- There is improved IntelliSense, including formula highlighting and bracket matching.

8. After you have finished writing the measure, select the matrix on the canvas and then place a check mark next to the new measure called [Total Sales] that appears in the Sales table on the right. Power BI places the measure into the matrix.

9. Select the matrix and then click the Tree Map visualisation in the visualisations list.

10. Open the Products table in the fields list on the right side.

11. Remove the check mark from Category and place a check mark next to SubCategory.

12. On the report canvas, resize the tree map so that it takes up the full screen, as shown below.

Total Sales by SubCategory

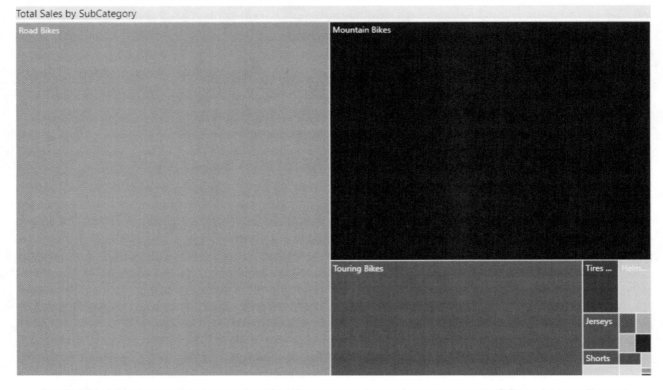

Note: The tree map is one of many new visualisations that are available in Power BI. The items in a tree map are sorted from largest to smallest, left to right. The boxes are proportional to the relative size of each item.

Here's How: Publish Your Report to PowerBI.com

Follow these steps to publish a report to PowerBI.com:

1. Save the Power BI workbook. Note that it is saved with a .pbix extension.
2. Click the Publish button in the menu at the top of the page. You need to be logged in to your Power BI account to publish a report. The first time you use PowerBI.com, you are prompted to create an account, as shown below.

✕

Power BI Desktop

Power BI Desktop and the Power BI service work seamlessly when you're signed in.

Sign in

Need a Power BI account? Try for free

3. If you don't yet have an account, click Need a Power BI Account? and follow the instructions to set up the account. If you do have an account, just sign in with your credentials. You get a success message when the file has been loaded to PowerBI.com. If you already have an account, log in using your credentials.

   Note: At this writing, you cannot create a Power BI account using a personal email address such as @gmail.com or @hotmail.com.

4. In a browser, navigate to http://powerbi.com and click the sign-in link in the top-right corner of the website.

5. Sign in with the same credentials you used in step 2. You can find your data model under Datasets and the tree map in the Reports section, as shown below.

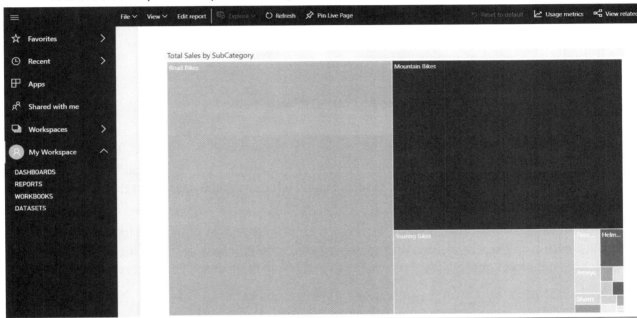

Here's How: Importing Excel Power Pivot Workbooks to Power BI Desktop

It is possible to import a Power Pivot workbook from Excel into Power BI Desktop, along with all the data connections, relationships, and measures. Unfortunately, any reports you have created in Excel are not migrated and need to be re-created in Power BI.

Note: It is possible to load an Excel Power Pivot workbook into Microsoft OneDrive for Business, synchronise the workbook to Power BI, and display the Excel workbook. You can read about this at http://xbi.com.au/XLPBI.

Follow these steps to import a Power Pivot workbook from Excel into Power BI Desktop:

1. In Power BI Desktop, select File, New.

2. In the new blank Power BI file, click File, Import, Excel Workbook Contents.

3. Navigate to the workbook you have created, click OK, and then select Import.

4. When you get the choice to copy the data from your queries or keep the connection (as shown below), click Keep Connection.

Import Excel Workbook Contents

There are queries and Data Model tables that depend on the
following worksheet tables in the original workbook:

- Hemisphere

- Increase

- YearTable

Do you want to copy the data from those tables to your Power BI
Desktop file or keep a connection to the original Excel workbook for
this data?

5.   The Excel workbook is then imported into Power BI Desktop. From there you can proceed to use
     Power BI Desktop instead of Excel and build your own visualisations on top of the Power Pivot data
     model.

Note: Power BI Desktop doesn't include the concept of linked tables. When you import into Power BI Desktop an Excel workbook that contains linked tables, you can either bring in the data as
a one-off migration or retain the link to the original linked table in the original Excel workbook.

22: Next Steps on Your DAX Journey

Okay, so you have almost finished reading all the chapters of this book. Now what? First of all, let me assure you that this is just the start, not the end, of your journey to learning to write DAX. As I have been saying all throughout the book, the most important thing is to practice, practice, practice. Start using your new skills at work and at play so that you build your depth of skill and knowledge. It will take you many months of using your new skills before you become an expert, but you are well on your way already. Now that you have a basic understanding of Power Pivot, you can incrementally learn and improve over time. But there are some things that will help you learn more and faster.

Third-Person Learning

I am a big believer in "third-person learning." I first heard of this term from Stephen Covey, at one of his seminars. The basic idea is that you learn more when you learn with the intent to teach others, and you learn more from the process of teaching others. For this reason, I really believe in the benefits of participating in user forums. As I mentioned at the start of the book, I have set up a forum at http://powerpivotforum.com. au, and it is free for anyone and everyone to ask questions and also to help others. If you want to really cement your new skills and knowledge, then sign up and ask for help, and, more importantly, answer questions and help others on the forum. When you help others, you cement your knowledge and become better and stronger with your DAX.

Blogs

There are a number of Power Pivot blogs that I recommend you subscribe to. Reading blogs is a great way to keep in touch with the latest thinking from people who spend their life working with Power Pivot. Here are some that I think are especially useful:

- My blog: http://xbi.com.au/blog
- Rob Collie's blog: http://powerpivotpro.com
- Scott Senkeresty's blog: http://tinylizard.com
- Marco Russo and Alberto Ferrari's blog: http://sqlbi.com

Books

There are a few really good DAX books that I recommend (and have mentioned previously). These are my favourites:

- Rob Collie and Avi Singh's *Power Pivot and Power BI*: http://xbi.com.au/DAXFormulas
- Alberto Ferrari and Marco Russo's *Microsoft Excel 2013*: Building Data Models with PowerPivot: http://xbi.com.au/TheItalians or http://xbi.com.au/books
- Other books: I keep a list of books I recommend on my website and update it over time, and you can always find an updated list at http://xbi.com.au/books

Live Training

Some people learn best in a class environment. If this sounds like you, you can attend a live training event in a location suitable for you. My company, Excelerator BI, offers live training courses in Australia. For details about upcoming events, see http://xbi.com.au/training.

For those that can't attend my training live in Australia, I also have a "semi-live" online training course that you can read about at http://xbi.com.au/scpbi. With this course, you get online videos and five weekly Q&A calls with me over five weeks.

Don't Forget Power Query

Early in this book I recommended that you load your data into Power Pivot using Power Query. Loading well-shaped tables into Power Pivot is just the tip of the iceberg of what can be done with this great tool. Power Query is a desktop ETL (extract, transform, and load) tool for Excel users. It allows you to connect to data from anywhere, clean up and change the shape of that data, and then load it into your workbooks. Once the data is loaded with Power Query, you can easily refresh the link at any time and bring in the latest updated data.

Online Training

I have a comprehensive online training course that will teach you how to be a Power Query superhero. Learn more about it at http://xbi.com.au/pqt.

I often blog about Power Query at http://xbi.com.au/blog, and you can also get great information from these websites and books:

- Ken Puls' blog: http://www.excelguru.ca/blog
- Chris Webb's blog: http://blog.crossjoin.co.uk
- Chris Webb's book *Power Query for Power BI and Excel*: http://xbi.com.au/ChrisWebbBook
- Ken Puls and Miguel Escobar's book *M is for Data Monkey*: http://xbi.com.au/DataMonkey

That's All, Folks

I hope you have enjoyed this book and that it has successfully started you on your journey to becoming a DAX superhero. If you liked this book, please tell your Excel friends and colleagues so they, too, can become DAX superheros.

Appendix A: Answers to Practice Exercises

This appendix provides the answers to the practice exercises scattered throughout the book. The answers are in the same order the exercises appear in the book and are numbered so you can easily match up the exercises and the answers.

SUM()

These practice exercises appear in Chapter 4. Did you remember to put your measures in the correct table? Did you put the measure in the table the data comes from? Did you format with an appropriate number format?

1.

```
Total Sales
    = SUM(Sales[ExtendedAmount])
```

or

```
Total Sales
    = SUM(Sales[SalesAmount])
```

2.

```
Total Cost
    = SUM(Sales[TotalProductCost])
```

or

```
Total Cost
    = SUM(Sales[ProductStandardCost])
```

3.

```
Total Margin $
    = [Total Sales] – [Total Cost]
```

4.

```
Total Margin %
    = [Total Margin $] / [Total Sales]
```

or

```
Total Margin %
    = DIVIDE([Total Margin $] , [Total Sales])
```

5.

```
Total Sales Tax Paid
    = SUM(Sales[TaxAmt])
```

6.

```
Total Sales Including Tax
    = [Total Sales] + [Total Sales Tax Paid]
```

7.

```
Total Order Quantity
    = SUM(Sales[OrderQuantity])
```

COUNT()

These practice exercises appear in Chapter 4.

8.

```
Total Number of Products
    = COUNT(Products[ProductKey])
```

9.

```
Total Number of Customers
    = COUNT(Customers[CustomerKey])
```

Note: Counting the "key" columns is generally pretty safe because, by definition, each one must have a value. Technically, you can count any column that has a numeric value in each cell, and you will get the same answer. Just be careful if you are counting a numeric column that may have blank values: COUNT() does not count blanks.

COUNTROWS()

These practice exercises appear in Chapter 4.

Note: Remember that COUNTROWS() takes a table, not a column, as input.

10.

```
Total Number of Products COUNTROWS Version
    = COUNTROWS(Products)
```

11.

```
Total Number of Customers COUNTROWS Version
    = COUNTROWS(Customers)
```

DISTINCTCOUNT()

These practice exercises appear in Chapter 4.

12.

```
Total Customers in Database DISTINCTCOUNT Version
    = DISTINCTCOUNT(Customers[CustomerKey])
```

13.

```
Count of Occupation
    = DISTINCTCOUNT(Customers[Occupation])
```

14.

```
Count of Country
    = DISTINCTCOUNT(Territories[Country])
```

15.

```
Customers That Have Purchased
    = DISTINCTCOUNT(Sales[CustomerKey])
```

MAX(), MIN(), and AVERAGE()

These practice exercises appear in Chapter 4.

16.

```
Maximum Tax Paid on a Product
    = MAX(Sales[TaxAmt])
```

17.

```
Minimum Price Paid for a Product
    = MIN(Sales[ExtendedAmount])
```

18.

```
Average Price Paid for a Product
    = AVERAGE(Sales[ExtendedAmount])
```

COUNTBLANK()

These practice exercises appear in Chapter 4.

19.

```
Customers Without Address Line 2
    = COUNTBLANK(Customers[AddressLine2])
```

20.

```
Products Without Weight Values
    = COUNTBLANK(Products[Weight])
```

DIVIDE()

These practice exercises appear in Chapter 4.

21.

```
Margin %
    = DIVIDE([Total Margin $] , [Total Sales] )
```

22.

```
Markup %
    = DIVIDE([Total Margin $] , [Total Cost])
```

23.

```
Tax %
    = DIVIDE(SUM(Sales[TaxAmt]), [Total Sales])
```

or

```
Tax %
    = DIVIDE([Total Sales Tax Paid], [Total Sales])
```

SUMX()

These practice exercises appear in Chapter 7.

24.

```
Total Sales SUMX Version
    = SUMX(Sales, Sales[OrderQuantity] * Sales[UnitPrice])
```

Note: In this sample database, the order quantity is always 1.

25.

```
Total Sales Including Tax SUMX Version
    = SUMX(Sales,Sales[ExtendedAmount] + Sales[TaxAmt])
```

26.

```
Total Sales Including Freight
    = SUMX(Sales,Sales[ExtendedAmount] + Sales[Freight])
```

27.

```
Dealer Margin
    = SUMX(Products,Products[ListPrice] - Products[DealerPrice])
```

AVERAGEX()

These practice exercises appear in Chapter 7.

28.

```
Average Sell Price per Item
```

```
= AVERAGEX(Sales, Sales[OrderQuantity]
* Sales[UnitPrice])
```

29.

```
Average Tax Paid
    = AVERAGEX(Sales, Sales[TaxAmt])
```

Note: Note how the expression can be a single column. It doesn't have to be an equation using multiple columns.

30.

```
Average Safety Stock
    = AVERAGEX(Products, Products[SafetyStockLevel])
```

Calculated Columns

This practice exercise appears in Chapter 8.

31.

```
= IF(OR('Calendar'[CalendarQuarter]=1, 'Calendar'[CalendarQuar-
ter]=2),"H1","H2")
```

Note: There are a number of ways to write this calculated column. If yours is different but works, then all is well and good.

CALCULATE() with a Single Table

These practice exercises appear in Chapter 9.

32.

```
Total Male Customers
    = CALCULATE([Total Number of Customers], Customers[Gender] = "M")
```

33.

```
Total Customers Born Before 1950
    = CALCULATE([Total Number of Customers], Customers[BirthDate]
<DATE(1950,1,1))
```

34.

```
Total Customers Born in January
    = CALCULATE([Total Number of Customers], MONTH(Customers[BirthDate])=1)
```

35.

```
Customers Earning at Least $100,000 per Year
    = CALCULATE([Total Number of Customers], Customers[YearlyIn-
come]>=100000)
```

CALCULATE() with Multiple Tables

These practice exercises appear in Chapter 9.

36.

```
Total Sales of Clothing
    = CALCULATE([Total Sales], Products[Category]="Clothing")
```

37.

```
Sales to Female Customers
    = CALCULATE([Total Sales], Customers[Gender]="F")
```

38.

```
Sales of Bikes to Married Men
    = CALCULATE([Total Sales],
        Customers[MaritalStatus]="M",
        Customers[Gender]="M",
        Products[Category]="Bikes"
    )
```

VALUES()

These practice exercises appear in Chapter 12.

39.

```
Number of Color Variants
    = COUNTROWS(VALUES(Products[Color]))
```

40.

```
Number of Sub Categories
    = COUNTROWS(VALUES(Products[SubCategory]))
```

41.

```
Number of Size Ranges
    = COUNTROWS(VALUES(Products[SizeRange]))
```

42.

```
Product Category (Values)
    = IF(HASONEVALUE(Products[Category]), VALUES(Products[Category])
    )
```

43.

```
Product Subcategory (Values)
    = IF(
        HASONEVALUE(Products[SubCategory]),
        VALUES(Products[SubCategory])
      )
```

44.

```
Product Color (Values)
    = IF(HASONEVALUE(Products[color]), VALUES(Products[color])
    )
```

45.

```
Product Subcategory (Values) edited
    = IF(
        HASONEVALUE(Products[SubCategory]),
        VALUES(Products[SubCategory]),
        "More than 1 Sub Category"
    )
```

46.

```
Product Color (Values) edited
  = IF(
        HASONEVALUE(Products[color]),
        VALUES(Products[color]),
        "More than 1 Color"
    )
```

ALL(), ALLEXCEPT(), and ALLSELECTED()

These practice exercises appear in Chapter 13.

47.

```
Total Sales to All Customers
    = CALCULATE([Total Sales] , All(Customers))
```

Note: This measure belongs in the Sales table, not the Customers table.

48.

```
% of All Customer Sales
    = DIVIDE([Total Sales] , [Total Sales to All Customers])
```

49.

```
Total Sales to Selected Customers
    = CALCULATE([Total Sales] , ALLSELECTED(Customers))
```

50.

```
% of Sales to Selected Customers
    = DIVIDE([Total Sales] , [Total Sales to Selected Customers])
```

51.

```
Total Sales for All Days Selected Dates
    = CALCULATE([Total Sales] , ALLSELECTED(Calendar))
```

Note: Did you know to use ALLSELECTED() and not ALLEXCEPT()?

52.

```
% Sales for All Days Selected Dates
    = DIVIDE([Total Sales] ,
    [Total Sales for All Days Selected Dates])
```

This is what your pivot table should look like:

MonthName			
January	February	March	April
May	June	July	August
September	October	November	December

CalendarYear
2001
2002
2003
2004

Row Labels	Total Sales	Total Sales for All Days Selected Dates	% Sales for All Days Selected Dates
Sunday	$2,321,342	$16,321,404	14.2%
Monday	$2,279,220	$16,321,404	14.0%
Tuesday	$2,315,978	$16,321,404	14.2%
Wednesday	$2,391,460	$16,321,404	14.7%
Thursday	$2,349,082	$16,321,404	14.4%
Friday	$2,307,355	$16,321,404	14.1%
Saturday	$2,356,967	$16,321,404	14.4%
Grand Total	**$16,321,404**	**$16,321,404**	**100.0%**

53.

```
Total Orders All Customers
    = CALCULATE([Total Order Quantity] , ALL(Customers))
```

54.

```
Baseline Orders for All Customers with This Occupation
    = CALCULATE(
        [Total Order Quantity],
        ALLEXCEPT(Customers, Customers[Occupation])
      )
```

55.

```
Baseline % This Occupation of All Customer Orders
  = DIVIDE(
        [Baseline Orders for All customers with this Occupation],
        [Total Orders All Customers]
      )
```

56.

```
Total Orders Selected Customers
    = CALCULATE([Total Order Quantity] , ALLSELECTED(Customers))
```

57.

```
Occupation % of Selected Customers
    = DIVIDE([Total Order Quantity],
          [Total Orders Selected Customers]
        )
```

58.

```
Percentage Point Variation to Baseline
    = [Occupation % of Selected Customers] -
[Baseline % this Occupation is of All Customer Orders]
```

FILTER()

These practice exercises appear in Chapter 14.

59.

```
Total Sales of Products That Have Some Sales but Less Than $10,000
    = CALCULATE([Total Sales],
      FILTER(Products, [Total Sales]
      <=10000 && [Total Sales] >0))
```

60.

```
Count of Products That Have Some Sales but Less Than $10,000
    = CALCULATE(COUNTROWS(Products),
      FILTER(Products, [Total Sales]
      <=10000 && [Total Sales] >0))
```

Time Intelligence

These practice exercises appear in Chapter 15.

61.

```
Total Sales Month to Date
    = TOTALMTD([Total Sales], 'Calendar'[Date])
```

62.

```
Total Sales Quarter to Date
    = TOTALQTD([Total Sales], 'Calendar'[Date])
```

Note: Did you set up your pivot table correctly? Something like this would be appropriate for QTD:

CalendarYear 2003		
Row Labels	**Total Sales**	**Total Sales QTD**
January	$438,865	$438,865
February	$489,090	$927,956
March	$485,575	$1,413,530
April	$506,399	$506,399
May	$562,773	$1,069,172
June	$554,799	$1,623,971
July	$886,669	$886,669
August	$847,414	$1,734,082
September	$1,010,258	$2,744,340
October	$1,080,450	$1,080,450
November	$1,196,981	$2,277,431
December	$1,731,788	$4,009,218
Grand Total	**$9,791,060**	**$4,009,218**

Note: Conditional formatting is good because it gives immediate feedback about whether things are working as expected.

63.

```
Total Sales FYTD 30 June
    = TOTALYTD([Total Sales], 'Calendar'[Date],"30/6")
```

64.

```
Total Sales FYTD 31 March
    = TOTALYTD([Total Sales], 'Calendar'[Date],"31/3")
```

65.

```
Total Sales Previous Month
    = CALCULATE([Total Sales], PREVIOUSMONTH('Calendar'[Date])
)
```

66.

```
Total Sales Previous Day
    = CALCULATE([Total Sales], PREVIOUSDAY('Calendar'[Date])
)
```

67.

```
Total Sales Previous Quarter
    = CALCULATE([Total Sales], PREVIOUSQUARTER('Calendar'[Date])
)
```

68.

```
Total Sales Moving Annual Total
    = CALCULATE([Total Sales],
            FILTER(ALL('Calendar'),
```

```
                           'Calendar'[ID] > MAX('Calendar'[ID]) - 365 &&
                           'Calendar'[ID] <= MAX('Calendar'[ID])
                      )
                 )
```

69.

```
     Total Sales Rolling 90 Days
         = IF(MAX('Calendar'[ID])>=90,
              CALCULATE([Total Sales],
                  FILTER(ALL('Calendar'),
                      'Calendar'[ID] > MAX('Calendar'[ID]) - 90 &&
                      'Calendar'[ID] <= MAX('Calendar'[ID])
                      )
                  )
              )
```

Harvester Measures

This practice exercise appears in Chapter 17.

70.

```
     Total Customers Born Before Selected Year
         = CALCULATE(
         [Total Number of Customers],
         FILTER(
             Customers,
             Customers[BirthDate] < DATE([Selected Year], 1, 1 )
         )
     )
```

Multiple Data Tables

These practice exercises appear in Chapter 19.

71.

```
     Total Budget = SUM(Budget[Budget])
```

This measure should be placed in the `Budget` table.

72.

```
     Change in Sales vs. Budget
         = [Total Sales] - [Total Budget]
```

This measure could be placed in either the `Sales` table or the `Budget` table. I normally place it in the `Sales` table because the name of the measure is `[Change in Sales vs. Budget]`.

73.

```
     % Change in Sales vs. Budget
         = DIVIDE([Change in Sales vs. Budget] , [Total Budget])
```

Also place this measure in the `Sales` table.

Table of Here's How Sections

Here's How: Enabling Power Pivot in Excel 3

Here's How: Data Load Using Power Pivot 6

Here's How: Data Load Using Power Query 8

Here's How: Renaming Tables and Columns 10

Here's How: Joining Tables in Power Pivot 13

Here's How: Making Changes to a Table That Is Already Loaded 17

Here's How: Deleting Steps in a Query 19

Here's How: Importing New Tables 19

Here's How: Changing the File Location of an Existing Connection 21

Here's How: Inserting a New Pivot Table 24

Here's How: Writing Measures 26

Here's How: Using IntelliSense 29

Here's How: Editing Measures 31

Here's How: Changing Display Names in Pivot Tables 40

Here's How: Applying Conditional Formatting 43

Here's How: Manually Adding a Measure to a Pivot Table 48

Here's How: Moving an Existing Measure to a Different Table 48

Here's How: Creating a Day Type Calculated Column 71

Here's How: Changing the MonthName Sort Order 94

Here's How: Using ALLEXCEPT() 108

Here's How: Marking a Table as a Date Table 122

Here's How: Manually Adding Data to Power Pivot from a New Linked Table 145

Here's How: Solving Practice Exercise 70 153

Here's How: Creating a Morphing Switch Measure 155

Here's How: Applying Banding 157

Here's How: Editing a Manually Created Table 159

Here's How: Deleting Interim Calculated Columns 162

Here's How: Creating a KPI 165

Here's How: Adding a Budget Table 167

Here's How: Creating a Budget KPI 174

Here's How: Converting a Pivot Table to Cube Formulas 175

Here's How: Writing CUBEVALUE() from Scratch 177

Here's How: Applying Filters to Cube Formulas 179

Here's How: Adding a Slicer Without a Pivot Table 179

Here's How: Connecting a Slicer to a Cube Formula 180

Here's How: Installing Power BI Desktop 182

Here's How: Importing Data to Power BI Desktop 182

Here's How: Creating Relationships 183

Here's How: Creating New Measures 184

Here's How: Publish Your Report to PowerBI.com 188

Here's How: Importing Excel Power Pivot Workbooks to Power BI Desktop 189

Index

Symbols

13 4-week period calendar 121
445 calendar 121
&&&& And operator 72
% of Total 100
|| OR operator 72

A

Access database 8
Active learning v
AdventureWorks vii
Age bands 156
Aggregation functions 34
Aggregators 34
Aggregators vs. X-functions 64
ALL 98
    with Calendar 134
    with Column 103
ALLEXCEPT 104, 108
ALLSELECTED 104
AND function 72
AVERAGE 47
AVERAGEX 70

B

Banding 156
    Upper & lower values 157
Baseline calculation 109
BLANK 88
Blogs 191
Books, suggested 191
Budget vs. actual 167
Building Data Models with Pow-
    erPivot 191

C

Cached copy 22
Caesar salad 74
CALCULATE 74
    Explicit 118
    Implicit 117
    with Advanced filter 78
    with ALL 98
    with multiple tables 77
    with no filter 87
    with Simple filter 74
Calculated columns
    for Filtering 71
    versus Measures 67
Calculated field 25
CALCULATETABLE 101

Calculation area 25
Calendar, reserved word vi, 123
Calendar table 120
    ID column 130
Changing a table 17
Check formula 27
Collie layout 16, 171
Collie, Rob 16, 41, 149, 191
Compression 58
CONCATENATEX 94
Conditional formatting 43
Context transition 85
    with FILTER 118
Convert to Formulas 175
COUNT 38
COUNTAX 70
COUNTBLANK 48
COUNTROWS 39
    with VALUES 92
COUNTX 70
Covey, Stephen 191
Cross-filtering 182
Cube formulas 175
    with Filters 179
    with Slicer 180
    Writing 176
CUBEMEMBER 177, 180
CUBEVALUE 177
Customers born before N 76

D

Daily vs monthly 170
Data bars 43
Data modelling 1
Data modelling engine 1
Data tables 16
    Multiple 167
    versus Flattened 57
Data view 10
DATEADD 140, 142
DATESBETWEEN 142
DATESINPERIOD 142
DATESMTD 142
DATESQTD 142
DATESYTD 142
Date table 122
DAX
    Researching 140
DAX Formatter 79
DAX Reference Guide PDF 143
Day type 71
Deleting steps 19
De-normalising 58
Diagram view 10

Dimensional modelling 15
Dimension tables 16, 57
Disconnected tables 149, 158
Display names 40
DISTINCTCOUNT 42
DIVIDE 49
Drag direction 14

E

Easy to read DAX 79
Editing linked table 159
ENDOFMONTH 142
ENDOFQUARTER 142
ENDOFYEAR 142
Enter data 145
Errata vii
Error checking 80
Escobar, Miguel 192
Evaluation context 82
Excel users iv
Exercise data vii

F

Fact tables 16
Ferrari, Alberto 79, 191
File location, changing 21
FILTER 111
    avoid IF 113
    in CALCULATE 114
Filter context 49
    Removing with ALL 98
Filter propagation 51
    Downhill only 52
    Versus manual 54
    with FILTER 116
Financial year 121
FIND 88
    inside IF 90
FIRSTDATE 142
First year 139
Fiscal year 121
Fit to screen 12, 169
Flattened tables 57
Foreign key 17
Formula bar 25
Forum vii

G

GETPIVOTDATA 175
Get & Transform 5
Granularity 167

H

Half year calculation 73
Harvester 149

Harvester measures 149
Harvest filter context 132
HASONEVALUE 94
Hemisphere 145
Hidden CALCULATE 86
House owner 88

I

IF 88
   versus Banding table 157
Imaginary temporary table 119
Implicit CALCULATE 86
Implicit measure 28
Importing table 19
Incremental learning iv
Initial filter context 51
IntelliSense 29
Interim calculated columns 160
   Deleting 162
Interim measures 105
Iterators 62
   FILTER 112

J

Jelen, Bill iv
Joining tables 13

K

Key performance indicator 164
Kimball methodology 15
KPIs 164
   Display bug 166

L

LASTDATE 142
LASTNONBLANKDATE 142
Leap years 137
   7-year system 139
Lifetime purchases 114
Lineage 119
List incomplete 18
Live Training 191
Loading data 5
   using Power Pivot 6
   using Power Query 8
Lookup tables 16
   versus Flattened 57

M

Master data tables 57
MAX 47
   Harvest filter context 132
MAXX 70
Measures
   Adding to pivot table 48

Defined 25
Dialog 26
Editing 31
Formatting 27
from SWITCH 155
Grand total 101
Harvester 150
Implicit 28
in Power BI Desktop 184
Interim 101
Modal dialog box 32
Morphing switch 155
Moving 48
Naming 27, 40
Reusing 35
Suspend writing 33
Testing 126
versus Calculated columns 67
MIN 47
   Harvest filter context 132
MINX 70
M is for Data Monkey 192
Months in year 92
Morphing switch measure 155
Moving annual total 138
MSDN 140

N

Naked columns 34
Names, display 40
Naming conventions viii
New measure 26
NEXTDAY 142
NEXTMONTH 142
NEXTQUARTER 142
NEXTYEAR 142
Nonstandard calendars 121
Number format 27

O

One-to-many 14
Online Training 192
OR function 72

P

PARALLELPERIOD 142
Percentage of Total 100
   as Measure 102
Percent of Selected 105
Pipe symbols 72
Pivot table 1
   Inserting new 24
PowerBI.com 181
   Publishing to 188

Power BI Desktop 181
   Importing data 182
   Importing from Excel 189
   Installing 182
   Measures 184
   Relationships 183
   Relationships view 182
Power BI Mobile 181
Power Pivot and Power BI 191
Powerpivotforum.com.au vii
Powerpivotpro.com 191
Power Query 5, 8
Power Query for Power BI and
   Excel 192
Practice exercises
   ALL, ALLEXCEPT 105
   AVERAGEX 70
   Calculated columns 73
   CALCULATE (multiple tables)
      77
   CALCULATE (single table) 76
   COUNT 38
   COUNTBLANK 48
   COUNTROWS 39
   DISTINCTCOUNT 42
   DIVIDE 50
   FILTER 115
   Harvester measures 153
   MAX MIN AVERAGE 47
   Multiple data tables 173
   SUM 36
   SUMX 63
   Time intelligence 127
   VALUES 96
PREVIOUSDAY 128, 142
PREVIOUSMONTH 128, 142
PREVIOUSQUARTER 128, 142
PREVIOUSYEAR 142
Primary key 17, 57
Puls, Ken 192

Q

Query, deleting steps 19
Query Editor
   Cached data 22

R

Reference tables 57
RELATED 144
RELATEDTABLE 144
   from many side 148
Relationships 13, 59
   Adding 56
Relationships view 13

Renaming columns 10
Renaming tables 10
Retain lineage 91
RETURN keyword 161
Return value 141
ROUNDDOWN 158
Row context 62
   versus Filter context 84
Russo, Marco 79, 191

S

SAMEPERIODLASTYEAR 123
Sample data vii
Select Case 88
Senkeresty, Scott 191
Shaping data 14
Show Value As 100
Singh, Avi 191
Slicer 106
   from Parameter 151
   without pivot table 179
Snowflake schema 16, 60
Sorting with numeric column 94
Sort order 94
SQLBI.com 191
Star schema 15, 59
STARTOFMONTH 142
STARTOFQUARTER 142
STARTOFYEAR 142
SUM 34
SUMX 62
   versus SUM 65
Supercharge Power BI iv
Surrogate key 122
SWITCH 88
   Measure 155
Syntax sugar 75
   FILTER 114

T

Territory builder 146
Text constant 33
Third-person learning 191
Time intelligence 120
   Custom 129
   List of functions 142
Tinylizard.com 191
TOTALMTD 127, 142
TOTALQTD 127, 142
TOTALYTD 125
Training 191
Transaction tables 57

U

Unfiltered 55

V

VALUES 91
   Single value 93
VAR for variable 160
VBA macro 41
Virtual tables 91
   Lineage 119
VLOOKUP alternative 16

W

Webb, Chris 192
Weekend calculation 72
Whole of table 129
Word wrap macro 41

X

X-functions vs. aggregators 64

Y

Year to date 125, 133
YYYYMM 168

Notes